Robert Burns
Cronies, Colleagues and Contemporaries

by
James L. Hempstead

Robert Burns: Cronies, Colleagues and Contemporaries

*For Effie, with whom I spent 56 years of happy married life,
until her death on 28 September, 2005.*

Published by Masonic Publishing Company,
30 Loanbank Quadrant, Glasgow.

Designed and Printed in Scotland by William Anderson & Sons Ltd.,
Commercial and Colour Printers, Glasgow G51 3HZ
From typeset copy supplied.

ISBN 0-9544268-5-1

CONTENTS

FOREWORD

I consider it a great privilege and honour to be invited to write a Foreword to this book, by James Hempstead, under the title of *Robert Burns: Cronies, Colleagues and Contemporaries.*

James joined Dumbarton Burns Club in 1958 and very soon his talent as a speaker and reader became evident, and he was a regular on the Burns Supper programmes for the next forty years. In 1971 he became President of the Club and also served as Secretary from 1978 to 1989. During his service as Secretary he introduced a Club Newsletter, and edited it for 20 years. He also was largely instrumental in setting up a collection of Burns books in the local Library.

My association with James commenced some 15 years ago when I was appointed editor of the *Burns Chronicle,* although I was already aware of his many talents. It proved a very happy association, and his continued support to the Chronicle was much appreciated. In a recently published Directory to all the articles and features published in the *Burns Chronicle,* since its inception in 1892 to 2005, James's contribution far outstrips all others, his total since 1974 being 37 articles, poems, etc., a record that will surely stand for many years to come.

In 1991 he was honoured by the members of Dumbarton Burns Club, who elected him their Honorary President, and in 1994 he was elected an Honorary President of the Robert Burns World Federation, in recognition of the excellent contribution he has made to Burns literature.

Part of James's great strength lies in the research he undertakes 'before putting pen to paper'. One has only to look at the Notes and Sources of this book to realise the amount of research he has undertaken in respect of each subject.

It is not the first time James has gone into print. No mean versifier himself, in 1992 he published a book of humorous verses called *Rhyme for Fun,* and this was followed in 1996 with *Robert Burns and Dumbartonshire,* in which he produced much that was new on Burns's West Highland Tour, and laid to rest some of the misconceptions that had clouded this enigmatic journey, hitherto. And in 2004, together with a colleague, they produced a *History of Dumbarton Burns Club.*

It is the first time that such a comprehensive study of Robert Burns's friends and acquaintances has ever been undertaken, and should find pride of place in any Burns library. The illustrations, many of them in colour, should add to the reader's pleasure.

Peter J. Westwood, Editor, *Burns Chronicle*

ACKNOWLEDGEMENTS

It is difficult to remember all those who have assisted me over the last thirty years, but I am mindful of the help I have received on numerous occasions from the staff of the Mitchell Library, Glasgow, and to them I extend my sincere thanks. I am also indebted to Mr. Graham Hopner, Information Services Librarian at Dumbarton Public Library, for his generous assistance from time to time, and especially for unearthing proof of William Corbet's marriage. I am also very grateful to Dumbarton Kilwinning Lodge No. 18 for permission to print an extract from their minutes, and to the late Mr. James Adie who, kindly undertook the research.

To my family, David, Morag and Iain, whose knowledge of computers is much greater than mine, I record my appreciation, for ironing out some of the difficulties which arose from time to time.

I should like to pay tribute to fellow Burnsian, Ian McLean, who can work magic with photographs for illustrations. Not only is he a wizard on photography, but his extensive knowledge in computing was invaluable in putting the whole package together. I am also most grateful to my good friend and fellow Burnsian, Mike Taylor, who, in the preparation of all material for the printer became my amanuensis, and for his invaluable assistance at the proof stages and also in the preparation of the Index. It is no exaggeration to say that without the help of these two friends, the date of publication would have been seriously delayed.

A word of thanks is due to Annette Wright, Honorary Secretary of Sandyford Burns Club, who furnished me so promptly with information regarding the renovated memorial stone of Alexander Findlater, and to Dave Smith, Secretary of Dumfries Howff Burns Club, who willingly met with my request for a copy of Burns's Dumfries Burgess Ticket, and photographs of Dumfries statue of Jean Amour. To Ron Howard of Edinburgh, who deserves more than a passing word of praise for the information he gave me on Peter Hill and his family.

To the Directors of Irvine Burns Club, who kindly granted permission to use the illustration on the dust cover. To Peter Westwood, I say, 'Thanks Peter for a very gracious Foreword.'

I am deeply conscious of the obligation I owe to Angus MacInnes, of Masonic Publications, who also introduced me to Andy Mushet of Anderson Printers, whose eye for layout, colour and detail, is reflected in the final excellent work.

To my dear late wife, Effie, as always, I owe a far greater debt of gratitude than I can ever express in words. It is a great pity she did not live to see the final work.

JAMES L. HEMPSTEAD   **Dumbarton 2008**

INTRODUCTION

The following sketches of Robert Burns's cronies, colleagues and contemporaries have appeared over the last thirty years in the pages of the *Burns Chronicle,* the official publication of the Robert Burns World Federation. The sketches have now been revised and supplemented, and brought together in one volume, in response to suggestions from a number of friends.

I acknowledge that I have covered ground already traversed by other writers, but a great deal of hitherto unpublished material has been found, and consequently, the reader will find much that is new. Research has also revealed that, in a number of instances, the lives of Burns's friends have been clouded by misconceptions and wrongful assumptions - a fate that has bedevilled the life story of the Bard himself, even to this day.

I have tried, wherever possible, to quote from the best authenticated sources - Burns's own letters and poems, and the letters and records of his cronies and contemporaries. I have also drawn on the works of numerous writers on Burns, but where evidence has conflicted, I have followed my own line.

JAMES L. HEMPSTEAD   **Dumbarton 2008**

ILLUSTRATIONS

ABBREVIATIONS

Throughout the text I have adopted the system of referring to the poems and songs as *(CW)*, followed by their page numbers in *The Complete Works of Robert Burns (1986)*, and the letters of the poet by *(CL)*, followed by their page numbers in *The Complete Letters of Robert Burns (1987)*, both volumes edited by James A McKay, and published by the Burns Federation.

ALLOWAY AND AYR

'Kirk - Alloway was drawing nigh,
Whare ghaists and houlets nightly cry.'

'Auld Ayr, whom ne'er a town surpasses,
For honest men and bonie lasses.'

JOHN MURDOCH

An Act passed by the Scottish Parliament in 1694 decreed that there should be a school in every parish, but in many parishes throughout Scotland the Act often went unheeded. Although Alloway was within the Parish of Ayr, where several schools had been established, it had to depend on private initiative to provide some form of education for the children of the village. For instance it is reported that a school was conducted in Kirk Alloway sometime between 1746 and 1757 but after a time fell into abeyance. In 1765 a school was established by Adam Campbell[1] at Alloway Mill, which was located near the mouth of the River Doon and about a mile from the village itself. William Burnes lost no time in enrolling his sons Robert and Gilbert, where they were given the rudiments of reading and spelling, although it is probable that they had already received some tuition from their father. Unfortunately the school closed down after a few months when Campbell left to take up a more remunerative post as Master of Ayr Workhouse, which had been opened in 1756.

Obviously William Burnes was very anxious that another school should be set up as soon as possible, and in early 1765 he took the lead in finding another schoolmaster. He was on friendly terms with two of the masters of Ayr Academy and they recommended a certain John Murdoch as a suitable person to teach his children. Burnes arranged for Murdoch to meet him at Simpson's Inn which was located close to the south end of the 'Auld Brig'[2] and to bring his writing book with him. The interview proved satisfactory and Murdoch was engaged to teach Robert and Gilbert and the children of four other families in the neighbourhood. He was a solemn youth, some 12 years older than his famous pupil, having been born at Ayr on 25 March, 1747. His father, also John Murdoch, was teacher and session clerk at Auchinleck.[3] Young Murdoch had been educated at Ayr Grammar School, then went on to complete his studies in Edinburgh before returning to his home town to look for a teaching post.

In a letter which Murdoch sent to the Irish antiquary, Joseph Cooper Walker, on 22 February, 1799, and reproduced by Dr. Currie,[4] he gives an account of his meeting with William Burnes and the conditions of his subsequent employment:

> 'In 1765, about the middle of March, Mr. W. Burnes came to Ayr and sent to the school, where I was improving in writing under my good friend Mr. Robinson, desiring that I would come and speak to him at a certain Inn, and bring my writing-book with me. This was immediately complied with. Having examined my writing, he was pleased with it (you will allow he was not difficult); and told me that he had received very satisfactory information from Mr. Tennant, the Master of the English School, concerning my improvement in English, and in his method of teaching. In the month

The Twa Brigs o' Ayr looking south, from the painting by Henry Duguid.
William Burnes crossed the 'Auld Brig' to meet Murdoch at Simpson's Inn,
which was at the south end.

of May following, I was engaged by Mr. Burnes, and four of his neighbours, to teach, and accordingly began to teach the little school at Alloway, which was situated a few yards from the argillaceous fabric above-mentioned. My five employers undertook to board me by turns and to make up a certain salary at the end of the year, provided my quarterly payments from the different pupils did not amount to that sum.'[5]

In the same letter he goes on to give an interesting account of the early education of Robert and Gilbert, the teaching methods which he employed and the school books which were most commonly in use. Of the two brothers, it was Gilbert who impressed Murdoch as being the most likely to court the Muses, and what is even more surprising, in view of later developments, is what transpired when he tried to teach the brothers a little church music:

'My pupil, Robert Burns, was then between six and seven years of age; his preceptor about eighteen. Robert and his younger brother, Gilbert had been grounded a little in English before they were put under my care. They both made a rapid progress in reading; and a tolerable progress in writing. In reading, dividing words into syllables by rule, spelling without book, parsing sentences, etc., Robert and Gilbert were generally at the upper end of the class, even when ranged with boys by far their seniors. The books most commonly used in the school were, the *Spelling Book*, the *New Testament*, the *Bible*, *Mason's Collection of Prose and Verse* and *Fisher's English Grammar*. They committed to memory the hymns and other poems of that

Sketch of Murdoch's house, c1894 which stood at 52 Sandgate, Ayr.
A plaque on the present building reads:
*Here stood the house of John Murdoch, schoolmaster, in which Robert Burns lodged in his
14th year and received lessons in English and French.*

collection, with uncommon facility. This facility was partly owing to the method pursued by their father and me in instructing them, which was to make them thoroughly acquainted with the meaning of every word in each sentence, that was to be committed to memory. By the bye, this may be easier done and at an earlier period than is generally thought. As soon as they were capable of it, I taught them to turn verse into its natural order; sometimes to substitute synonymous expressions for poetical words, and to supply all the ellipses. These, you know are the means of knowing that the pupil understands his author. These are excellent helps to the arrangement of words in sentences, as well as to a variety of expression.

Gilbert always appeared to me to possess a more lively imagination, and to be more of the wit than Robert. I attempted to teach them a little church-music. Here they were left far behind by all the rest of the school. Robert's ear, in particular, was dull, and his voice untunable. It was long before I could get them to distinguish one tune from another. Robert's countenance was grave, and expressive of a serious, contemplative, and thoughtful mind. Gilbert's face said 'Mirth with thee I mean to live', and certainly, if any person who knew the boys had been asked which of them was the most likely to court the Muses, he would surely have never guessed that Robert had a propensity of that kind.' [6]

Murdoch has often been mocked as a pedant, arising mainly from his description of William Burnes's cottage as 'an argillaceous fabric,' 'a mud edifice' and 'a tabernacle of clay.' James Mackay gives a possible reason for this when he writes that 'he was writing, in relative old age, to a man of some rank in society and established literary reputation.' [7]

The little house then selected for use as a school was located on the roadside directly opposite the cottage. It was still standing a hundred years later but was demolished in 1878.[8] The fees paid by the parents guaranteed Murdoch sixpence a day in addition to full board and lodging.

In his autobiographical letter to Dr. Moore, dated 2 August 1787, *(CL 248)*, Burns makes only casual reference to his early school days, but he dealt in more detail with the effect his early reading, under Murdoch, had on him:

> 'Though I cost the schoolmaster some thrashings, I made an excellent English scholar; and against the years of ten or eleven, I was absolutely a critic in substantive verbs, and particles ... The earliest thing of composition that I recollect taking pleasure in was 'The Vision of Mirza', and a hymn of Addison's beginning, 'How are thy servants blest, O Lord!'. I particularly remember one half-stanza which was music to my boyish ears -
>
> > 'For though in dreadful whirls we hung
> > High on the broken wave;'
>
> I met with these pieces in Mason's English Collection, one of my school-books.'

In a letter which Gilbert sent to Mrs. Dunlop many years later, and usually referred to as 'Gilbert's Narrative,' he gives a further account of their early education.

> 'The education of my brother and myself was in common, there being only twenty months between us, in respect of age. Under Mr. John Murdoch we learned to read English tolerably well, and to write a little. He taught us too the English grammar. I was too young to profit much from his lessons in grammar, but Robert made some proficiency in it, a circumstance of considerable weight in the unfolding of his genius and character, as he soon became remarkable for the fluency and correctness of his expression, and read the few books that came in his way with much pleasure and improvement; for even then he was a reader when he

could get a book. Murdoch, whose library at that time had no great variety in it, lent him *The Life of Hannibal*, which was the first book he read (the school books excepted) and almost the only one he had an opportunity of reading while he was at school; for the *Life of Wallace* which he classes with it in one of his letters, he did not see for some years afterwards when he borrowed it from the blacksmith who shod our horses.'[9]

Of all the schoolbooks to which Burns was introduced by Murdoch, it was a *Collection of Prose and Verse* which exerted the most influence on his young mind. The book was the work of Arthur Masson (Burns and Murdoch both misspelt his name as 'Mason') and contained selections from Shakespeare, Milton, Dryden, Addison, Thomson, Gray, Akenside and Shenstone as well as a number of minor poets, whose works are now almost forgotten. It also contained an assortment of moral, didactic and historical prose; and a selection of moral letters by Elizabeth Rowe. The influence which this book had on the youthful Burns cannot be overstated. The numerous quotations which appeared later in his correspondence came from poems which he had obviously memorised from this anthology.

By the end of 1765 William Burnes found that the cottage at Alloway was becoming too small for his steadily growing family. He was also anxious to keep his family together, rather than have them leave home to become hired servants on some distant farm. At Whitsun 1766, he took possession of the seventy acre farm of Mount Oliphant which lay two miles southeast of Alloway. For the next two years Robert and Gilbert continued to attend Murdoch's school at Alloway until early in 1768, when Murdoch obtained a teaching post in Dumfries. Gilbert recounts how Murdoch visited the farm before he left the district to take up his new appointment:

'Murdoch came to spend a night with us, and to take his leave when he was about to go into Carrick. He brought us a present and memorial of him, a small compendium of English Grammar, and the tragedy of *Titus Andronicus* and by way of passing the evening, he began to read the play aloud. We were all attention for some time, till presently the whole party was dissolved in tears. A female in the play (I have but a confused recollection of it) had her hands chopt off, her tongue cut out, and then was insultingly desired to call for water to wash her hands. At this, in an agony of distress, we with one voice desired he would read no more. My father observed that if we would not hear it out, it would be needless to leave the play with us. Robert replied that if it was left he would burn it. My father was going to chide him for this ungrateful return to his tutor's kindness; but Murdoch interposed, declaring that he liked to see so much sensibility; and he left the *School for Love* a comedy (translated I think from the French) in its place.'[10]

Some years prior to Murdoch taking up the teaching post at Alloway, William Burnes had started work on a theological manual, which was designed to give religious guidance to his children. It took the form of a dialogue between father and son in which the son puts questions to the father. William's *Manual of Religious Belief* was first published in 1875, almost a hundred years after his death, and shows that although it was compiled by him, it was transcribed by Murdoch. It would appear that Murdoch shared William Burnes's liberal religious views and that the manuscript was transcribed during the schoolmaster's stay in Alloway.

Silhouette of Gilbert Burns.

Many years later Murdoch recalled the happy hours he had spent with the Burnes's family in the cottage at Alloway. 'In this mean cottage, to which I myself was at times an inhabitant, I really believe there dwelt a larger portion of content, than in any palace in Europe. 'The Cotter's Saturday Night' will give some idea of the temper and manner that prevailed there.' [11]

William Burnes had apparently made a profound and lasting impression on Murdoch. In his letter to Walker he paid a moving and sincere tribute to William's character and integrity:

'I have always considered William Burnes as by far the best of the human race that ever I had the pleasure of being acquainted with - and many a worthy character I have known. I can cheerfully join with Robert in the last line of his epitaph - borrowed from Goldsmith:

'And ev'n his failing lean'd to vitue's side.'

He was an excellent husband, if I may judge from his assiduous attention to the ease and comfort of his worthy partner; and from her affectionate behaviour to him, as well as her unwearied attention to the duties of a mother.

He was a tender and affectionate father; he took pleasure in leading his children in the path of virtue; not driving them, as some parents do, to the performance of duties to which they themselves are averse. He took care to find fault but seldom, and therefore when he did rebuke, he was listened to with a kind of reverential awe. A look of disapprobation was felt, a reproof was severely so; and a strip of the *tawz*, even on the skirt of the coat, gave heart-felt pain, produced a loud lamentation, and brought forth a flood of tears.

He had the art of gaining the esteem and good-will of those that were labourers under him. I think I never saw him angry but twice; the one time, it was with the foreman of the band, for not reaping the field as he desired; and the other time, it was with an old man for using smutty innuendoes and *double entendres*. Were every foul-mouthed old man to receive a seasonable check in this way, it would be to the advantage of the rising generation. As he was at no time overbearing to inferiors, he was equally incapable of that passive, pitiful, paltry spirit that induces some people to keep 'booing and booing' in the presence of a great man. He always treated superiors with a becoming respect; but he never gave the smallest encouragement to aristocratical arrogance. But I must not pretend to give you a description of all the manly qualities, the rational and Christian virtues, of the venerable William Burnes. Time would fail me. I shall only add that he carefully practised every known duty, and avoided every thing that was living a life void of offence towards God and towards man. O for a world of men of such dispositions! We should then have no wars. I have often wished, for the good of mankind, that it were so customary to honour and perpetuate the memory of those who excel in moral rectitude, as it is to extol what are called heroic actions:- then would the mausoleum of the friend of my youth overtop and surpass most of the monuments I see in Westminster Abbey.

Although I cannot do justice to the character of this worthy man, yet you will perceive from these few particulars, what kind of person had the principal hand in the education of our poet. He spoke the English language with more propriety (both with respect to diction and pronunciation) than any man I ever knew, with no greater advantages. This had a very good effect on the boys, who began to talk and reason like men much sooner than their neighbours.' [12]

In 1772, having taught for some years in a school in Dumfries, Murdoch returned to Ayr to succeed as English master, David Tennant, who had been promoted to Latin master. Gilbert recalls:

'The remembrance of my father's former friendship, and his attachment to my brother, made him do every thing in his power for our improvement. He sent us Pope's works, and some other poetry, the first that we had an opportunity of reading, excepting what is contained in *The English Collection*, and in the volume of *The Edinburgh Magazine* for 1772; excepting also those excellent new songs that are hawked about the country in baskets, or exposed on stalls in the streets.

The summer after we had been at Dalrymple school, my father sent Robert to Ayr, to revise his English grammar, with his former teacher. He had been there only one week, when he was obliged to return, to assist at the harvest. When the harvest was over, he went back to school, where he remained two weeks; and this completes the account of his school education, excepting one summer quarter, some time afterwards, that he attended the parish school of Kirk-Oswald (sic), where he lived with a brother of my mother's to learn surveying.

During the last two weeks that he was with Murdoch, he himself was engaged in learning French, and he communicated the instructions he received to my brother, who, when he returned, brought home with him a French dictionary and grammar, and the *Adventures of Telemachus* in the original. In a little while, by the assistance of these books, he had acquired such a knowledge of the language, as to read and understand any French author in prose. This was considered as a sort of prodigy, and, through the medium of Murdoch, procured him the acquaintance of several lads in Ayr, who were at that time gabbling French, and the notice of some families, particularly that of Dr. Malcolm, where a knowledge of French was a recommendation....

Thus you see Mr. Murdoch was a principal means of my brother's improvements. Worthy man!' [13]

Murdoch himself has left an interesting account of this period:

'In 1773, Robert Burns came to board and lodge with me, for the purpose of revising English grammar, etc., that he might be better qualified to instruct his brothers and sisters at home. He was now with me day and night, in school, at all meals, and in all my walks. At the end of one week I told him that he was now pretty much master of the parts of speech, etc., I should like to teach him something of French pronunciation, that when he should meet with the name of a French town, ship officer, or the like, in the newspapers, he might be able to pronounce it something like a French word. Robert was glad to hear this proposal, and immediately we attacked the French with great courage. Now there was little else to be heard but the declension of nouns, the conjugation of verbs, etc. When walking together, and even at meals, I was constantly telling him the names of different objects as they presented themselves in French; so that he was hourly laying in a stock of words, and sometimes little phrases. In short, he took such pleasure in learning, and I in teaching, that it was difficult to say which of the two was most zealous in the business, and about the end of the second week of our study of the French, we began to read a little of the *Adventures of Telemachus,* in Fénélon's own words.'

Murdoch interrupts his narrative to record, in his quaint way, that Robert was obliged to return home to assist in the work of the harvest:

'But now the plains of Mount Oliphant began to whiten, and Robert was summoned to relinquish the pleasing scenes that surrounded the grotto of Calypso, and, armed with a sickle, to seek glory by signalising himself in the field of Ceres - and so he did; for although but about fifteen, I was told that he performed the work of a man.'

Although he had lost his prodigious pupil to the farm, Murdoch continued to keep in touch with Robert and the family and in his letter he pays tribute to the affection and devotion of Agnes Burnes.

'Thus was I deprived of my very apt pupil, and consequently, agreeable companion, at the end of three weeks, one of which was spent entirely in the study of English, and the other two chiefly in that of French. I did not, however, lose sight of him; but was a frequent visitant at his father's house when I had my half holiday, and very often went accompanied with one or two persons more intelligent than myself, that good William Burnes might enjoy a mental feast. Then the labouring oar was shifted to some other hand. The father and the son sat down with us, when we enjoyed a conversation, wherein solid reasoning, sensible remark, and a moderate seasoning of jocularity, were so nicely blended, as to render it palatable to all parties. Robert had a hundred questions to ask me about my French, etc., and the father, who had always rational information in view, had still some question to propose to my more learned friends, upon moral or natural philosophy, or some such interesting subject. Mrs. Burnes too was of the party as much as possible:

Burns Cottage in Winter from an old postcard.

'But still the house affairs would draw her thence,
Which, even as she could with haste dispatch,
She'd come again, and with a greedy ear
Devour up their discourse.'

And particularly that of her husband. At all times, and in all companies, she listened to him with a more marked attention than to any body else. When under the necessity of being absent while he was speaking, she seemed to regret as a real loss, that she had missed what the good man had said. This worthy woman, Agnes Brown, had the most thorough esteem for her husband of any woman I knew.' [14]

The house in the Sandgate where Robert lodged with Murdoch in 1773, was still standing at the beginning of the twentieth century, but was later demolished. A stone plaque was subsequently affixed to the south gable of the premises which took its place at 58 Sandgate, and this records that 'Here stood the house of John Murdoch, schoolmaster, in which Robert Burns lodged in his fourteenth year and received lessons in English and French.'

In 1776 John Murdoch left Ayr under a cloud. As a result of a petition which was laid before the magistrate by James Neill, procurator fiscal, he was dismissed from his post on 14 February, 1776. The complaint set forth that he did 'particularly within the house of Mrs. Tennant, inn-keeper in Ayr, as well as in the house of Patrick Auld, weaver in Ayr,

Drawing of Agnes Burns, the poet's mother.

utter the following, or such like, unworthy, base reproachful, and wicked expression - viz that he, Dr. William Dalrymple, was revengeful as hell, and as false as the devil; and that he was a liar, or a damned liar; that he the said John Murdoch, also called Dr. Dalrymple a hypocrite, or accused him of hypocrisy.'[15]

It would appear that Murdoch was intoxicated when he made those accusations, as Gilbert records that 'one evening that he (Murdoch) had been overtaken in liquor, he happened to speak somewhat disrespectfully of Dr. Dalrymple, the parish minister, who had not paid him that attention to which he thought himself entitled. In Ayr he might as well have spoken blasphemy.'[16] The Reverend Dr. William Dalrymple, who baptised Robert

Burns, was the senior minister of the collegiate charge of Ayr and was held in high esteem by his parishioners.

Following his dismissal from his teaching post in Ayr, Murdoch went to London, where he set himself up as a teacher of English and French. Shortly after he had settled in the capital, he made a tour of France, no doubt to improve his pronunciation of the French language. When in France he made the acquaintance of Colonel Fullarton, who was then secretary to the British Embassy in Paris. On his return to London he began to teach English and French, and Colonel Fullarton introduced several foreigners of rank to him, who received tutoring in English. Among them was the French statesman Talleyrand, who was then on a diplomatic visit to London. It is also of interest that one of his pupils in his old age was Mrs. Elizabeth Everett, granddaughter of the poet.[17]

In reply to a letter sent to Murdoch by Burns from Lochlie, on 15 January, 1783 *(CL 54)* which took him almost five years to answer, he wrote:

> 'If ever you come hither, you will have the satisfaction of seeing your poems relished by the Caledonians in London full as much as they can be by those in Edinburgh. We frequently repeat some of your verses in our Caledonian Society; and you may believe I am not a little vain that I have had some share in cultivating such a genius ...
> Pray let me know if you have any intention of visiting this huge, overgrown metropolis. It would afford matter for a large poem.'

Burns never went to London, but his younger brother William did, to work as a journeyman saddler. Burns wrote to Murdoch from Ellisland on 16 July 1790 *(CL 55)* asking him to get in touch with William and gave him William's employer's address in the Strand. About a fortnight before the letter reached Murdoch, however, William had, by some means found Murdoch's address and paid him a visit, when no doubt happy memories were revived of his early teaching days at Alloway.

The day after he received Burns's letter, Murdoch, having heard that William was ill, called at his lodgings only to find that he had died three days earlier of a putrid fever. A few days later his remains were interred in St. Paul's churchyard - Murdoch had the melancholy duty of acting as chief mourner at the funeral and sending to the poet news of his brother's death.[18]

It would appear that, in addition to teaching French and English, Murdoch also had a shop and library in Hart Street, Bloomsbury, where he sold stationery and published books. He assisted John Walker, the lexicographer, in performing for publication the third edition of his dictionary, which was published in 1802, and to have written the 'Rules to be observed by the natives of Scotland for attaining a just pronunciation of English', which are included in it. His own works are a *Radical Vocabulary of the French Language 1783; Pronunciation and Orthography of the French Language 1788; and a Dictionary of Distinctions in Three Alphabets, 1811.*[19]

Teaching French and English, compiling books and selling stationery, Murdoch seems to have done fairly well for a time, but the French Revolution flooded London with refugee priests, many of whom turned to teaching their native language for support. This cut heavily into Murdoch's income and in his latter years, illness reduced him to the brink of destitution. A small sum was raised for him by some admirers of the poet, but was barely sufficient and he died on 20 April, 1824 at the age of seventy-seven. [20]

That John Murdoch's teaching had a profound influence on the education of Robert Burns there can be little doubt. His methods certainly encouraged the virtues of clarity and precision. As one writer observed 'That Burns, in later life never had any difficulty in saying precisely what he meant, he probably owed to Murdoch's severe drill'. His training in spelling and grammar were such that there never was a trace of the rustic in his speech, written or spoken. While it is true that Murdoch did not introduce Burns to any Scottish vernacular literature, he nevertheless gave him a grounding in English literature, especially the poets from Shakespeare to Shenstone. Murdoch was also responsible for introducing Burns to the French language, although it would appear that the teacher also was in the learning process. In a letter which Burns sent to Murdoch dated 15 January 1789 (CL 54/55), he described Murdoch as 'a masterly teacher' and in the same letter wrote 'I have not forgotten, nor never will forget the many obligations I lie under to your kindness and friendship'. Gilbert, as we have seen, confirmed that 'Mr. Murdoch was a principal means of

Mount Oliphant Farm, from the painting by Monro S. Orr.

Alloway's 'Auld Haunted Kirk' and Kirkyard.

my brother's improvement. Worthy man!' John Murdoch certainly occupies a worthy niche in the life story of Robert Burns.

William Burnes expressed a wish to be buried in Alloway's Kirkyard. His grave is just inside the entrance gate, and bears the following tribute which his son Robert paid him in the epitaph he wrote for the tombstone:

> O ye whose cheek the tear of pity stains,
> Draw near with pious rev'rence, and attend !
> Here lie the loving husband's dear remains,
> The tender father, and the gen'rous friend;
> The pitying heart that felt for human woe,
> The dauntless heart that feared no human pride,
> The friend of man – to vice alone a foe;
> For, "ev'n his failings lean'd to virtue's, side."

TARBOLTON AND IRVINE

'In Tarbolton, ye ken, there are proper young men
And proper young lasses and a' man.'

'Irvine's bairns are bonie a.'

DAVID SILLAR

Old print of Spittleside.

The farm of Spittleside is situated about half a mile north of the village of Tarbolton, and it was there in 1760 that David Sillar was born. He was the third of four sons of Patrick Sillar, who was tenant of the farm. Allan Cunningham described David Sillar as a 'good scholar',[1] but there is no evidence to suggest that he received more than a grounding in reading, writing and arithmetic. What he seems to have possessed, however, was a modicum of native wit and an above average desire for learning. In his early years he worked as a herd boy, and later as a ploughman on his father's farm. Like many a young man of his day he courted the muse, and in a poem entitled 'Epistle to the Critics', he writes about his early life and education.

> Then know when I these pieces made,
> Was toiling for my daily bread;
> A scanty learning I enjoy'd,
> Sae judge how I hae it employ'd.
> I ne'er depended for my knowledge
> On school, academy or college,
> I gat my learnin' at the flail,
> An' some I catch'd at the plough-tail;
> Amang the brutes I own I'm bred,
> Since herding was my native trade.

> Some twa three books I read wi' care,
> Which I had borrow'd here an' there,
> The actions an' the ways o' men
> I took great pains an' care to ken,
> Frae them, their manners, an' their looks,
> Their words, their actions, an' frae books;
> On these for knowledge I relied,
> Without anither for my guide,
> Latin an' Greek I have never knew sic,
> An sae how can my works be classic?

One writer has stated that Sillar 'was not over fond of manual work and from an early date he had been preparing himself for the duties of a schoolmaster.'[2] This seems to be borne out by the fact that in 1781 he acted as interim teacher in the parish school during a vacancy. He subsequently applied for the post but was unsuccessful, the appointment being given to John Wilson, immortalised by Burns as 'John Hornbook o' the Clachan.' By this time, no doubt feeling confident in the role of teacher, Sillar opened an 'adventure' school at Commonside on the outskirts of Tarbolton, but it was abandoned after a short period through lack of support.

In the absence of direct information, it would appear that Sillar's friendship with Robert Burns originated in 1780, or early in 1781. The latter date is the more likely as it was in 1780 that Burns and a few of his cronies formed the Tarbolton Bachelors' Club, of which Sillar did not become a member until May of the following year.[3] Had they been acquainted at the time of the Club's inception, it is almost certain that Sillar would have been one of the founder members.

Old postcard of Bachelors' Club, shows the Cross Keys Inn (centre background)
which stood on the south side of Loudon Street, opposite the Cross.
It was demolished in 1821 when Earl Grey Street was constructed.

In a letter which Sillar sent to Robert Aiken, the Ayr lawyer, ('Orator Bob'), he has left a vivid picture of Burns as he knew him in the Lochlie period.

'Mr. Robert Burns was some time in the parish of Tarbolton prior to my acquaintance with him. His social disposition easily procured him acquaintance, but a certain satirical seasoning, with which he and all poetical geniuses are in some degree influenced, while it set the rustic circle in a roar, was not unaccompanied by its kindred attendant - suspicious fear. I recollect hearing his neighbours observe he had a great deal to say for himself, and that they suspected his principles. He wore the only tied hair in the Parish, and in the church, his plaid, which was of a particular colour, I think 'fillemot', he wrapped in a particular manner round his shoulders. These surmises and his exterior had such a magical influence on my curiosity, as made me particularly solicitous of his acquaintance. Whether my acquaintance with Gilbert was casual or premeditated, I am not now certain. By him I was introduced not only to his brother, but to the whole of that family, where, in a short time, became a frequent, and I believe, not unwelcome visitant.

After the commencement of my acquaintance with the Bard, we frequently met upon Sundays at Church, when, between sermons, instead of going with our friends or lasses to the inn, we often took a walk in the fields. In these walks I have frequently been struck by his facility in addressing the fair sex, and many times, when I have been bashfully anxious how to express myself, he would have entered into conversation with them with the greatest ease and freedom, and it was generally a deathblow to our conversation, however agreeable, to meet a female acquaintance. Some of the few opportunities of a noontide walk that a country life allows her labourious sons, he spent on the banks of the river, or in the woods in the neighbourhood of Stair, a situation peculiarly adapted to the genius of a rural bard. Some book (especially one of those mentioned in his letter to Mr. Murdoch) he always carried, and read when not otherwise employed. It was likewise his custom to read at table. In one of my visits to Lochlea, in time of a sowen supper, he was so intent on reading, I think 'Tristram Shandy', that his spoon, falling out his hand, made him explain, in a tone scarcely audible, 'Alas, poor Yorick.' !!!' [4]

In the concluding part of the letter Sillar comments on Burns's religious beliefs, which were then considered by some of the Tarbolton folk as bordering on heresy. This was before the great outpouring of the Mossgiel period, when he fired his satirical broadsides against the Auld Lichts.

'He had in his youth paid considerable attention to the arguments for and against the doctrine of original sin, then making considerable noise in the neighbourhood of Ayr, and having perused Dr. Taylor's book on that subject, and also a book called 'Letter concerning the Religion essential to Man', his opinions, when he came to Tarbolton, were consequently favourable to what you Ayr people call the 'moderate side'. The religion of the people of Tarbolton at this time was purely that of their fathers, founded on the 'Westminster Confession' and taught by one generation to another, uncontaminated by reading, reflection, and conversation; and though divided into different sectaries, the 'Shorter Catechism' was the line which bounded all their controversies. The slightest insinuation of Taylor's

Bachelors' Club today.

opinions made his neighbours suspect, and some even avoid him, as an heretical and dangerous companion. Such was Burns, and such were his associates, when, in May 1781, I was admitted a member of the Bachelors' Club.'[5]

The book by Dr. Taylor, to which Sillar refers, was *The Scriptural Doctrine of Original Sin Proposed to Free and Candid Examination,* a third edition of which had been published in 1750.

Scott Douglas has left the following note on Sillar, with reference to the Bachelors' Club: I quote from a letter of Mr. Sillar, 29th September, 1828, the lines :

> Of birth or blood we do not boast,
> Nor gentry does our club afford;
> But ploughmen and mechanics we,
> In Nature's simple dress record.
>
> Let nane e'er join us who refuse,
> To aid the lads that haud the ploughs,
> To choose their friends and wale their wives,
> To ease the labours of their lives.

These lines, therefore (hitherto ascribed to Burns) are in fact the lawful property of Mr. Sillar.[6]

It is difficult to accept the claims that the two verses were written by Sillar. When Dr. Currie printed the 'History of the rise, proceedings and regulations of the Bachelors' Club', only the first four lines of verse headed the preamble. While it is true that the rules, etc. of the club were not put down in writing until the Autumn of 1782, it is generally agreed that they are the work of Burns. The second verse, as quoted above, is so inferior that one suspects that it was added by Sillar, when he wrote to Scott Douglas in 1828.[7]

Following Sillar's introduction to Burns by Gilbert, they became boon companions. Both shared a love of versifying and music, and undoubtedly, it was those interests that brought them together. It was about this time that Burns took up the fiddle, probably due to the influence of Sillar, who played the instrument reasonably well. Burns never really mastered it, although he could scrape out a tune, usually to the great discomfort of those who were within earshot. Sillar, on the other hand, was sufficiently accomplished to try his hand at composing, and one of his airs so impressed Burns that he set the words of 'A rosebud by my early walk' to it. *(CW 318)*. The song was written in honour of Jenny Cruikshank, the twelve year old daughter of William Cruikshank, classical master at the High School in Edinburgh. Burns's words are ageless, but Sillar's tune has become a museum piece. It is in Strathspey time, but contains too many unvocal intervals which renders it unfit for the average voice.[8] Burns sent it to James Johnson and it was included in the *Scots Musical Museum*, but the tune is almost unknown today and is never sung.

In his autobiographical letter to Dr. Moore, Burns wrote:

> 'A country lad rarely carries in an amour without an assisting confident - I possessed a curiosity, zeal and intrepid dexterity in these matters which recommended me a proper Second in duels of that kind; and I daresay, I felt as much pleasure at being in the secret of half the amours of the parish, as ever did Premier at knowing the intrigues of half the courts of Europe.' *(CL 252)*.

One of the amours to which Burns acted as confident, or 'blackfoot', as it was known, was between David Sillar and Peggy Orr, who was nursemaid at Stair House, the residence of Mrs. Catherine Stewart, which stood on the banks of the river Ayr, about three miles south of Tarbolton. Legend has it that Burns introduced Peggy to Sillar following a church service, and both accompanied her back to Stair House, where within a short time they were welcome visitors in the kitchen. While not forgetting the main purpose of their visits, it seems that the evenings were enlivened by Sillar playing the fiddle and the poet reciting some of his own compositions, copies of which he left behind for the further enjoyment of Peggy and the housekeeper, Mary Crosbie. One or two copies eventually came into the hands of Mrs. Stewart, who was so captivated by them, that on Burns's next visit to Stair, he was invited into the drawing room where he engaged in conversation with the lady of the house. Writing to Mrs. Stewart some five years later, when he was planning to leave Scotland, he said, 'One feature of your character, I shall ever with grateful pleasure remember, the reception I got when I had the honour of waiting on you at Stair' *(CL 125)*. In 1791, when he compiled for the collection now known as the Afton MS, he wrote in the dedication, 'To the first person of her sex and rank that patronised his humble lays.' *(CL 126)*.

On each of their visit to Stair, Sillar pursued his ardent courtship of Peggy supported and encouraged by his 'blackfoot'. Their united efforts eventually were successful when Peggy accepted Sillar's proposal of marriage. The ceremony was sealed in the kitchen of Stair House, according to the custom of those days, such as exchange of a broken coin, hand clasping, and solemn vows made in the presence of Mrs. Crosbie and Burns as witnesses.[9] Unfortunately the contract was short-lived as Peggy rued her engagement and expressed a wish to be released from it. This was readily granted by Sillar who, under the circumstances, could see no prospect of future happiness with Peggy.

Tarbolton in those days was not short of versifiers. In addition to Burns and Sillar, there was Saunders Tait (see page 52), an itinerant tailor, whose rough doggerel verses chronicled all the events of the neighbourhood, and castigated anyone who provoked his displeasure. He was a popular and 'weel-kent' figure in the village and his rhyming effusions were highly applauded by the rustics, giving credence to the statement made by Sillar, when he described Tarbolton folk as 'uncontaminated by reading, reflection and conversation.' Both Burns and Sillar became the objects of Tait's scurrilous verse. Obviously there was an element of jealousy, as Tait would not take too kindly to anyone who was likely to usurp his position as 'village laureate'. Burns, it seems, had 'made a sang on him', now unfortunately lost, but it would be safe to assume that it contained a measure of Burns's 'satirical seasoning'. In reply Tait directed his spleen in most abusive verse, not only against the young poet from Lochlie, but against William Burnes, whom he flayed mercilessly over that unfortunate man's dispute with his landlord, David McLure.

Sillar's 'crime' was that in conversation with John Wilson ('Dr. Hornbook of the Clachan'), he had likened Tait's muse to a tumbling cart. This was a very primitive vehicle, with wooden axles and wooden wheels, not bound with iron, and being seldom greased, made a terrible grating noise. The simile so angered Tait that in revenge he replied with sixteen verses of uncouth vulgar rhyme, called 'Sillar and Tait' or 'Tit for Tat', which begins with the couplet:

> My pipe wi' wind I maun gae fill'er,
> And play a tune to David Sillar

There then follows a crude account of Sillar's 'ongauns' with a girl called Susie, and also includes an accusation that he and Burns are responsible for six girls in the parish being in a 'certain condition'. While it is impossible to accept that Burns and Sillar were such village

Stair House.
Home of Mrs. Catherine Stewart where Burns acted as 'blackfoot' to Davie Sillar when he wooed
Peggy Orr one of the housemaids. It was here that Mrs. Stewart read some of Burns poems and
was one of his first patrons.

Lotharios as suggested by Tait, the old adage, 'there's no smoke without fire' cannot be entirely discounted. Tait may have been expressing the consensus of opinion of Tarbolton folk when he wrote:

> There's nane can sound the bawdy horn
> Like you and Burns.[10]

The social hours which Burns and Sillar enjoyed in each other's company were interrupted in Midsummer, 1781 when Burns went to Irvine to learn flax-dressing. Scott Douglas states that 'David Sillar assured Mr. Robert Chambers that this notion originated from William Burnes, who thought of becoming entirely a lint-farmer, and, by way of keeping as much of the profits as he could within his own family, of making his son a flax-dresser.'[11]

This statement is at variance with Gilbert Burns's account of the venture. He said that Robert wished to be in a position to marry, but could see no prospect of doing so as long as he remained a farmer:

> 'He and I had for several years taken land of my father for the purpose of raising flax on our own account. In the course of selling it, Robert began to think of turning flax-dresser, both as being suitable to his grand view of settling in life, and as subservient to the flax-raising. He accordingly wrought at the business of flax-dressing in Irvine for six months, but abandoned it at that period, as neither agreeing with his health nor inclination.'[12]

Towards the end of 1783, Sillar left Tarbolton and settled in Irvine, where he set up business as a grocer in a shop at the base of the Tolbooth and next to the Council Chambers. He was then in his twenty-third year and, writing to a friend on 21st January, 1786, he recorded his arrival in the seaport town:

> It is twa years, an' something mair
> Sin' I left Kyle i' this same shire,
> An' cam' to trade an' think an' fare,
> Like ither men,
> 'Side Irvine banks, an' country fair,
> O'Kinnikem (District of Cunninghame).

Why he chose to go into business in Irvine, and as a grocer, is not known. No doubt the experience and knowledge of the town which Burns had gained, during his heckling venture would be related to Sillar, and may have influenced his decision. It is more likely, however, that he was attracted to Irvine as it was then the second largest town in Ayrshire, with a population of around 4000, and second only to Greenock as the busiest seaport in the West of Scotland.

In the summer of 1784 Burns penned the principal part of what was to become the 'First Epistle to Davie, a Brother Poet, Lover, Ploughman and Fiddler' *(CW 86)*. Gilbert Burns furnished some particulars of the history of the poem to Dr. Currie in 1798:

House of John Wilson ('Dr. Hornbrook o' the Clachan') in Tarbolton (one-storied house beyond the tavern).

'Among the earliest of his poems was the 'Epistle to Davie'. Robert often composed without any regular plan. When anything made a strong impression on his mind, so as to arouse it to poetic exertion, he would give way to the impulse, and embody the thought in rhyme. If he hit on two or three stanzas to please him, he would then think of proper introductory, connecting, and concluding stanzas; hence the middle of a poem was often first produced. It was, I think, in summer 1784 when, in the interval of harder labour, he and I were weeding in the garden (kail-yard) that he repeated to me the principal part of the epistle. I believe the first idea of Robert's becoming an author was started on this occasion. I was much pleased with the epistle, and said to him that I was of opinion it would bear being printed, and that it would be well received by people of good taste; that I thought it at least equal, if not superior, to many of Allan Ramsay's epistles, and that the merit of these, and much other Scotch poetry, seemed to consist principally in the knack of the expression, but here, there was a strain of interesting sentiment, and the Scotticism of the language scarcely seemed affected, but appeared to be the natural language of the poet.' [13]

Gilbert's account seems to indicate that the poem was not completed until later that year, and the fact that it was not sent to Sillar until January, 1785 appears to confirm this. James Kinsley states that it was probably not drafted as an epistle to Sillar. Certainly the 'principal part' of the epistle is devoted to the disparity between poverty and riches, and the consolation the poet could expect if he ever had to go a-begging. Kinsley also is of the opinion that the following lines were probably an addition:[14]

> There's a 'the pleasures o' the heart,
> The lover an' the frien',
> Ye hae your Meg, your dearest part,
> And I my darling Jean. *(CW 88)*.

The inclusion of the above verse may have been a last minute decision by Burns, as Jean Armour was then established as the poet's 'Deity'. Most writers have accepted that Meg, named in the lines was Margaret or Peggy Orr, who was the object of Sillar's courtship at Stair House. This is extremely unlikely as Sillar's affair with Peggy ended, presumably when he left Tarbolton in 1783, and is more or less confirmed by his marriage soon after settling in Irvine. His first wife (he was married twice) was a widow, whose maiden name was Margaret Gemmill, and probably she was the Meg to whom Burns was referring.[15]

On 30th October, 1786 David Sillar attended the inaugural meeting of the Mauchline Conversation Society. Dr. Currie left this account of its formation:

'After the family of our bard removed from Tarbolton to the neighbourhood of Mauchline, he and his bother were requested to assist in forming a similar institution there. The regulations of the Club in Mauchline were nearly the same as those of the club at Tarbolton, but one laudable alteration was made. The fines for non-attendance had at Tarbolton been spent on enlarging their scanty potations. At Mauchline it was fixed that the money so arising, should be set apart for the purchase of books... Though the records of the society at Tarbolton are lost, and those of the society at Mauchline have not been transmitted, yet we may safely affirm, that our poet was a distinguished member of both these associations.' [16]

The original minute book of the Mauchline Conversation Society was discovered in Victoria, New South Wales in 1893, and interesting extracts were published in the *Kilmarnock Standard* for 25th June of the same year. These show that the Burns family had been settled for two years in Mossgiel before the formation of the society, and it would appear that the poet was not a member, as he is not mentioned as having attended any of the meetings. The minute book covers the period from 30th October, 1786 to 20th November, 1797, and shows that Gilbert Burns and David Sillar were active members

Irvine Townhead with Tolbooth c. 1804.

throughout that time. Both were founder members, as was Sillar's brother, John. The society met monthly, and a president was chosen for each meeting. Sillar was president on nine occasions, when the society debated the following subjects, which seem to have concentrated mainly on matters surrounding love and marriage.

October 29, 1787   'Whether real love can be said
                            to be a universal passion or not.'

September 2, 1788   'Whether a man ought to defer marriage
                            until he find a woman capable to be his
                            bosom friend or not'.

June 1, 1789   'Whether it would be better for the
                            generality of men to marry in early life
                            when love first suggests to them the idea, or
                            to defer it till maturer age, when circumstances
                            in the world may be more favourable'.

March 14, 1791   'Which is most an object of desire, an enlightened
                            understanding or a feeling heart?'

The Cross. Kilmarnock, c1890. The statue shown was that of Sir James Shaw who was born at Mosshead, near Riccarton in 1764. He rose to be Lord Mayor of London in 1805, and was created a Baronet in 1809. After the death of Robert Burns in 1796, he supported his widow and assisted in gaining employment for his sons. The monument, which was raised by public subscription, was unveiled on 4th August, 1848.

July 4, 1791	'Whether love in the present state of society is generally more productive of pain or pleasure.'
November 26, 1792	'Whether trouble of mind or trouble of body is most prejudicial to the constitution.'
March 19, 1793	'Whether the present war with France may be supposed to turn out for or against the cause of liberty.'
January 26, 1795	'Whether prosperity or adversity is most likely to cause keenness of pursuit after their business in the minds of men in general.'
June 6, 1796	'Whether when a man is courting a woman it is better to pay his visits in a public or in a private manner.' [17]

Apparently the distance between Irvine and Mauchline was no obstacle to Sillar as he was present at all meetings in all seasons. He probably made the journey on horseback and stayed overnight with a friend or at one of the local inns.

It might have been expected that when Sillar went to Irvine to 'trade, an' think, an' fare like ither men', he would have abandoned poetry altogether in order to concentrate on business, but this does not seem to have been the case. In his first few years in the town he spent much of his time courting the muse, as many of his published poems are related to Irvine and its environs. It is doubtful if he ever entertained any thought of publishing his verses, until prompted by the extraordinary success of Burns's first edition. Sillar obtained fourteen subscribers for Burns's volume, which was published by John Wilson of Kilmarnock in July, 1796. Three years later, *Poems by David Sillar* appeared from the same press. The poems were dedicated to Hugh Montgomerie Esq. of Skelmorlie ('Sodger Hugh') afterwards Earl of Eglinton, and were prefaced by the following introduction:

'Mankind in general, but particularly those who have had the advantage of a liberal author, who has been denied that privilege, to attempt either instruction or amusement. But however necessary a learned education may be in Divinity, Philosophy, or the Sciences, it is a fact that some of the best Poetical Performances amongst us have been composed by illiterate men. Natural genius alone is sufficient to constitute a poet; for the imperfections in the works of many poetical writers, may, he believes, with more justice to want of genius. He leaves every person to judge of his by his writings. The following pieces were composed just as the objects they treat of struck his imagination;

and, if they give others the same pleasure in reading, which they gave him in composing, he will have the satisfaction of obtaining his principal end in publishing.

The design of the author in his publication is by no means to offend, but to instruct and amuse, and although some, with greater judgement and sagacity, might have steered a more prudent course for themselves, yet he is conscious, however he may be treated, of having kept clear of personal reflections. The approbation of the judicious though few, will always support him under the censure of the superstitious and prejudiced, and inspire him with a proper disregard for popular applause. For the liberal encouragement his respectable and numerous subscribers have given him, the author returns his sincere thanks.'

> For back'd by them, his foes, thro' spite
> May girn their fill, but daurna bite.

His poems bear witness to the truth of his own axiom - that the ill success of poets proceeds as often from lack of genius as from a deficiency of education.[18] The verses, though sensibly composed, lack force and many are marred by indelicacies, unredeemed by the saving grace of humour. They are not, however, without a leavening of wisdom, as illustrated in his advice to the 'Lassies of Irvine' -

> The time o' youth's a pleasin' time.
> For lasses young an' dainty,
> Before they pass out owre the line,
> Hae aften lads in plenty:
> But if they chance to pass their prime,
> Braw wooers then grow scant aye;
> Then dinna, tho' your sun does shine,
> Think ye'll get leave to rant aye
> Wi' lads ilk day.

In many of his poems Burns sang in praise of Scotch Whisky, but Sillar obviously had little respect for it. In a poem of twenty stanzas, he writes of its ill effects, and even goes the length of naming it as one of the worst curses of Scotland. If his verses do not display the same poetic forte as his gifted friend, they are, at least, seasoned with good common sense, as the following stanzas show -

> Poets wi' muckle wit an' skill,
> Hae sung the virtues o' Scot's yill;
> An' wi' the worth o' Highland gill
> Out ears hae rung;

The bad effects o' whisky still
    Remain unsung.

I'm sair surprised how whisky poison,
Frae men o' sense, has got sic fraisin'
They might hae sung wi' greater reason,
    Gude caller water,
Which cheaper is in any season,
    An' slockens better.

But whisky, warst o' Scotland's curses,
Than it I ken o' nane that worse is
It mak's poor bodies draw their purses,
    Though hunger stare,
An, pawn their duds for't aff their arses,
    An' rin threadbare.

The only epistle of Sillar to Burns, which has survived, was obviously written following Burns's successful entry into Edinburgh;

While Reekie's bards your muse commen',
An' praise the numbers o' your pen,
Accept this kin'ly frae a frien'
    Your Dainty Davie,
Wha ace o' hearts does still remain,
    Ye may believe me.

Let *Coila's* plains wi' me rejoice
An' praise the worthy Bard whose lays,
Their worth and beauty high doth raise
    To lasting fame;
His works, his worth, will ever praise
    An' crown his name.
      * * * * * * *

I ne'er was muckle gi'en to praisin',
Or else ye might be sure o' fraisin',
For troth, I think, in solid reason,
    Your kintra reed
Plays sweet as Robin Fergusson,
    Or his on Tweed (Ramsay)

But tho' the tout o' Fame may please you
Let na the flatterin' ghaist o'erheeze you;
Ne'er flyte nor fraise tae gar fo'k rouse you
    For men o' skill,
When ye write weel; will always praise you
    Out o' gude will.
      * * * * * * *

Your *Luath, Caesar* bites right sair,
An' when ye paint the *Holy Fair,*
Ye draw it to a very hair,
    Or when ye turn,
An' sing the follies o' the fair,
    How sweet ye mourn!

Sae to conclude, auld frien' an' neebor,
Your muse forgetna weel to feed her,
Then steer through life wi' birr an' vigour
    To win a horn,
Whase soun' shall reach ayont the Tiber
    'Mang ears unborn.

It was in reply to these verses from Sillar that Burns wrote Second Epistle to Davie', which Sillar prefixed to his volume of poems.

Auld Neebor,
I'm three times doubly owre your debtor,
For your auld-farrent, frien'ly letter
Tho' I maun say't, I doubt ye flatter
    Ye speak sae fair,
For my puir, silly, rhymin' clatter
    Some less maun sair.

Hale be your heart, hale e your fiddle,
Lang may your elbuck jink an' diddle
Tae cheer you thro' the weary widdle
    O' war'ly cares,
Till bairns' bairns kindly cuddle
    Your auld gray hairs.

* * * * * * *

Leeze me on rhyme! It's aye a treasure
My chief, amaist my only pleasure,
At hame, a-fiel', at work or leisure,
    The muse, poor hizzie!
Tho' rough an' raploch be her measure,
    She's seldom lazy.

Haud tae the muse, my dainty Davie,
The warl' may play you monie a shavie;
But for the muse, she'll never leave ye,
    Tho' o'er sae puir,
Na, even tho' limpin' wi the spavie
    Frae door tae door.

When Sillar's book of poems was published in 1789, Burns was settled in Ellisland, and the two friends do not appear to have met again. A very brief correspondence ensued, and although Sillar's letters have not survived, three of Burns's letters are extant. In the earliest one, written on 5th August, 1789, Burns expresses his vexation at the impersonal nature of Sillar's last letter. It also shows the interest Burns took in the publication of Sillar's book of poems, and the effort he was making to get subscribers:

'My dear sir,
    I was half in thoughts not to have written you at all, by way of revenge for the two d-mn'd business letters you sent me - I wanted to know all about your Publication, what were your views, your hopes, fears, etc. etc. in commencing Poet in Print - in short, I wanted you to write to Robin like his old acquaintance, Davie; and not in the style of Mr. Tare to Mr. Trot -

Mr. Trot,
Sir,
This comes to advise you that your fifteen barrels of herrings were, by the blessing of God, shipped safe on board the Lovely Janet, Q.D.C., Duncan McLeerie Master, etc., etc., etc.,
I hear you have commenced, Married Man, so much the better though perhaps your Muse may not fare the better for it - I know not whether the NINE GIPSEYS are jealous of my Lucky, but they are a good deal shyer since I could boast the important relation of Husband.

I have got I think about eleven Subscribers for you My acquaintance in this place is yet, but very limited else I might have had more. When you send Mr. Auld in Dumfries his, you may with them pack me eleven; should I need more, I can write you, should these be too many, they can be returned. My best compliments to Mrs. Sillar, and believe me to be, Dear David.

Ever yours
Robert Burns'

(CL 536)

The next letter was also sent from Ellisland on 22nd January, 1790. It was a brief, hurried note in which Burns enclosed £2.4/- for the eleven copies of the poems which he had collected from subscribers in the Dumfries area. *(CL 536).*[19]

Sillar, like Burns, corresponded with John Lapraik, the unfortunate bard of Muirkirk. In one of his epistles to him he touches on controversial subjects, and expresses thoughts and beliefs that were anything but agreeable to the rigidly orthodox. In another poem entitled 'Satan's Complaint, or the Vision', he attempts to vindicate the character of 'Auld Nick', which must have exposed him to considerable censure.

The publication of his poems met with little success, and the work of preparing them for the press, probably contributed to the failure of his grocery business. He became bankrupt and was imprisoned in the Tolbooth for a paltry debt of five pounds. An appeal to one of his brothers, who was then a prosperous merchant in Liverpool, met with a refusal. It is said that this cruel denial of aid, from a source where he had expected understanding and support, left an indelible impression on his mind and completely changed his outlook on life. It was at this time, in his extremity that he applied to Burns for help. His request came at a most unfortunate time as Burns was then in financial straits himself. All he could offer was his sympathy, as he explained in his letter to Sillar, probably written in the early summer of 1791:

'My dear Sir,
I am extremely sorry to hear of your misfortune, and the more so, as it is not in my power to give you any assistance. I am just five shillings rich at present, tho' I was considerably richer three days ago, when I was obliged to pay twenty pounds for a man who took me in to save a rotten credit. I heedlessly gave him my name on the back of a bill, wherein I had no concern, and he gave me the bill to pay. To write you a long letter of news, etc., would but insult your present unfortunate feelings: I trust your many rich and powerful friends will enable you to get clear of that flinty-hearted scoundrel, whose name I detest.

Yours,
Robert Burns' *(CL 576)*

Following his failures in business and his brief imprisonment, Sillar went to Edinburgh. What his purpose was in going to the capital is not known. One writer has suggested that he may have been seeking employment as a copying clerk.[20] Had he known of the advice which Burns gave to John Wilson, who had considered similar employment, he would never have entertained such a prospect. *(CL566)*. Sillar failed to find whatever he was seeking in Edinburgh and returned to Irvine where he set up a school, chiefly for the instruction of young seamen in the science of navigation. His knowledge of this subject must have been for some time rather limited, but by application and perseverance his venture soon became a success. In the course of a few years, his school provided him with an income of £100. In the Burgh Records for 1794 he is described as 'David Sillar, Schoolmaster', and in the same year he was appointed Quartermaster at a salary of £5 per annum. In 1797 he must have felt himself sufficiently qualified to apply for the vacant post as teacher of English, writing and arithmetic at the Academy, but his application was unsuccessful. [21]

His success in life was now established but greater fortune was to follow. His younger brother, who had succeeded his father at Spittleside, died during the term of the lease which had still a few years to run; it reverted to David, along with a considerable amount of money. As he decided to continue with his school in Irvine, it suggests, perhaps that the sum of money he inherited was not enough to provide a sufficient income on which to live. At any rate, it was agreed that Mrs. Sillar (his second wife) should manage the farm at Spittleside, while he returned there at week-ends.

His eldest brother, Robert left the farm at an early age to learn the business of soap boiling with a relative in Ayr. After a few years there, he journeyed south to Liverpool, where he entered into business as general merchant. He was so successful that John, the next eldest, was persuaded to join him. Within a year or two, they were both engaged in a lucrative trade with Africa, and John latterly went there to look after that end of the business. He died in Africa, and as a Mr. Walker, his partner, was involved, it was many years before David received a settlement of John's estate. Finally, the sum of £12,000, which had been held in Chancery, was divided between Walker's heirs and David. Meanwhile, about 1811, Robert died, and being a bachelor, like John, the whole of his monies and effects passed to David. As he was particularly reticent on the subject, the exact amount of the fortune he inherited is not known, but it must have been considerable. He was now a rich man, but was frequently heard to say, that five pounds from his brother at the time of his imprisonment, would have done him more good than all the wealth he had ultimately left him.[22] Following brother Robert's death, Sillar gave up his school in Irvine and resided at Spittleside until 1814, when he returned to Irvine.

Some writers have portrayed Sillar as parsimonious, having accepted the canard that when asked to contribute towards the Burns Monument on the banks of the Doon, he replied,

'I cannot well do so. You starved him when alive, and you cannot with good grace erect a monument to him now.' This lie was nailed, finally in 1959, when John McVie published irrefutable proof that Sillar's name was included in the list of subscribers to the Monument Fund, as having subscribed the sum of £1.1s. He gave two donations of £50 to Irvine Academy, and because of his generosity he was made a director for life. He also lent money to various people, including £4,000 to the Earl of Eglinton and £2,000 to the daughters of Mrs. Stewart of Stair, Burns's first patroness.[23] Those who knew him intimately regarded him as a man of stern justice, sometimes generous, but not ostentatious in the giving. He was aware that his good fortune attracted many who had ignored him previously, but he held to those who had been his friends in the less fortunate period of his life.

Sillar prided himself that, except on two occasions, he had never attended any place of worship in Irvine, other than the Established Church under the Rev. James Richmond. His two 'lapses' were in response to a request by Mrs. Stewart of Stair, who wished to have some account of the Buchanites, who were at that time causing quite a stir in Irvine. Accordingly he attended two of their meetings, and the Rev. Hugh White of the Relief Church, who had observed him taking notes, spoke to him at the close of the service. He expressed the hope that the notes were in the same spirit as that in which they had been given. Sillar said the notes had been taken with the sole object of giving information to a friend and offered them to Mr. White to read. This he did and returned them to Sillar, with the observation that they were a fair report of the meeting. Unfortunately Sillar's letter to Mrs. Stewart, giving his account of the Buchanites, has not survived, and it is reported that he often regretted that he had not retained a copy.

When Sillar returned to Irvine in 1814, he bought a house at Kirkgatehead, at the corner of Hill Street, unfortunately demolished many years ago. He took an active interest in local affairs and was for some time a councillor of Irvine Town Council. He also served as a magistrate for about two years. Two characteristic anecdotes, associated with his term as magistrate, have fortunately been preserved and show that he had not lost the wit and spirit of humanity that had endeared him to Burns. At one of the annual evening parties, given on the election of the Magistrates and Town Council, the Rev. Mr. Campbell gave as a toast 'The medical profession', to which was given an immediate reply. This was followed by another 'the learned legal profession', after which a dead pause ensued, in expectation that some of the legal gentlemen present would acknowledge the honour paid to them. At length when the patience of the company was almost worn thin, Sillar rose, and with much solemnity of manner, briefly addressed the chair, 'May I be permitted a few words. One toast has been given, and an appropriate reply was elicited, but another has been proposed, which no one has volunteered to acknowledge. I suppose the profession are consulting as to which of them should reply, none of the learned body being fond of speaking without a fee.'

When presiding one day in the Small Debt Court, a case came before the Court from a neighbouring parish, in which a surgeon was pursuer and the kirk session defenders. The surgeon, who had been called to attend a pauper belonging to the parish, and had performed an operation which was the means of saving the person's life, claimed remuneration. The session resisted the claim, the minister pleading that justice did not demand them to provide medical aid to their poor, and there was no law to compel them to do so. The Court found in favour of the session, and Sillar, in addressing the minister said, 'The decision is given in your favour, but the coat that you wear, and the office you hold, lead me to hope that your law and your justice will in future be tempered with mercy.' [24]

It has been suggested in some quarters that, following Burns's inability to give financial aid to Sillar, the friendship cooled. Burns's letter 1791 is certainly rather curt and suggests that he and his friend are apart by something more than the distance between Ellisland and Irvine. It is doubtful if there was any further correspondence. Following Burns's death, however, Sillar always upheld the memory and name of his late friend, and loved to discourse on their early days together. Along with Dr. John Mackenzie he was instrumental in forming the Irvine Burns Club in 1826, and at the first dinner he acted as croupier, a position which was then second to the president. He was prevented from becoming president the following year, owing to an illness which was protracted and resulted finally

Sam Hay.
He was the genial curator of Batchelor's Club from 1974 until his death in 1987.
He liked nothing better to impart his wide knowledge of Burns and Tarbolton to audiences.
He was also Provost of Tarbolton in 1971.

Interior of the Burns Bachelor Club.

in his death on 3rd May, 1830; he was then in his seventieth year. He was buried in Irvine Parish Churchyard and his grave is marked with a headstone. It is the second stone, which is a facsimile of the original, and was erected by Irvine Burns Club in 1962. The inventory of his estate revealed movable assets to the value of £314, five shares in Irvine Gas Company, several houses and heritable bonds to the value of £6,000.[25]

David Sillar was twice married and had several children by his first wife, but was survived by only one - Dr. Zachariah Sillar, who in 1830 resided at Ravenscroft, near Irvine. Later he practised as a physician in Liverpool. It is interesting to note that when Dr. Sillar was made a Burgess of Irvine in 1817, his father's name appears on the Burgess Ticket as Treasurer of the Burgh.[26]

Although Burns called Sillar a 'brother poet', it cannot be seriously advanced that he deserved that title. It would be more accurate to include him among those who, in the wake of Burns's success, flooded Scotland with indifferent Scottish verse. Probably Sillar's poems were as good as many and better than most. Following the isolation years at Mount Oliphant, Burns was eager for male companionship, and the formation of the Bachelors' Club filled that need and provided him with an audience and a sense of belonging. Sillar, obviously, was the companion whom Burns found most worthy of his friendship, which was then of immense value to him and greatly assisted in his development as a poet.

DR. JOHN MACKENZIE, M.D.

The young doctor who was called to Lochlie Farm in 1783 to attend William Burnes in his final illness, was John Mackenzie of Mauchline. A native of Ayrshire, he had studied medicine at Edinburgh University and on completion of his studies, was persuaded by Sir John Whiteford of Ballochmyle to establish a medical practice in Mauchline.[1] He rented premises at the Cross, where he set up a consulting room and drug store, with a sign informing the public that he was both 'Doctor and Midwife'.[2]

It was upon his first visit to Lochlie that he met Robert Burns. He was about the same age as the poet and despite what seemed an unfavourable start, a warm friendship followed their meeting. In a letter to Professor Josiah Walker, written in 1810, Mackenzie gave an interesting account of his visit to Lochlie and his impression of the Burns family:

Portrait of John MacKenzie by William Findlay after an oil painting
by William Tannock.

'When I first saw William Burnes (sic) he was in very ill health, and his mind suffering from the embarrassed state of his affairs. His appearance certainly made me think him inferior, both in manner and intelligence, to the generality of those in his situation; but before leaving him, I found that I had been led to form a very false conclusion of his mental powers. After giving a short, but distinct account, of his indisposition he entered upon a detail of the various causes that had gradually led to the embarrassment of his affairs; and these he detailed in such earnest language, and in so simple, candid, and pathetic manner, as to excite both my astonishment and sympathy. His wife spoke little but struck me as being a very sagacious woman, without any appearance of forwardness, or any of that awkwardness in her manner which many of those people show in the presence of a stranger. Upon further acquaintance with Mrs. Burnes, I had my first opinion of her character fully confirmed. Gilbert and Robert Burns were certainly very different in their appearance and manner, though they both possessed great abilities and uncommon information. Gilbert partook more of the manner and appearance of the father, and Robert of the mother. Gilbert in the first interview I had with him at Lochlea (sic) was frank, modest, well informed and communicative. The poet seemed distant, suspicious, and without any wish to interest or please. He kept himself very silent in a dark corner of the room; and before he took part in the conversation, I frequently detected him scrutinising me during my conversation with his father and brother. But afterwards, when the conversation, which was on a medical subject, had taken the turn he wished, he began to engage in it, displaying a dexterity of reasoning and ingenuity of reflection, and a familiarity with topics apparently beyond his reach, by which his visitor was no less gratified than astonished.'

Mackenzie, like many others after him, was impressed by Burns's great intellect and his brilliant powers of conversation. In the same letter, he continues:

'From the period of which I speak, I took a lively interest in Robert Burns; and, before I was acquainted with his poetical powers, I perceived that he possessed very great mental abilities, an uncommonly fertile imagination, a thorough acquaintance with many of our Scottish poets, and an enthusiastic admiration for Ramsay and Fergusson. Even then, on subjects with which he was acquainted, his conversation was rich in well chosen figures, animated and energetic. Indeed, I have always thought that no person could have a just idea of the extent of Burns's talents, who had not an opportunity to hear him converse. His discrimination of character was great beyond that of any person I ever knew; and I have often observed to him, that it seemed to be intuitive. I seldom ever knew him to make a false estimate of character, when he formed the opinion from his own observation, and not from the representation of persons to whom he was partial.' [3]

Procession of the St. James Masonic Lodge, Tarbolton.
Engraving by D.O.Hill from *The Land of Burns.*

It seems obvious from the passage just quoted, that the doctor admired Burns and enjoyed his company. No doubt their friendship was further cemented when the poet moved to Mossgiel farm, early in 1784, as it lay just one mile north of the village of Mauchline. Mackenzie was shrewd enough to realise that Burns was something more than just a tenant farmer, and quick to recognise the man of genius under a rustic garb.

Burns was not long settled in Mossgiel when he suffered a recurrence of the heart complaint which would result finally in his death. Both Professor Snyder and Maurice Lindsay state that Mackenzie attended the poet in his illness, and although there is no documentary evidence to support their claim, in all probability he did. Maurice Lindsay goes further, however, and claims that Mackenzie 'has been much criticised for prescribing not only the wrong treatment of Robert's illness, but one which, in all probability, accelerated the progress of the disease. He instructed his patient to plunge into cold baths and to get rid of the melancholy by still harder farm work.[4] In view of the uncertainty of Mackenzie's involvement, it does seem to be taking an unfair liberty to place the responsibility for the treatment at Mackenzie's door. The poet was almost twenty-five years of age when he first met the Mauchline doctor, and since his early teens, had suffered from palpitation of the heart, and a threatening of fainting and suffocation in bed at night. It seems more likely that Burns had recourse to the cold water treatment long before he met Mackenzie.

The poet and the doctor had a common interest. Both were enthusiastic Masons and were members of St. James Lodge, Tarbolton. Burns was elected Deputy Master at a meeting on 27th July, 1784 in Manson's Inn. Each year a procession was held on St. John's Day, 24th June, and on the eve of the 1786 procession, Burns sent a rhyming invitation to Mackenzie.

> Friday first's the day appointed
> By the Right Worshipful anointed,
> To hold our grand procession;
> To get a blad o' Johnie's morals,
> And taste a swatch o' Manson's barrels
> I' the way of our profession.
> The Master and the Brotherhood
> Would a' be glad to see you;
> For me I would be mair than proud
> To share the mercies wi' you.
> If Death, then, wi' skaith, then
> Some mortal heart is hechtin
> Inform him, and storm him,
> That Saturday you'll fecht him. *(CW 237)*

Some explanation of the lines is necessary and this was given by 'Johnie' (Mackenzie himself) in a letter to Dr. Robert Chambers, when the biographer was collecting material for his life of the poet. He wrote, 'The phrase 'Johnie's morals' originated from some correspondence Burns and I had on the origin of morals; and 'Manson's Barrels' to the small beer of a very superior kind that the brethren got from him at the dinner. The lines 'If death, then, wi' skaith, then', etc were in consequence of my expressing a doubt whether I could attend the lodge on that day, from the number of patients that I had to visit at the period'.[5] Unfortunately, the correspondence which Mackenzie had with Burns on the origin of morals has not survived.

Mackenzie is also credited with writing on some controversial topic under the title of Common Sense, and because of this, his name has been linked with the following verse in 'The Holy Fair' -

> In guid time comes an antidote
> Against sic poison'd nostrum;
> For Peebles, frae the water-fit,
> Ascends the holy rostrum:
> See, up he's got the word o' God,
> An meek an' mim has view'd it,

> While 'Common Sense' has taen the road,
> An' aff, an' up the Cowgate
> Fast, fast that day. *(CW 132)*

Tradition has it that on the day of the Mauchline annual Communion, held on the second Sunday of August, 1785, Mackenzie had arranged to meet Sir John Whitefoord and accompany him to Dumfries House, in Auchinleck parish, to dine with the Earl of Dumfries. Having taken Communion at an early 'table', and listened to some of the harangues from the 'tent' he was seen making his way up the Cowgate, en route for Ballochmyle, as the Rev. William Peebles of Newton-on-Ayr (the water fit) was about to mount the rostrum.[6]

Mackenzie obtained a copy of 'The Holy Fair' from Burns and passed it to the Rev. Dr. Hugh Blair, the moderate minister of the High Kirk of St. Giles, who also held the Chair of Rhetoric at Edinburgh University. He happened to be visiting Lord Barskimming, Lord Chief Justice of the Court of Session, at his country seat at Barskimming, just outside Mauchline. Blair was one of the Edinburgh literati, and was the arbiter of 'good taste' in the capital. He was partly responsible for the exclusion of 'The Jolly Beggars' *(CW 182 - 191)* and a poem called 'The Prophet and God's Complaint', now unfortunately lost.

Lochlie Farm where Dr. MacKenzie first met Burns.

Mackenzie reported Blair 'was much pleased' with 'The Holy Fair' and said 'it was the production of a great genius, and that it contained some of the finest and justest descriptions he had ever seen'.[7] Burns altered the fourth line of the twelfth stanza from 'tidings o' salvation' to 'damnation' on Blair's suggestion.

Mackenzie's practice extended for a considerable distance around Mauchline, and he was physician to such notable persons as Sir John Whitefoord of Ballochmyle, and Colonel Hugh Montgomerie of Coilsfield, who later became the Earl of Eglinton. It is reported that he attended the Countess of Loudon, who was born in 1677, during the reign of Charles II, and whose life extended to one hundred years.[8] Mackenzie, however, was no ordinary physician. In addition

Professor Dugald Stewart
He was sent a copy of the Edinburgh Edition by Dr. Blackstock and was so impressed that he invited Burns to dine with him. Much to Burns' surprise Lord Daer also was of the company and Burns was so taken by the Lord that he wrote the famous poem "On Dining wi' a Lord".

to his skill as a doctor, he seems to have been a man of considerable intelligence, a liberal thinker, and an excellent conversationalist. He was a welcome guest in the homes of many of the gentry and nobility in the area, and a frequent visitor to Catrine House, the country home of Dugald Stewart about two miles distant from Mauchline. Stewart was Professor of Moral Philosophy at Edinburgh University, and spent most of his leisure time at Catrine whenever he was free of his University duties. During his visits, Mackenzie spoke so highly of Burns's accomplishments that the Professor expressed a desire to meet him. The meeting took place on 23rd October, 1786, when Mackenzie and Burns were invited to dine with the Professor at Catrine House.

Also present on the occasion was Lord Daer, who was the second son of the fourth Earl of Selkirk. He was a radical Whig, whose political principles were very similar to those embraced by Burns. The poet commemorated the occasion in the humorous 'Lines on Meeting wit Lord Daer' *(CW 254)*. Enclosing the poem in a letter to Mackenzie, he said:

> 'I never spent an afternoon among great folks with half that pleasure as when, in company with you, I had the honour of paying my devoirs to that plain, honest, worthy man, the Professor ...I think his character, divide into ten parts, stands thus - four parts Socrates - four parts Nathaniel - and two parts Shakespeare's

Brutus. The foregoing verses were really extempore, but a little corrected since. They may entertain you, with the help of that partiality with which you are so good as to favor the performances of ... Robert Burns.' *(CL 113).*

In the poem, the poet described Lord Daer:

> The fient a pride, nae pride had he,
> Nor sauce, nor state, that I could see.
> Mair than an honest ploughman. *(CW 254)*

Dugald Stewart, on his part, was struck with Burns's manners, which he said were 'simple, manly, and independent; strongly expressive of conscious genius and worth'. He was also greatly impressed with the poet's command of language. On this point, he noted 'Nothing, perhaps, was more remarkable among his various attainments, than the fluency, and precision, and originality of his language.' [9]

The Mauchline doctor not only introduced Burns to Professor Stewart, and brought his works to the notice of the Rev. Dr. Blair, but when the poet went to Edinburgh in November, 1786 to try for a second edition of his poems, Mackenzie recommended him to Sir John Whitefoord and the Hon. Andrew Erskine, who became his patrons.[10] Sir John had been forced to sell Ballochmyle in 1785, following the failure of the Ayr bank of Douglas and Heron, in which he was a shareholder, and had removed to

Irvine. Engraving by D.O.Hill., from *The Land of Burns*.

Edinburgh with his family. He was a friend of Lord Glencairn, who became Burns's principal patron. The Hon. Andrew Erskine was the brother of the Earl of Kellie and a well known wit and versifier. He had settled in Edinburgh following a period of service in the army, and was on good terms with James Boswell, who was over-generous when he described him as 'both a good poet and a good critic'. Erskine collaborated with George Thomson in the early stages of the *Select Scottish Airs*.[11]

Burns was not long in Edinburgh when he learned that Sir John Whitefoord had spoken in defence of his moral character. The news was contained in a letter from Mackenzie. It appears that the poet had been maligned in the course of conversation by a detractor, intent on raking up the story of his affair with Jean Armour. This prompted Burns to write to Sir John on 1st December, 1786. In his letter he wrote:

> 'Mr. Mackenzie, in Mauchline, my very warm and worthy friend, has informed me how much you are pleased to interest yourself in my fate as a man, and (what to me is incomparably dearer) my fame as a poet.
>
> I was surprised to hear that anyone, who pretended in the least to the manners of a gentleman should be so foolish, or worse, as to stoop to traduce the morals of such a one as I am, and so inhumanly cruel too, as to meddle with that late most unfortunate, unhappy part of my story. With a tear of gratitude, I thank you, Sir, for the warmth with which you interposed in behalf of my conduct.' *(CL 52)*.

Very few letters were exchanged between the poet and the doctor. This is understandable as they were in regular contact with each other after Burns moved to Mossgiel. The only letter which he sent to Mackenzie from Edinburgh was on 11th January, 1787, following a meeting with Sir John. He wrote:

> 'I saw your friend and my honoured patron, Sir John Whitefoord, just after I read your letter, and gave him your respectful compts. He was pleased to say many handsome things of you, which I heard them with the more satisfaction, as I knew them to be just.' *(CL 114)*.

When Burns returned to Mauchline at the end of February, 1788, after his second visit to Edinburgh, he found Jean Armour banished from her parents' home 'all for the good old cause'. She was about to give birth to the second twins, and had been given refuge by Willie Muir and his wife at Tarbolton Mill. Burns immediately rented an upstairs room in the Back Causeway belonging to Archibald Muckle, a Mauchline tailor, and it was in this room that twin daughters were born on 3rd March.[12] Both girls died shortly afterwards. Some writers have suggested that Dr. Mackenzie was the first to give shelter to Jean when she was driven from her father's house. While this may be true, unfortunately

Eglinton Castle, c 1796.
In 1925 it became too large and expensive to maintain, and the family vacated it. It soon became a
ruin and in 1975 the ruins were removed. It is now a public park.

it cannot be substantiated, although it seems that the doctor attended to Jean at the births.[13] In the following month of April, 1788 Burns acknowledged Jean Armour as his wife.

When Mackenzie first came to Mauchline and set up in practice, he lodged in the Sun Inn, one of the more respectable inns in the village. It was owned by John Miller, 'auld John Trot' of Burns's 'Mauchline Wedding' *(CW 151)* and father of Helen and Elizabeth, two of the 'Mauchline Belles'. The young doctor paid court to Helen, and in due course they were married on 9th August, 1791.[14] Helen brought with her a considerable dowry, which had been settled on her by her brother, who had made his fortune in India.[15] It is almost certain that Mackenzie lodged in the Sun Inn until his marriage. Thereafter he and his wife occupied a house in the Back Causeway, immediately adjoining Archibald Muckle's property and opposite Nance Tinnock's hostelry. He also used part of the building as a surgery, which was known locally as the 'Doctor's shop'. In 1788 he acquired a bond on the property and became sole owner in 1815.[16] It was probably about 1788 that he removed from his 'shop' at Mauchline Cross to the Back Causeway. It is interesting to note that one of the four tenants named in a title deed of 1831 was Dr. Dugald Stewart Hamilton (son of Gavin Hamilton) who bought Mackenzie's practice in 1801.[17]

As has already been stated, Mackenzie numbered among his patients Colonel Hugh Montgomerie of Coilsfield. He was a Member of Parliament for Ayrshire from 1784 to

1789, and again in 1796, but almost immediately succeeded his cousin as twelfth Earl of Eglinton.[18] About this time he removed from Coilsfield and took up residence in the Castle. He had formed a very high opinion of Mackenzie as a physician, so much so that he persuaded the doctor to leave Mauchline in 1801, and set up practice in Irvine, which was conveniently near to Eglinton Castle. In consideration, the Earl agreed to pay Mackenzie a life rent annuity of £130, which the doctor accepted in lieu of all fees for his professional services to the Earl and his family. The bond of annuity makes interesting reading:

> 'Mr. John Mackenzie, surgeon in Mauchline, has for these several years past, attended as my family surgeon, and that I have had greatest reason to be highly satisfied with the professional abilities and the very greatest care and attention which the said John Mackenzie has shown to me in a dangerous and critical indisposition, and that therefore, anxious to have the benefit of the said Mackenzie's assistance, I proposed to him to remove from his present residence in Mauchline and settle himself and family in Irvine, in my immediate neighbourhood, which he has accordingly agreed to do upon my making him a fair and reasonable compensation for the loss of his practice in Mauchline and the risk he runs in settling in a new place.' [19]

Dr. John MacKenzie's Masonic Apron.
In the possesion of Irvine Burns Club.

Mackenzie soon established himself in the busy seaport town of Irvine and his practice prospered. He took an active interest in town council affairs and held the offices of Treasurer and Dean of Guild. He also served at various times as a Bailie. In Irvine he made the acquaintance of David Sillar, friend of Burns and 'a brother poet', who had settled in the town in 1783. Mackenzie's great interest in Burns and his works never diminished in the long interval since the Mauchline days, when he and the poet were in close contact with each other. In 1826 he helped found the Irvine Burns Club. A meeting was held on 2nd June of that year, at which it was resolved by the twelve gentlemen present, to form a committee 'for the purpose of establishing a Club or Society for commemorating the birth of Robert Burns'. Mackenzie's name headed the signatories to the document. The first Burns celebration was held on 25th January, 1827, in the King's Arms Hotel, with Dr. Mackenzie in the chair and David Sillar as croupier.[20]

John Mackenzie served the people of Irvine faithfully for twenty-six years. Although engaged in municipal affairs, he found time to keep abreast of the modern advances in medical science which were then being made. In 1824 he made his own contribution when he submitted his thesis on 'De Carcinomate' to his Alma Mater.[21] This suggests that, even then, doctors were trying to find a care for this deadly disease.

On 2nd March, 1827, his wife, Helen died at Seagate House, Irvine, and in the same year he retired from practice and removed to Edinburgh where he spent his remaining years until his death on 3rd January, 1837 at 4 Shandwick Place at an advanced age.[22]

John Mackenzsie was a man of liberal outlook and, like Robert Burns, was a keen observer of contemporary life. He was among the first to recognise the genius of the young farmer at Lochlie and, following the publication of the Kilmarnock volume, introduced him to some of his influential patients and friends. Burns, for his part, liked and trusted Mackenzie and referred to him as 'his warm and worthy friend', which certainly reflects the true nature of their relationship. The doctor did as much as anyone to ensure that Burns's entry into Edinburgh would be as easy and successful as possible. For that he occupies a special place in the life story of Robert Burns.

'EPISTLE TO DR. JOHN MACKENZIE'

In 1886, William F. Watson, an Edinburgh bookseller and, obviously an admirer of Robert Burns and his works, bequeathed to the Scottish National Portrait Gallery a collection of paintings, drawings and manuscripts. Included among the paintings were the valuable Reid miniature of Burns and the equally valuable silhouette by John Miers. In 1930, on the recommendation of the Royal Commission on Museums and Galleries, Watson's collection of holograph letters and other manuscripts was transferred on loan to the National Library of Scotland.

About 1936, the Keeper of the Manuscripts at the National Library drew the attention of James C Ewing, then editor of the *Burns Chronicle,* to **MS 585, No. 1086,** of the Watson Collection. It is a holograph document, written in the hand of Dr. John Mackenzie, on foolscap paper, watermarked '1815'. It is a thirteen-verse epistle, addressed 'Dear Thinker

Robert Burns, from an etching by Ian Strang.
Commissioned by Dumbarton Burns Club in 1926,
to commemorate the return of Burns's Burgess Ticket to
the town. The artist has based his portrait on the Skirving chalk drawing of Burns.

Trinity Church, Irvine from the river c1900.

John' (Mackenzie). It would appear that the doctor copied it out for a friend, as an inscription at the end of the poem reads, 'Dr. Mackenzie to Mr. Thomson (may have been George Thomson) with most respectfulls (sic) compliments'. The MS is headed 'A Correct Copy'.

James Kinsley in *The Poems and Songs of Robert Burns* lists the epistle (title and two lines of first verse only) in an appendix of poems that 'have been admitted at various times to the canon of Burns's works, either wrongly or on inadequate evidence'. James MacKay, in *Burns A-Z the Complete Word Finder*, prints the epistle in full under an appendix of 'dubious and spurious works'. Both quote James Barke (1955, pp 263-5) as their reference, but point out that Barke gives no authority for his text.

In a brief article in the *Burns's Chronicle* (1937), James Ewing printed the epistle in full. It was the first time it had appeared in print, and it is almost certain that it was James Barke's source. Ewing obviously had examined the document and is of the opinion that it is probably not a true copy, as it bears evidence of having been written in haste and points to the mis-spelling of the signature:

A CORRECT COPY

Dr. Thinker John,

Your creed I like it past expression;
I'm sure, o' truth, it's nae transgression
To say the great Westminster Session,
    Wi' a' their clatter
In Carraches or large Confession   (catechisms)
    Ne'er made a better.

For me, I ken a weel ploughed rigg,
I ken a handsome hizie's leg
When, springing taper straught & trig,   (straight)
    It fires my fancy,
But *system-Sandy* mills to bigg   (to form platonic
    Is nae that chancy.   friendships)

Sma skill in *holy war* I boast,
My wee bit spunk o' *Latin's* lost,
An' Logie gies me ay the hoast
    An' cuts my win',   (wind)
Si I maun tak the rear-guard post
    Far, far behin'.

I see the poopet ance a week,   (pulpit)
An' farefu' every sentence cleek,   (catch)
Or if frae — a smirking keek   (Jean?)
    Spoil my devotion,
My carnal een I instant steek   (Close his eyes)
    Wi' double caution.

Still, tho' nae staunch polemic head
O lang-win'd Athanasian breed,
I hae a wee bit cantie *creed*
    Just ae my ain,
An' tho' uncouthly it may read,
    It's unco plain.

Tho' human-kind be sae at odds,

Poor waspish, animated clods,
There's just twa patent turnpike roads
    They a' maun gang
To dark futurity' abodes –
    The *right* an *wrang*.

If, in spite of a' its crooks an' thraws,
The heav'n ward road your fancy draws,
If *ye resemble* ought their laws
    An' ways that's there
Then march awa and never pause:
    Your conduct's fair.

But if ye think, within yoursel,
You'll fairly tak your chance o' hell
An honestly your notion tell,
    Free, unashamed,
Then faith, I see nae how that well
    Ye can be blam'd.

But here the conduct I call evil:
Some at their heart wad sair the d-v-l,   (serve)
Yet groan, & drone, an' sigh, and snivel,
    An' pray & cant.
An' be to heaven as fair an' civil
    As ony saunt.   (saint)

Thae rotten hearted twa-fac'd wretches,
Wi a' their hypocritic fetches,
I would rejoice in well-splice'd stitches
    O' hempen string
Out owre a tree, the sons o' bitches,
    To see them swing.

Ye see my skill's but very sma,
Some folk may think I've nane ava,
But we shall gie our pens a claw
    Some ither time,
An' hae about between us twa
    At prose an' rhyme.

Farewell, dear death-defying John!
Aft hunt-the-gowke for you he's gone,   (fool's errand)
But some day he'll come down the loan
    Wi spurtlin shanks,   (stick-like)
An' grip ye till he gar you groan,
    By way of Thanks.

But then, before that come to pass:
May ye toom many a social glass,   (empty)
An' bless a dear warm hearted lass
    That likes you some;
Then after fifty simmers grass
    E'en let him come!

Signed Rab Ryhmer (*sic*)
18th April, 1786.

The first verse suggests that the writer had received a communication from the doctor setting out his views on some moral issue. Professor Walker informs us that Mackenzie's favourite topic was the 'origin of morals',[1] and we have it from Mackenzie himself that he and Burns had exchanged letters on the subject; the epistle may have been part of the correspondence. The epistle is signed 'Rab Rhymer', which was a pet-name Burns used more than once, notably in the second line of the first verse of the poem, 'On dining with Lord Daer' – 'I rhymer Rab alias Burns' *(CW 254)*.

All the foregoing evidence points to Burns as the author, and it comes as no surprise that he addressed the epistle to 'Dear Thinker John'. Written in 'Standard Habbie' verse form, a measure much favoured by Burns, the poem is on the poet's familiar topic of religion and hypocrisy. It bears all the hallmarks of Burns's work: the sly humour, the easy conversational style, the fluency and the unmistakable craftsmanship. In the absence of a Burns holograph, it is impossible to make an authoritative judgement, but the theme and the style appear so convincingly Burns, that the epistle would be worthy of a place in the full canon of his works.

SAUNDERS TAIT

At Whitsun, 1777, William Burnes and his family removed from Mount Oliphant to the farm of Lochlie in the Parish of Tarbolton. Robert was then eighteen years of age and probably welcomed the move. Apart from brief visits to Dalrymple, Ayr and Kirkoswald to improve his education, his life at Mount Oliphant had been that of 'the cheerless gloom of a hermit with the increasing toil of a galley slave'. *(CL 250)*. **Brother Gilbert, writing of this period, said; 'Nothing could be more retired than our general manner of living at Mount Oliphant: we rarely saw anybody but the members of our own family... My father was for some time almost the only companion we had'.[1]**

Lochlie farm lay two and a half miles north-east of Tarbolton, and after the isolation of Mount Oliphant, Robert sought companionship among the lads of the village. This was the formative period of his life, and it was at Lochlie that he defied his father and attended a dancing class in Tarbolton, 'to give his manners a brush'. It was there that he and several similar minded youths formed the Bachelors' Club - a debating society for mutual improvement, and it was in a lodge at Tarbolton that he was passed and raised as a Mason.

It was also in Tarbolton that he came across Saunders Tait, a local rhymster and versifier, who enjoys the unique reputation as being the only contemporary poetaster, who never had a good word to say about Burns. During the time the Burns family were at Lochlie, Tait lashed them unmercifully, in fierce, rough doggerel verse. He probably viewed with alarm the rise of

Ballochmyle House, c 1850.
In 1780 the house and estate were owned by Sir John Whitefoord, but having suffered severe financial losses in the failure of the Douglas and Heron Bank he was forced to sell to the Alexander family.

a new young poet, whose talents far exceeded his own. Unfortunately, most of Burns's work of his Tarbolton days has been lost. In his autobiographical letter to Dr. Moore, (CL 248) he wrote 'None of the rhymes of those days are in print, except 'Winter, a Dirge', (the eldest of my printed pieces), The Death of Poor Mailie' and 'John Barleycorn'. Tait's rhymes, however, have survived, and it would appear that Burns must have written some uncomplimentary verses about him as is evident from Tait's poem called 'Burns in his Infancy'.

> Now I maun trace his pedigree
> Because he made a sang on me.

Saunders Tait was born at Innerleithen, about 1715, as he tells us in verses called, 'The Author's Nativity':

> Leithen so pretty,
> When first I drew braith,
> There my mither Betty
> She clad me in claith,
> A shirt, a coat and vest,
> Breeks, stockins and shoon,
> My hair neatly dressed
> And a wee hat aboon.

It was probably at Innerleithen that he learned the trade of tailoring, which in those days was closely allied to that of an itinerant packman. Mantua-making was also part of the business of a tailor and, on selling a length of cloth, it was not unusual for him to remain in the house of the customer until the garment was made up. 'Whup the Cat', as he was known, visited all the farm villages over a wide area, but ultimately settled down in the village of Tarbolton, where he became a kenspeckle figure.

According to a contemporary, Saunders was a stout, well-informed man of middle stature. He appears to have been a smart and active sort of person, with an inexhaustible fund of humorous anecdotes. His company was eagerly sought after for weddings, rockings and other merrymaking parties. As he went his rounds, he collected all the gossip and scandal of the countryside, which usually found its way into his rhymed lampoons. He was a ready chronicler of all local squabbles and peculiar events, and although regarded as something of an eccentric, he had considerable influence in the village.

He owned several small properties and took an active interest in local affairs, being at one period a bailie. In one of his rhymed effusions, he enumerates his public offices:

> I'm Patron to the Burgher folks,
> I'm Cornal to the Farmers' Box,
> And Bailie to guid hearty cocks,
> That are a' grand:
> Has heaps o' hooses built on rocks
> Wi' lime and sand.

The first line of the above verse refers to the building of the Secession or Burgher Church in Tarbolton in 1777, to which the parish minister and local gentry were strongly opposed. At one stage, the work was delayed because of a scarcity of hewn stone. A public meeting was held to consider the situation, and Saunders undertook to manage to deal with the problem. He managed to resolve it within a few days by a roundabout scheme, which nobody thought would be successful, thereby enhancing his reputation as a man of influence and shrewdness.

The second line of the verse refers to the Universal Friendly Society of Tarbolton in which for a long time he held the rank of *Colonel*. The Society held frequent parades with the object of recruiting new members, and Saunders is known to have marched at the head of a long procession through the village, proudly wearing his cocked hat. At that time Friendly Societies were established in Ayrshire, for the purpose of alleviating the widespread poverty then existing. It would appear from William Aiton's Agricultural Report of 1811, however, that many of them had lost sight of their original objects. He writes:

> 'Friendly or penny societies have been formed in many parts of Ayrshire, and promise to be antidotes against poverty. Masons, weavers, shoemakers and other societies had been formed many years ago, in most of the towns in the county, and some supply has been drawn from them, to some of their indigent members. But, unfortunately, they generally throw away much of their revenue in purchasing flags, spontoons, gorgets, crowns, coats of mail, sceptres, robes, trains, and other fooleries, and in making fool-like parades, through towns, drinking on the street, etc. One is burdened with a coat of mail, and termed a *Champion*; one with a crown, a fool's coat, and a train supported by half a dozen idle boys, is termed a *King*, and holds a piece of a painted timber as his sceptre, others are *Colonels, Captains, Lords*, or rather the whole make themselves *downright fools,* for a time, and dissipate the fund which ought to be applied to charitable purposes. It is in vain to look to these ridiculous institutions for relief to the poor. They are in fact beggar-making societies, which ought to be abolished.'

In 1794, when Major Montgomerie, afterwards Earl Eglinton, raised a regiment of West Lowland Fecibles, Tait, though well advanced in years, was one of the first to enlist. In Kay's Edinburgh Portraits, where a portrait and memoir of the Earl are given, the following notice of Saunders Tait is appended by way of a footnote:

'Among the others who 'followed to the field' was an eccentric personage of the name of Tait. He was a tailor, and in stature somewhat beneath the military standard; but he was a poet, and zealous in the cause of loyalty. He had sung the deeds of the Montgomeries in many a couplet, and having animated the villagers with his loyal strains, resolved to encourage his companions in arms to victory by the fire and vigour of his verses. It is said that he could not write; nevertheless he actually published a small volume of poems. These have long ago sunk into oblivion ... He was bachelor and occupied an attic of very small dimensions. At the 'June Fair', when the village was crowded, Saunders, by a tolerated infringement of the excise laws, annually converted his 'poet's corner' into a temple for the worship of Bacchus, and became a publican in a small way... his apartment was always well frequented, especially by the younger portion of the country people, who were amused by his oddities.

Hugh Montgomerie, ('Sodger Hugh'), Twelfth Earl, of Eglinton. Caricature by Kay.

Poor Saunders, unluckily, was more in repute for his songs than his needle ... it is told that on some particular occasion he had made a coat in one day, but then his 'steeks' were prodigiously long, and with him fashion was out of the question, abiding as he always did by the 'good old plan'. The result was that while his brethren of the needle were paid eighteen pence a day, Saunders acknowledged his inferiority by claiming no more than sixpence. Whether the duties were too fatiguing, or whether his compatriots had no relish for poetical excitements, we know not, but true it is that in the dusk of a summer evening, some few weeks after the departure of the Fencibles, Saunders was seen entering the village leading a goat which he had procured in his travels, and followed by a band of youngsters, who had gone to meet him on his approach.' [2]

Tait, like many another minor versifier of the period, ventured into 'guid black prent'. His book was published in Paisley in 1790 by John Neilson, for and sold by the author only, for the small charge of 1/6, although it contained 304 pages octavo... From certain verses in the volume, it appears that he spent a short time in Paisley as a journeyman tailor with a man called Daniel Mitchell in John Street, and it is assumed that it was during this brief period that his book went through the press. He sang of 'Lady Ballochmyle's Chariot', and the deeds of the Montgomeries are recorded in such verses as 'Coilfield's Hawks and Greyhounds'. In another set of verses entitled 'The Illumination of Tarbolton on the Recovery of His Majesty' (George III), he praises the loyalty and liberality of Major Montgomerie, while the establishment of the Catrine cotton mills in 1787 by Claud Alexander of Ballochmyle, in partnership with David Dale of Glasgow, was also celebrated in the following very mediocre verses:

> To the pretty lads buys our laird's estates,
> And wins their money in foreign parts;
> They make our tradesmen to rant and rair,
> And build cotton-mills on the banks o' Ayr.
>
> There's Claud Alexander in Ballochmyle
> May Providence upon him smile,
> And never let his purse run bare,
> While he's upon the banks o' Ayr.

From the footnote in Kay's *Edinburgh Portraits,* already referred to, it is obvious that Tait was on very good terms with the Alexander family of Ballochmyle. It must have been a source of deep chagrin to Burns that the beautiful song he sent to Wilhelmina Alexander was never acknowledged, while an inferior versifier like Tait was made welcome at Ballochmyle.

Tait's book of verse is certainly more impressive for its quantity than its quality, and his rhymes are invariably crude in expression and almost always feeble in structure. He reserved his most scurrilous abuse, however, for the Burns' family. Whatever may have been the cause of his spleen, it is obvious from such vitriolic verses as 'Burns in his Infancy', 'Burns in Lochly', 'Burns's Hen Clockin' in Mauchline',[3] and others, that he detested the name of Burns.

While tenant of Lochlie Farm, William Burnes became involved in a prolonged litigation with his landlord, David McLure. The lease was imperfectly drawn up and was the principal cause of the dispute. For more than a century, very little of the details of the litigation was known, but Saunders Tait had made several references in his verses to the affair... The legal documents, giving McLure's version of the dispute, came to light in 1896, about the same time as W. E. Henley was writing his famous essay on Burns. Henley wrote, 'I need scarce say that Saunders Tait produced a 'Burns at Lochly' in which he fell on his enemy tooth and claw. His statements are as specific as McLure's and are substantially in agreement with some of them'.[4] He then quotes the following:

To Lochly ye came like a clerk.
And on your back was scarce a sark,
The dogs did at your buttocks bark,
But now ye're braw,
Ye poucht the rent ye was so stark
Made payments sma'.

Other references to William Burnes are taken from the same:

McLure he put you in a farm
And coft you coals your arse to warm,
And meal and maut - Ye did get barm,
And then it wrought,
For his destruction and his harm
It is my thought.

In another poem called 'A Compliment', Tait alleged that, in addition to being £500 in arrears of rent, the Burns' family had smuggled away the goods sequestrated by McLure.

The horse, corn, pets, kail, kye and lures,
Cheese, pease, beans, rye, wool, house and flours,
Pots, pans, crans, tongs, brace-spits and skeurs,
The milk and barm,
Each thing they had was a' McLure's -
He stock's the farm.

It was not until 1935 that the legal documents were discovered which gave William Burnes's side of the dispute, and these were printed in full by John McVie in the *Burns Chronicle* of 1935. In an excellent article he proves every one of Tait's statements to be false and shows that the rhyming tailor merely reiterated the McLure line.[5]

Saunders Tait did not long survive his short term of service with the Fencibles. Being ill, and realising that his end was approaching, he was taken to the house of a friend, William Wallace of Millburn, a short distance from Tarbolton, and died there towards the close of the century.

His posthumous reputation, such as it is, survives only because of the reflected genius of Robert Burns. Had their paths never crossed, it is almost certain that Tait's coarse doggerel verses would have been consigned, long since, to discreet and everlasting oblivion.

CAPTAIN RICHARD BROWN

In the summer of 1781, Robert Burns went to Irvine to learn flax dressing. He and his brother, Gilbert, were anxious to improve conditions on the farm at Lochlie, and had rented about three acres from their father for the purpose of growing flax. At that time, flax was a paying crop, and obviously Burns thought that it could be more profitable if heckled by themselves for the spinners. He also wished to be in a position to marry and settle down, but saw no prospect of being able to do so while he remained a labourer on his father's farm. Writing of these circumstances, Gilbert tells us, 'The stocking of a farm required a sum of money, Robert had no probability of being master of for a great while. He began, therefore, to think of trying some other line of life.'[1]

Burns stayed in Irvine about eight months, but the experiment was a failure, as he relates in his autobiographical letter to Dr. Moore, written in 1787:

> 'My twenty-third year was to me an important era. - Partly thro' whim, and partly that I wished to set about doing something in life, I joined with a flax-dresser in a neighbouring town to learn his trade and carry on the business of manufacturing and retailing flax. - This turned out a sadly unlucky affair. - My Partner was a scoundrel of the first water who made money by the mystery of thieving; and to finish the whole, while we were giving a welcome carousal to the New Year, our shop, by the drunken carelessness of my partner's wife, took fire and was burnt to ashes; and left me like a true Poet, not worth sixpence. From this adventure, I learned something of a town-life.' *(CL 253)*

Irvine, in those days, had a population of around 4,000 and was the second largest town in Ayrshire. It was also one of the principal centres of flax-dressing in Scotland, but manufacturing as yet was not carried on to any great extent. At the time of the Union in 1707, it had ranked as the first seaport in the West of Scotland, and although it had lost its supremacy to Greenock, it still had a fine harbour and carried on a busy export and import trade, mainly with Ireland. Many of its young men became sailors, or went to the West Indies and America as planters and storekeepers.

Irvine opened up a whole new world to Burns. Hitherto most of his adult life had been spent in the backwater of Lochlie. Although he was almost twenty-three years of age he was in many respects immature. His sojourn in Irvine changed all that; it was there that he attained his manhood.

The person who exercised the most influence on him during his stay in the town, and who enlightened him in the ways of the world, was the sailor, Richard Brown. In the same letter to Dr. Moore, the poet devotes more space to him than to any other individual, which is an indication of the high value he placed on Brown's friendship. He writes:

'... the principal thing which gave my mind a turn was, I formed a bosom friendship with a young fellow, the first created being I had ever seen, but a hapless son of misfortune. - He was the son of a plain mechanic, but a great Man in the neighbourhood taking him under his patronage, gave him a genteel education, with a view to bettering his situation in life. - the Patron dying just as he was ready to launch forth into the world, the poor fellow in despair went to sea; where after a variety of good and bad fortune, a little before I was acquainted with him, he had been set ashore by an American Privateer on the wild coast of Connaught, stript of everything.' *(CL 254)*

'Glasgow Vennel', Irvine, where Burns lodged during his stay in Irvine; the 'vennel' has been fully restored and the house is now a museum.

Brown was a native of Irvine and six years older than Burns, having been born on 2nd June, 1753. The Irvine Parish Register records that he was the son of William Brown and Jane Whamie, but little else known of his early life, apart from what Burns tells us. It is clear that the young man from Lochlie regarded him with an affection bordering on hero worship. He continues in the letter:

'The gentleman's mind was fraught with courage, independence, Magnanimity, and every noble, manly virtue. - I loved him, I admired him, to a degree of enthusiasm, and I strove to imitate him. - In some measure I succeeded: I had the pride before, but he taught it to flow in proper channels. - His knowledge of the world was vastly superior to mine, and I was all attention to learn. - He was the only man I ever saw who was a greater fool than myself when WOMAN was the presiding star; but he spoke of a certain fashionable failing with levity, which hitherto I had regarded with horror. - Here his friendship did me a mischief; and the consequence was, that soon after I resumed the plough, I wrote the WELCOME enclosed.' *(CW 112)*

To say that Burns was taken with his new friend is putting it mildly. It should be remembered, however, that his health was in a very poor state at that time. A letter to his father, written from Irvine on 27th December, 1781 *(CL 41)*, is evidence of the morbid state of his mind, especially when he declares that he is 'quite transported at the thought that ere long, perhaps very soon, I shall bid an eternal adieu to all the pains, and uneasiness and disquietudes of this weary life; for I assure you I am heartily tired of it'. Meeting with the warm-hearted and widely travelled Brown must have acted like a tonic, and perhaps explains, to some degree, the fulsome compliments which Burns bestowed on him.

A very different interpretation is put on the friendship by one writer, who states:

'Let me recommend a close study of the relationship between these two young men - the sailor twenty-nine and the poet twenty-three when they first met - to those itchy-minded modern writers who cannot bear to imagine that the object of their researches is utterly and unexceptionally homosexual. There is certainly something equivocal about Brown's character'. Later the same writer, without offering a single shred of positive proof, continues the subject with these words, 'Let me finally pass on my scandalous suggestion about Burns and Brown to any non idolater, who cares to follow it up and to speculate further.'[2]

Burns has been accused of many things and some with justification, but bearing in mind his life-long love of the lasses, and the many scrapes his sexual indiscretions landed him in, it is utterly ridiculous even to hint that his relationship with Brown was homosexual. It is a 'scandalous suggestion' and so preposterous that it can be dismissed out of hand.

The statement that Brown did Burns 'a mischief' was later strenuously denied by Brown, who claimed that when the two met, Burns had nothing to learn on the subject of illicit love. It does seem unfair on Burns's part to make Brown the scapegoat for his lapse with Betty Paton, which occurred almost three years after he left Irvine. When he tells us that Brown's 'mind was fraught with every noble, manly virtue', it would appear contradictory and, at the least ungracious, to accuse Brown of leading him astray, and

A West Indiaman of late 18th century.

to be so indiscreet as to set it down in writing to an entire stranger. With the benefit of hindsight, it could be argued that Burns would have gone down the same road, irrespective of the influence of Richard Brown.

There is little doubt, however, that Brown exerted a greater influence on Burns than anyone hitherto, with the exception of his father and possibly school teacher, Murdoch. Brown seems to have 'straightened out' the young man from Lochlie, who admits, 'I had the pride before, but he taught it to flow in proper channels'. Further proof of Burns's admiration and gratitude is to be found in a letter which he sent to Brown, six years later, on 30th January, 1787. By this time Brown had become captain of a West Indiaman, belonging to the Thames. Burns wrote:

> 'I have met with few things in life which has given me more pleasure than Fortune's kindness to you since those days in which we met in the vale of misery, as I can honestly say, that I never met with a man who more truly deserved it, or to whom my heart more truly wish'd it. - I have been much indebted, since that time, to your story and sentiments, for steeling my heart against evils of which I have had a pretty decent share. - My will-o'-wisp fate, you know: do you recollect a Sunday we spent in Eglinton woods? You told me, on repeating some verses to you, that you wondered I could resist the temptation of sending

verses of such merit to a magazine: 'twas actually this that gave me an idea of my own pieces which encouraged me to endeavour at the character of a Poet.'
(CL 418)

The verses which Burns repeated to Brown would be chosen from those written prior to his twenty-third birthday, before the full flood of the Mossgiel period. They may have included 'Winter, a Dirge' *(CW 50)*, 'John Barleycorn' *(CW 60)*, 'Death and Dying words of Poor Mailie' *(CW 62)*, and the song, 'Corn Rigs' *(CW 46)* which vibrates with physical passion. This song would no doubt appeal to Brown.

It is to the credit of Brown he had the good sense to appreciate the poetic ability and possible future potential of Burns, and was the first to suggest that the verses had sufficient merit to warrant going into 'print'. Perhaps of greater importance, it was he who fired Burns's ambition 'to endeavour at the character of Poet'. Just how much he owed to Brown's influence and encouragement can be judged from the fact that in the Preface to the Kilmarnock Edition, he pays an indirect acknowledgement to the sailor friend he met in Irvine. The passage reads:

'Though a Rhymer from his earliest years, at least from the earliest impulses of the softer passions, it was not till very lately, that the applause, perhaps the partiality, of Friendship, wakened his vanity so far as to make him think anything of his was worth showing.' *(CW 29)*

Robert Burns reciting some of his verses to Captain Brown in Eglinton Wood.
From the mural in the Burns Room in Irvine Burns Club.

Black Bull Inn, Argyle Street, Glasgow.
It was the terminus for coaches arriving from Perth, Edinburgh, Kilmarnock and Dumbarton. Site is now occupied by Marks and Spencer's chain store. A plaque on the west wall of the building commemorates Burns's visits in 1787 and 1788.

It is significant, too, that when Brown died in 1833, one of the very few presentation copies of the Kilmarnock Edition was found among his effects.

In December, 1787, the two began a correspondence which lasted two years, in the intervals of Brown's voyages. Their only recorded meeting was in the Black Bull Inn, Glasgow, sometime in the middle of February, 1788, when they were joined by the poet's younger brother, William. From the letters, it is evident that the lapse of seven years had not diminished Burns's admiration for the sea captain, nor the value that he placed on the friendship. In a letter to him from Mossgiel on 24th February, 1788, he wrote:

> 'I have met with few incidents in my life which gave me so much pleasure as meeting you in Glasgow. There is a time of life beyond which we cannot form a tie worth the name of Friendship. - 'Oh youth! enchanting stage, profusely blest!' - Life's a fairy scene almost all that deserves the name of enjoyment, or pleasure, is only a charming delusion; and in comes ripening Age, in all the gravity of hoary wisdom, and chases away the dear bewitching Phantoms.'
> *(CL 420)*

Further proof of the friendship is contained in a letter, sent to Brown from Mauchline, on 21st May, 1789:

> '... wishing you would always set me down as your bosom friend - wishing you long life and prosperity and that every good thing may attend you - wishing

Mrs. Brown and your little ones as few of the evils of this world as are consistent with humanity ... Farewell, God bless you! my long-loved dearest friend !!!'
(CL 421).

In 1789, Richard Brown was master of the brig, Mary and Jean, of 191 tons, built at Greenock, in 1786, for the owner, John Campbell, Senr. of Glasgow, and sailing between Greenock and Grenada.[3] Is it merely a coincidence that the names of the ship and its owner have a Burns' connotation? In 1785 he married Eleonara Blair of Girtridge Mill in the Parish of Dundonald, who was ten years his junior, and about 1788, he made his home in Port Glasgow, with his wife and young family. When he gave up the sea, he became a prosperous shipowner and lived in one of the finest houses in the district. He was noted for being hospitable, generous and kind, and took a lively interest in educational and church movements. He was also a keen sportsman and was often out shooting on the moors above the town. The Greenock Ayrshire Society, which was formed about the time of Burns's death, had his enthusiastic support, and it is almost certain that he was a founder member of Greenock Burns Club, formed in 1801.

Many biographers have claimed that the friendship ended in a violent quarrel, apparently over the charge made by Burns in his letter to Dr. Moore. There is, however, no positive

'For GRENADA,

THE New Ship MARY & JEAN RICHARD BROWN, Maſter, will be ready to receive goods at Greenock by the 1ſt of next month, and clear to ſail the 10th of March. She has the beſt accommodation for paſſengers, and will land them at any of the iſlands to windward.

Apply to John Campbell, ſen. in Glaſgow, or the Maſter at Greenock.

N. B. A BLACKSMITH, wHling to Indent for a number of years, and well recommended, will meet with good encouragement. *Glaſgow, Jan. 15th,* 1788.

Enlarged copy of notice which appeared in the *Glasgow Mercury* on 30th January, 1788.
From the same paper we learn that the *Mary and Jean* did not sail until 20th March - ten days late.

Burns listening to Capt. Brown, relating some of his experiences.

proof to support such a claim. Indeed it is difficult to see how it could have happened, as Burns's letter to Moore was not published until 1800, four years after the poet's death. Although Brown hotly denied having led Burns astray, he continued to hold Burns in high regard, both as a poet and a man. An interesting minute of the Greenock Burns Club, dated August 1804, reports on a meeting at which there were over fifty members present. A speaker had given a talk on the life and character of Robert Fergusson. This was followed by a discussion in the course of which a member remarked that 'Burns had copied Fergusson's intemperate habits as well as his poems'. Captain Brown rallied to Burns's defence, stating 'that had the poet been the dissolute person his biographer had made him out, he would neither have had the time, inclination, nor ability to produce such inspired poetry, etc.' [4]

Burns's venture into flax dressing was an abject failure and he returned to Lochlie no better off. Spiritually, however, his sojourn in Irvine had set him on the right road to realising himself. To Richard Brown must go some of the credit, for having directed the footsteps of the young man from Lochlie along the road, which led to fame and finally immortality.

JOHN RANKINE

John Rankine was tenant of the prosperous farm of Adamhill, which lay in the Parish of Craigie about two miles west of Lochlie farm, then tenanted by William Burnes and his family. It would appear that Robert Burns and John Rankine became acquainted during the latter part of the Lochlie tenancy. Rankine was then about fifty years of age and father of a grown-up family. He was quick-witted, fun loving and a practical joker. Although rough in his ways, he was intensely human, and as a notorious wag, he was on good terms with many of the livelier county gentlemen. He and Burns had 'taken' to each other, no doubt finding that they shared a love of fun, and a common interest on many aspects of life.

Burns must have looked forward to his visits to Adamhill, as a welcome escape from the melancholy atmosphere of Lochlie, where his father was beset with worries of litigation and declining health. Rankine's youngest daughter, Annie, recalled the poet's first visit to Adamhill; when he came into the parlour he avoided treading on a small carpet which was in the centre of the floor.[1] Obviously he was not accustomed to such luxury at Lochlie.

While at Lochlie, Burns had a passionate affair with Elizabeth Paton, who was a servant at the farm. In a letter to Robert Chambers, Miss Isabella Begg, the poet's niece, records what her mother told her about Elizabeth Paton[2]:

> 'She had an extremely handsome figure, but very plain looking; so active, honest and independent creature, she had become a great favourite with her mistress. She was rude and uncultivated to a great degree; a strong masculine understanding with a thorough contempt for every sort of refinement.'

When the Burns' household at Lochlie was broken up, following William Burnes's death, Elizabeth Paton returned to the family home at Lairgieside, which was near John Rankine's farm at Adamhill. Burns continued to visit her and in November, 1784, the result of her liaison with him became apparent. It appears that Rankine heard about her 'condition' and forwarded the news to Burns, which provoked the poetic response, 'reply to an Announcement by John Rankine'. *(CW 85)*. The two stanzas beginning 'I am the keeper of the law' are not without interest. The last line of the first verse, 'the breaking of ae point, tho' sma' Breaks a' the gither', are a paraphrase of James, chapter 2, verse 10, 'For Whosoever shall keep the whole law, and yet offend on one point, he is guilty of all'. The second stanza, however is most revealing:

> I hae been in for't ance or twice,
> And winna say o'er far for thrice,
> Yet never met wi' that surprise -
> That broke my rest,
> But now a rumour's like to rise -
> A whaup's i' the nest.

It seems to imply that it was not Burns's first experience in seduction, though it was the first time that pregnancy had resulted. On the other hand, it may just be a case of sexual bravado, or 'he was simply brazening out his humiliation'.[3]

The metaphor was continued shortly thereafter with the much more fulsome 'Epistle to John Rankine enclosing some poems'. *(CW 82)*. It was also a response to the Paton affair. Rankine's character is set forth at the beginning of the poem as a rude, hard-drinking old sinner.

> O rough, rude, ready-witted RANKINE,
> The wale o' cocks for fun an' drinkin',
> There's monie godly folk are thinkin'
> Your dreams and tricks
> Will send you, Korah-like, a-sinkin'
> Straight to Auld Nick's.

> Ye hae sae monie cracks an' cants,
> And in your wicked drucken rants,
> Ye mak a devil o' the Saunts,
> An fill them fou
> And then their failings, flaws, an' wants
> Are a' seen thro'.

In the third and fourth verses, he appeals to Rankine to spare 'the lads in black', lest his 'curs't wit' will uncover their hypocrisy and leave them like 'ony unregenerate heathen Like you or I'. In the fifth verse he tells him that he has enclosed some 'rhymin' ware', and reminds Rankine to let him have a copy of the sang which he had promised. It is not until the seventh verse that the main theme of the epistle develops - the poet's affaire with Elizabeth Paton, couched in humorous, if indelicate allegory of a poacher bringing a partridge to ground -

> Twas ae night lately, in my fun,
> I gaed a rovin' wi' the gun,
> An' brought a paitrick to the grun' -

A bonie hen:
And as the twilight was begun,
Thought nane wad ken.

Unfortunately for Burns, somebody told the 'Poacher-Court' (Kirk session) 'The hale affair', for which he was fined a guinea. This is the only indication that Burns was disciplined by the kirk, as no records exist that he was officially censured at that time.

Snyder considered the poem outstanding - 'Burns never wrote with more verve than when composing the thirteen stanzas of this clever but blackguardly epistle. Never again was he so successful in this vein'. It was included in the Kilmarnock volume and in subsequent editions, despite the opinion of the Revd. Dr. Hugh Blair, who advised Burns to exclude it from the first Edinburgh edition on the grounds of indecency[4]:

> 'The Description of shooting the hen is understood, I find to convey an indecent meaning tho' in reading the poem, I confess I took it literally, and the indecency did not strike me. But if the Author meant to allude to an affair with a Woman, as it is supposed, the whole Poem ought undoubtedly be left out of the new edition.'

Although the epistle would be considered indecent to many in eighteenth century Scotland, it would hardly raise an eyebrow in our modern free-thinking society. It must be remembered that it was addressed to Rankine, who was just the type of person to enjoy verses recounting a sexual adventure. It is, however, another example of Burns's ability to produce brilliant verse out of a very earthy subject.

The Revd. Dr. Hugh Blair (1718- 1800).
Minister of the High Church, Edinburgh. In 1762 he was appointed to the new Chair of Rhetoric at Edinburgh University. Portrait by J. Kay.

In the first verse, Burns refers to Rankine's 'dreams and tricks', and in a footnote explains that 'a certain humorous dream of his was then making a noise in the countryside'. One writer has stated that 'At that time, the dreams of Rankine were of greater local fame than the verses of Burns'.[5] On one occasion he had been invited to a dinner party at a manse where a number of ministers were present. Some of them were taking him to task on some of his foibles. He fenced with them for a little while, but then became very silent, from which they assumed he had been bested. One of the company, however, endeavoured to rouse him and enquired in a very sympathetic tone why he looked so serious - had any calamity befallen him? Rankine replied that on the previous night, he had been troubled with a rather serious dream, which kept running in his mind and dampened his spirits. He said 'I dreamed I was dead and went to Heaven, and there I met the Archangel Gabriel who speired whaur I cam frae, and I telt him frae Ayrshire in Scotland. He then asked me what news I brought frae that part o' the world, and I said there was naething worthy o' special notice, except that recently there had been an unco number o' deaths amang the clergy there'. Gabriel seemed puzzled and replied 'I'm sorry indeed to hear such sad news, but not one of them has made his appearance here.'[6]

A story in similar vein is told of Lord Kames, who was in the habit of calling all his familiar acquaintances, 'brutes'. 'Well, ye brute, how are ye to-day?' was his usual form of greeting. Once in company, his Lordship, having indulged in his rudeness more than usual, turned to Rankine and asked, 'Brute, are ye dumb? Have ye no queer sly stories to tell us?' 'I have no story', replied Rankine, 'but last night I had an odd dream. I dreamed I was dead, and for keeping other than good company on earth, I was sent downstairs. When I knocked at the low door, wha should open it but the deil; he was in a rough humour, and said 'Wha may ye be, and whaur do ye come frae.' 'My name is John Rankine and my dwelling-place was Adamhill.' 'Gae awa wi' ye', replied Satan, 'ye canna come in here: ye're one o' Lord Kames's brutes - hell's four o' them already.'[7]

Some of Rankine's tricks and practical jokes have, fortunately, survived. The special prank which Burns refers to in the first verse of the Epistle, and which no doubt amused him, was the one which Rankine played on an unsuspecting 'sanctimonious professor', whom he had invited to a jorum of toddy in his farmhouse. The hot-water kettle had, by prearrangement, been primed with proof whisky, so that the more 'water' Rankine's guest added to his toddy for the purpose of diluting it, the more potent the liquor became.[8]

AB Todd who was the editor of the *Cumnock Advertiser* for over 30 years, and a close friend of John Rankine's grandson, Hugh Merry, gives the following account of an evening at Adamhill, as handed down to Merry:[9]

> 'Tarbolton Kirk Session were informed that the local Assistant Minister, the Revd. John McMath, had got drunk at Adamhill in the company of John Rankine and Robert Burns. The Session arranged to visit the farm to enquire into the incident and Rankine plotted to save McMath. He gave the visitors refreshments which he repeatedly topped up with 'hot water' from a kettle by the fire. Unknown to the visitors he had filled the kettle, not with water, but with whisky. Eventually, when all the Session were drunk, he had them loaded on to an open cart and dropped off at

their homes in Tarbolton, in full view of the public.'

There may have been some truth in the complaint against McMath, as he was obliged to demit his charge in 1791 because of his excessive drinking.

About the same time as he wrote the Epistle, Burns also penned 'Lines Addressed to Mr. John Rankine' *(CW 85)* by way of an epitaph, the theme of which has a striking similarity to one of Rankine's dreams. In it he compliments Rankine as the one 'honest man' in a 'mixi-maxi motley squad'.

> Ae day, as Death, that gruesome carl,
>> Was driving to the tither warl'
> A mixtie-maxtie motley squad,
>> And monie a guilt-besotted lad:
> Black gowns of each denomination,
>> And thieves of every rank and station,
> From him that wears the star and garter,
>> To him that wintles in a halter:
> Asham'd himself to see the wretches,
> He mutters, glowrin at the bitches:-
>> By God I'll not be seen behint them,
> Nor 'mang the sp'ritual core present them,
>> Without at least ae honest man,
> To grace this man'd infernal clan!'
> By Adamhill a glance he threw,
>> 'Lord god!' quoth he, 'I have it now,
> There's just the man I want, i faith!'
>> And quickly stoppit Rankine's breath.

Annie Rankine, who was the youngest daughter of the family, claimed that she was the heroine of Burns's song 'The Rigs o'Barley.' It is one of his most successful love songs and was included in the Kilmarnock edition of 1786. It is reported that following its publication, she met Burns and told him that she had not expected to be celebrated in print; and he had replied, 'Oh aye, I was just wanting to give you a cast amang the lave' (rest).[10] Annie married John Merry, an innkeeper in Old Cumnock, where she died in 1843.

Burns presented Rankine with a silver-mounted snuff box, and he was the recipient of several poems, apart from those addressed to him. While it must be admitted that 'rough, rude, ready-witted' Rankine was not the most desirable companion for a young man of 25, he was, nevertheless, very appreciative of Burns's burgeoning talents and encouraged him to court the muse. He was so different in character from Burns's father, that it is not surprising that the young poet should be attracted to someone who was so fun-loving as himself.

Lord Kames (1695- 1782).
Well known for his works in law and metaphysics. He was a judge of the Court of Session and had a fine sense of humour and fond of a practical joke. Caricature by J. Kay.

Rankine's memory was long respected in the district. He outlived the poet by almost fourteen years, dying on 2 February, 1810 and was buried in Galston churchyard. There is no evidence that the poet kept up his association with his old friend after he moved to Dumfries, although it is claimed that he wrote the following lines, while on his death-bed and they were forwarded to Rankine immediately after his death:[11]

'He who of Rankine sang, lies staff and deid,
And a green grassy hillock hides his heid:
Alas! Alas! A devilish change indeed!' (CW 86)

Burns was an ardent Mason throughout his entire adult life. There is no doubt that the tenets of the Masonic order of brotherhood and social equality would appeal to Burns' own belief, so nobly expressed in 'a Man's a Man for a' that'. The aristorcracy, scholars, philosophers, gentlemen, professors, farmers and tradesmen all mix together in the Scottish Masonic Fraternity.

In 1782 a dispute arose and the old members of St. James's Kilwinning Lodge, who had amalgamated with St. David's sometime previously, broke away and reformed the St. James's Lodge. It is reported that Burns was one who had followed his brothers into the reconstituted Lodge and he was elected Depute Master of St. James 27th July 1784. It must have given him a great deal of satisfaction on 25th March 1787 when as Depute Master he admitted Claude Alexander, brother of the bonny lass, and others, as honorary members. Later, when had got to know him better, he said of him, 'When Fate decreed that his purse should be full, Nature was equally positive that his head should be empty.'

When he reached the capital Burns was made a member of Canongate Kilwinning Lodge No. 2 Edinburgh. Listed among the members of this Lodge were Lord Elcho, Lord Torphichen, the Earl of Eglinton, Earl of Glencairn, Patrick Miller of Dalswinton, Lord Pitsligo, Professor Dugald Stewart, William Nicol, schoolmaster, William Creech, publisher and Alexander Nasmyth, who painted Burns' portrait.

Burns received honorary membership from Louden Kilwinning, at Newmilns on 27th

Manson's Inn, Tarbolton.
It was the meeting place of St. David's Masonic Lodge, No 174,
and it was there that Burns was passed and raised on 1st October 1781.

March 1786 and from St. John's Kilwinning, Kilmarnock on 26th October 1786. In company with his friend Ainslie, Burns received the Royal Arch degree from St. Abbs Lodge No. 70 on 19th May 1787 at Eyemouth. On the conclusion of his West Highland Tour, he visited Dumbarton where he was made an Honorary Burgess. During his short stay in the town it is almost certain that he visited the local Lodge, as the Master Robert Lindsay was a subscriber to his Edinburgh Edition. On 27th December 1791 when Burns moved to Dumfries he became a member of St. Andrew's Lodge No. 179. He attended a Lodge meeting three months before his death.

MAUCHLINE

**'But Mauchline Race or Mauchline Fair
I should be proud to meet you there'**

JAMES SMITH

Following the death of William Burnes in 1784, the family moved to Mossgiel Farm, which lies within the Parish of Mauchline and about one mile uphill from the village. The move had been eased by Gavin Hamilton, the Mauchline lawyer, who had given the family a sub lease of Mossgiel and befriended them following the father's bankruptcy. Robert was then twenty-five years of age, head of the house and full of resolve to make a success of the farm, along with brother Gilbert. Unfortunately, the purchase of bad seed and a late harvest proved disastrous, and overset all his good intentions. As he wrote in a letter to Dr. Moore, 'I returned like a dog to his vomit, and the sow that has washed to her wallowing in the mire.' *(CL 255)*

Gavin Hamilton, the Mauchline lawyer who befriended Burns.
A drawing by Otto Leyde.
Scottish National Portrait Gallery

It is not surprising, therefore, that he sought diversion from the drudgery and worries of Mossgiel in the life of the village. He had a genius for friendship and very soon he found himself the leader of a small band of harum –scarum youths, who fell under the spell of his magnetic personality. His two closest friends at this level were James Smith, who kept a haberdashers's shop on the north side of the Cross, and John Richmond, a clerk in Gavin Hamilton's office. Both were six years younger than Burns, and with him formed a rebellious trio, who cocked a snoot at convention and outraged all those 'douce folk who live by rule'.

Smith was born in Mauchline on 1st March, 1765, and it would appear that his childhood was not a particularly happy one. When he was ten years old, his father, Robert Smith, a local merchant, was killed by falling from his horse. After a reasonable period of mourning, his mother Jean, married James Lamie, kirk elder and colleague of William Fisher (Holy Willie). Young James was strictly brought up by his stepfather, and it is almost certain that he rebelled against the narrow Auld Licht doctrine embraced by Lamie. At the earliest opportunity he left the family home and went into lodgings. His only sister, Jean, would, no doubt be equally resentful of Lamie's strictures.

The only description of Smith is contained in the opening three stanzas of the verse epistle, which Burns penned to him in the Spring of 1786. It was subsequently included in the *Kilmarnock Edition. (CW 169)*

> Dear Smith, the slee'st pawkie thief,
> That e'er attempted stealth or rief,
> Ye surely hae some warlock-brief
> Owre human hearts;
> For ne'er a bosom yet was prief
> Against your arts.
>
> For me, I swear by sun an' moon,
> And ev'ry star that blinks aboon,
> Ye've cost me twenty pair o' shoon,
> Just gaun to see you;
> And ev'ry ither pair that's done,
> Mair taen I'm wi' you.
>
> That auld, capricious carlin, Nature,
> To mak amends for scrimpit stature,
> She's turned you off, a human-creature
> On her first plan;
> And in her freaks, on ev'ry feature,
> She's wrote the Man.

Although the compliments expressed in these verses are exaggerated in a happy and humorous way, they are, nevertheless sincere, and convey the depth of affection which Burns had for his young friend. The last verse, which neatly rounds of what many of his biographers consider to be his finest epistle, returns to the opening theme:

> Then Jamie, I shall say nae mair,
>   But quat my sang,
> Content wi' YOU to mak a pair,
>   Where'er I gang.

It was in this epistle that Burns gave the first hint that he was considering publication of his poems:

> This while my notion's ta'en a sklent,
> To try my faith in guid, black prent.

When proposals for publishing were subsequently issued, Smith proved most energetic in promoting the sales by securing forty-one subscriptions.

The value which Burns placed on Smith's friendship is further exemplified in a number of his letters. In one to Richmond, who was then working in Edinburgh, *(CL 76)* he states, 'I am extremely happy with Smith; he is the only friend I have now in Mauchline.' On 30th July, 1786, just prior to his projected departure for Jamaica, he wrote again to Richmond:

> 'My hour is now come--- You and I will never meet in Britain more--- I have orders within three weeks at farthest to repair aboard the Nancy, Capn. Smith from Clyde to Jamaica, and to call at Antigua,---This except to our old friend Smith, whom God long preserve, is a secret about Mauchline.' *(CL 77)*

The letter was written during the period when William Armour, anticipating that some money might come to Burns from the publication of his poems, had secured a warrant to put him in jail, until he could 'find security for an enormous sum'. Burns went into hiding to escape service of the warrant. His 'contact' at this time was Smith, who kept him informed of all that was happening in the Armour 'camp'. Burns never forgot the loyalty of his young friend. Writing to Robert Ainslie, two years later, he said, 'I pay you no compliment when I say that, except my old friend Smith, there is not any person in the world I would trust so far.' *(CL 33)*

There is no doubt that Burns was happy in Smith's company. Although the young Mauchline draper did not possess any literary or poetic talent, the one thing he did share with Burns and Richmond was a disposition to flaunt the narrow conventions of Mauchline society. Professed fornicators, they formed the 'Court of Equity', a mock court, whose object was to try those fornicators who denied their guilt. One of the 'hearings' has been commemorated by Burns in a lively humorous poem called, 'The 'Libel Summons' or 'Court of Equity' *(CW 222)*, in which he handles Scots legal and ecclesiastical phraseology in brilliant fashion. The officers of the Court are described thus:

> First POET BURNS he takes the CHAIR,
> Allow'd by a', his title's fair;
> And pass'd nem. con. Without dissension,
> He has a DUPLICATE pretension. ---
> Next, Merchant SMITH, our worthy FISCAL,
> To cow each pertinacious rascal;
> In this, as every other state,
> His merit is conspicuous great;
> RICHMOND the third, our trusty CLERK,
> The minutes regular to mark;
> And sit dispenser of the law
> In absence of the former twa.

Mauchline

In an article on Mauchline in the *Burns Chronicle* of 1896, J. T. Gibb states that, 'Kirsty Wilson had a son to James Smith, "slee'est James" as the Poet calls him, who was called by the name of William' . . . He served as a boy with Gilbert Burns at Mossgiel and in his latter days was the village postman.[1] He died about 1862. Entries in the Mauchline Kirk Session records reveal that on three Sundays in the summer of 1783, James Smith did public penance in church for the sin of fornication. There is nothing in the minutes to indicate the identity of the woman involved, although the two dates mentioned above would seem to be chronologically related, and suggest that the woman could have been Kirsty Wilson.

Several biographers have claimed that Smith fled from Mauchline in 1786 under censure of the Kirk. This is not borne out by the Kirk Session Records and some doubt exists as to his culpability. An entry in the minutes of 3rd December, 1786, reads:

> 'Compeared Agnes Curry. Acknowledges herself with child, and being exhorted to be ingeneous in naming the real father, declares that Mr. James Smith, late merchant in Mauchline is the father. The session appoint William Fisher and James Lamie to talk to Smith and report.'

Smith, by this time had removed to Linlithgow, where he had entered into partnership with a man called Miller, in a calico printing business on the banks of the Avon. He appeared before the Session on 10th December and denied that he was the father. He was desired by the Moderator ('Daddy' Auld) to attend when called. Smith replied that he would attend if he could, but he did not doubt of getting justice done whether present or absent. The Session, no doubt appreciating his difficulty in travelling from Linlithgow, later agreed to his request that Mr. Andrew Noble, Session Clerk, act as his agent. Agnes Curry made several subsequent appearances before the Session, along with another witness. She disclosed in evidence that she was a servant of Smith's mother. Mrs. Carswell in her Life declares that Agnes was more than twice Smith's age, but nowhere in the minutes is her age given.[2]

Last mention of the affair is made on 16th May, 1787. The entry in the minutes reads:

> 'The Session, according to their usual method, propose as soon as may be that the parties be confronted; and for this purpose shall be ready to call a meeting so soon as Mr. Smith comes to the country . . .'

It would appear that the confrontation never took place, as there is no evidence that James Smith or Agnes Curry ever did public penance in church.

Smith left Mauchline for Linlithgow in the latter part of 1786, and it was about this time that Burns wrote a humorous epitaph on a 'Wag in Mauchline'. *(CW 231)* It is generally believed that the wag was Smith, but as Henley so wisely observes, the epitaph need not be interpreted too literally.

> Lament him, Machline husbands a',
> He often did assist ye,
> For had ye staid hale weeks awa',
> Your wifes they ne'er had missed ye!
>
> Ye Mauchline bairns as on ye pass
> To school in bands thegither,
> O, tread ye lightly on his grass,
> Perhaps he was your father!

Backcauseway, Mauchline.
From a painting by Monro S. Orr, The house, on the immediate left,
is the one in which Burns and Jean Armour started married life.

Burns favoured Smith with a number of letters, and fortunately, six of these have survived. They are of particular interest as they furnish vital information on important aspects of the poet's life. When Burns was feeling miserable and distracted over the apparent desertion of Jean Armour, and considering fleeing the country, it was to Smith he wrote on 1st August, 1786, as his confidant:

'Against two things I am as fixed as fate--- staying at home, and owning her conjugally. The first, by Heaven, I will not do ! – the last, by hell I will never do!—A great God bless you, and make you happy, up to the warmest weeping wish of parting friendship! . . If you see Jean, tell her I will meet her; so help me God in my hour of need.' *(CL 117)*

Ten days later Burns addressed another letter to his friend in which he gave details of his altered plans for emigration to Jamaica. *(CL 118)* On his return to Mauchline, following his triumphant visit to Edinburgh, he again wrote to Smith on 11th June, 1787, *(CL 118)* expressing his disgust at the 'mean servile compliance' of the Armour family. It was to Smith too on 30th June of the same year, that he gave a lively account of his journey down Loch Lomondside. This letter, or more correctly, the latter half of it, and first published by Dr. Currie, contains almost all the information, however sparse, that Burns gave of his West Highland Tour. *(CL 119)*

The final two letters are the most important of the series, as they touch on the enigma of Burns's marriage to Jean Armour. Smith was the first to learn of the union. In his letter of 28th April, 1788, Burns wrote:

'...to let you into the secrets of my pericranium, there is a certain clean-limbed, handsome, bewitching young hussy of your acquaintance, to whom I have lately and privately given a matrimonial title to my corpus. I intend to present Mrs.Burns with a printed shawl, an article of which I daresay you have a variety; 'tis my first present to her since I have irrevocably called her mine, and I have a kind of whimsical wish to get the said first present from an old and valued friend of hers and mine, a trusty Trojan, on whose friendship I count myself possessed of a life-rent lease...Mrs. Burns ('tis only her private designation) begs her best compliments to you...' *(CL 121)*

While Burns informed Smith that 'lately and privately' he had married Jean, he was not forthcoming on the details or the exact date. The phrasing of the letter seems deliberately ambiguous, and tends to suggest that he never went through a formal marriage service. By Scots law of the day, a declaration of marriage in the presence of witnesses constituted a legal union, though in the eyes of the Kirk it was still an irregular marriage.

A subsequent letter to Smith, dated 26th June, 1788, suggests that Burns had not fulfilled this legal requirement. He wrote:

'I have waited on Mr. Auld about my Marriage affair, and stated that I was legally fined by a Justice of the Peace--- He says that if I bring an attestation of this by the two witnesses, there shall be no more litigation about it.--- As soon as this comes to hand, please write me in the way of familiar Epistle that, 'Such things are.' *(CL 122)*

In other words Smith was asked to testify, but not on oath, that he had been a witness to the marriage, when two months previously he had received a letter from Burns letting him into the secret. That Burns dissembled in this matter there can be little doubt, especially as Smith had not lived in Mauchline for over two years. The two letters quoted tend to destroy the claim made in the Train Manuscripts that 'Jean Armour and Rob Burns were privately married in the writing office of Gavin Hamilton, Mauchline, by John Farquhar, Esq., of Gilmilnscroft, J.P.'.[3] An aura of mystery surrounds the marriage and two centuries of research have failed to dispel it.

Smith's venture into calico printing was not a success and in 1788 he left the country, but not before the two friends had enjoyed a reunion in Linlithgow. It is generally believed that he went to Jamaica, that haven of Scots in the eighteenth century, and from whose unhealthy climate Burns had been happily spared. Nothing further was heard of Smith and he left no trace.[4] Cromek speaks of him being dead in 1805.[5]

Smith was the closest of all Burns's Mauchline friends and proved a sheet anchor during the Armour crisis. Although there was a wide gulf between his mediocre abilities and the genius of the poet, there was, nevertheless, a strong bond of fellowship between them. A happy freedom marked their relationship, and nowhere is this more evident than in the letters which Burns addressed to his friend. Perhaps the greatest tribute paid to Smith was when Burns described him as a 'trusty Trojan, whose friendship I count myself possessed of a life-rent lease'. *(CL 122)* Unfortunately that life-rent lease expired all too soon.

The Square, Mauchline.
From a painting by Monro S. Orr. The house at the end of the block was where Mary Morrison lived.

THE BELLES OF MAUCHLINE

In 1784 Robert Burns and brother Gilbert took over the tenancy of Mossgiel farm, situated just outside the village of Mauchline. The arrival of the poet must have caused a flutter in the hearts of the lasses. He wore the only tied hair in the parish and, when attending church, he wrapped his fillemot plaid round his shoulders in an unusual fashion, in defiance of convention. [1] While in Tarbolton he had attended a dancing class to 'brush up his manners', and could address the fair sex 'with the greatest ease and freedom' [2] With his long dark hair and smouldering eyes he must have set the tongues wagging. Obviously he made the acquaintance of the village lasses, as the following lines, written probably in late 1784, confirm.

> In Mauchline there dwells six proper young belles,
>> The pride of the place and its neighbourhood a',
> Their carriage and dress, a stranger would guess,
>> In Lon'on or Paris they'd gotten it a',
> Miss Millar is fine, Miss Markland's divine,
>> Miss Smith she has wit, and Miss Morton is braw,
> There's beauty and fortune to get wi' Miss Morton;
>> But Armour's the jewel for me o' them a'. *(CW 79)*

No doubt Burns was conscious of the stir his arrival had created. To add fuel to the gossip, he assumed the role of the rake in a song, which was written probably just after settling in to Mossgiel. It is nothing more than a piece of playful bombast, showing Burns posing as a village Lothario.

> O leave novels, ye Mauchline belles,
>> Ye're safer at your spinning-wheel;
> Such witching looks are baited hooks
>> For rakish rooks like Rob Mossgiel;
> Your fine Tom Jones and Grandisons,
>> They make your youthful fancies reel;
> They heat your brains, and fire your veins,
>> And then your prey for Rob Mossgiel.
>
> Beware a tongue that's smoothly hung,
>> A heart that warmly seems to feel;
> That feeling heart but acts a part–
>> 'Tis rakish art in Rob Mossgiel
> The frank address, the soft caress,

> Are worse than poisoned darts of steel:
> The frank address, and politesse,
> Are all finesse to Rob Mossgiel.

Sometimes Burns was inclined to invest his lady friends with qualities they did not possess in any great degree. Gilbert tells us that 'there was often a great disparity between his fair captivator, and her attributes'. [3] It would appear that this was also true of most of the Mauchline Belles. Several old persons who had lived in Mauchline in Burns's time and were still alive in 1858, retained vivid recollections of the six belles. According to them there was only one who could be considered a beauty. Of the rest, one was blind in one eye, another was badly marked with smallpox, and three were considered to have no more than ordinary attractions. It is even more surprising to learn that Jean Armour was regarded as the plainest of them all. [4]

The first of the belles to be mentioned in the poem was HELEN MILLER ('Miss Miller is fine'), eldest daughter of John Miller, landlord of the Sun Inn, which stood on the south side of Loudon Street, opposite the Cross. It was removed when Earl Gray Street was constructed in 1821. [5] Helen would have been considered beautiful had it not been that she was blind in one eye. Whether it was a defect from birth or the result of an accident is not known, although it is of interest that her brother Sandy was totally blind by the time he was middle aged. Helen, however, seems to have been endowed with her fair share of personal charms. She was regarded as a 'guid catch', as brother Sandy, who had made his fortune in India, had settled a large dowry on Helen and her younger sister, Elizabeth.

On 28th August, 1791, Helen married the village doctor, John Mackenzie, 'the warm and worthy friend of Robert Burns'. When Mackenzie set up practice in Mauchline he lodged in the Sun Inn and it was there that he met Helen. It is generally believed that they started their married life in a house in the Back Causeway, part of which also served as a surgery. The house which Mackenzie ultimately owned, has been preserved and now houses the caretaker of the Burns House Museum, immediately adjoining.

In 1801 Mackenzie sold his practice and moved to Irvine to be near Eglinton Castle, seat of the Earl of Eglinton, who had settled an annuity on the doctor in order to retain his services. Helen died at Seagate House, Irvine on 2nd March, 1827, and is buried in Irvine Parish Kirkyard. Immediately following her death, Mackenzie retired and went to Edinburgh, where he spent the remainder of his life until his death on 3rd January, 1837.

One feels that Burns was indulging in poetic licence when he described the next belle in the poem, JEAN MARKLAND, as 'divine'. She has been described as neat, rather than handsome, with a fine figure and a pleasant manner. One suspects that the word 'divine' has little more significance other than rhyming with 'fine'.

Jean, who was born at Mauchline on 20th October, 1765, was the daughter of George Markland, a general merchant, who had a shop at the head of the Cowgate, near the Cross, which dealt in groceries and drapery. He also kept several cows and traded as a dairyman. Apparently a very unpleasant rivalry existed among some of the Mauchline traders at that time. Whatever may have been the reason, several of Markland's competitors were extremely hostile towards him. [6]

This hostility came to a head in 1779, when Markland lodged a complaint with the Kirk Session against the wife of a fellow trader. He claimed that she had not only defamed him, but had said 'that he would not thrive, and that all his cattle would die', expressions that savoured very much of witchcraft. It came out in evidence that the accused had expressed the wish 'that George Markland's cow might die, as their other two had done which he had lost.' Her reason for expressing such an evil wish against a neighbour was the bad treatment she had received from Markland and his family. The Session found that nothing had been proved to sustain such a serious charge, and the complaint was dismissed. The accused than turned accuser and lodged a libel 'against Agnes Shaw, spouse of George Markland and against Jean Markland, their daughter, for having said that 'she had killed two of their cows, and that they should be bled above the eyes.' This was a commonly held superstition that such a bleeding rendered a witch powerless, and undid any evil she had done. The Session were reluctant to take up the case, but were obliged to do so. The evidence broke down, however, especially that given by Poosie Nancie, who had been called as a witness. It appears that she swore, but not in the required way. [7]

The whole episode was nothing more than mean petty squabble, unworthy of repetition except for the interest given to it by Jean Markland's involvement. It also reveals too, the deep-rooted belief in witchcraft which existed at that time. The poem, 'To a Louse' is reputedly to have been written by Burns about a 'crowlin' ferlie' seen on Jean's bonnet during a church service. It includes the incomparable opening lines of the final verse which are now renowned world-wide: *(CW111)*

> O wad some Power the giftie gie us
> To see oursels as ithers see us !

On 16th September, 1788, Jean married James Findlay, the Excise Officer at Tarbolton, who had instructed Burns in his excise duties earlier in the year. Robert Chambers claims that it was Burns who introduced Findlay to Jean. James Findlay was born in 1755. We first hear of him in the Excise at Ayr in 1786, next at Tarbolton in 1787 and 1788 and again at Ayr in 1789. In 1792 he was transferred to Greenock as Tide Surveyor. He retired in 1825 and died at Greenock in 1834. Jean died there in 1851,aged 86, having survived her husband by seventeen years. [8]

Burns was more truthful in his description of JEAN SMITH when he wrote, 'Miss Smith she has wit'. Jean, like her brother James, was small in stature, dark eyed and lively. Although not favoured with any degree of beauty, she was possessed of considerable wit and was the clever one of the belles. She was born on 3rd April, 1767,[9] the only daughter of Robert Smith, a local merchant, whose house stood on the north side of Mauchline Cross. It was demolished in 1821 to make way for the new road to Kilmarnock. At the time of her father's death in 1775, she was only eight years of age. Her mother remarried, her second husband being James Lamie, strict ultra Calvanistic elder of Mauchline Parish Kirk, and colleague of 'Holy Willie' Fisher. It can well be imagined that the spirited and fun loving Jean would not take too kindly to her narrow minded stepfather.

On 8th September, 1794 Jean married James Candlish,[10] who was born in the same year as Burns, in the little hamlet of Purclewan, about two miles from Mount Oliphant. His father, Henry McCandlish was the village blacksmith, and is credited with having lent a copy of *The Life of Wallace* to the youthful Burns. James McCandlish (he later dropped the Mac) and Burns first met when they attended Dalrymple Parish School in the summer of 1772. They met again the following year at Ayr Grammar School, when Burns spent a brief three weeks revising English grammar, under his former teacher, John Murdoch. Later, Burns described Candlish as 'the earliest friend except my brother that I have on earth, and one of the worthiest fellows that ever any man called by the name of Friend.' *(CL 319)*

The parents of James Candlish had intended him for the ministry, and he had commenced his theological studies, but finding himself in conflict with the accepted doctrine, he switched courses in favour of medicine. He attended Glasgow University, where he successfully completed his medical studies and was licensed as a physician. Of a very shy disposition, he decided not to enter general practice, and about 1788 he settled in Edinburgh as a teacher of medicine at Edinburgh University. While a student at Glasgow he taught languages at Mauchline, presumably during University recesses, and it was there that he met Jean Smith.

James Candlish died suddenly on 29th April, 1806, at the early age of forty-six. His death was most unexpected, and Jean found herself and her four surviving children left without any provision for the future. She left Edinburgh and went to Glasgow, where she conducted a successful school for young ladies. There were three sons and four daughters of the marriage. The youngest was the Rev. Dr. Robert Smith Candlish of the Free Church, who took a prominent part in the Disruption of the Church of Scotland in 1843. It was at his home in Edinburgh that his mother, Jean, died on 20th January, 1854, at the advanced age of eighty-seven, having survived her husband by forty-eight years and outlived all the other belles.[11] She is buried in the family grave in the Old Calton Cemetery, Edinburgh. [12]

'A Dance in a Barn' Pen and wash drawing by David Allan.
Original by Otto Leyde. National Gallery of Scotland.

The fourth belle, whose name appears in the poem, was ELIZABETH MILLER, of whom Burns wrote, 'Miss Betty is braw'. Daughter of John Miller and younger sister of Helen, she was born in 1768,[13] and was better known under the diminutives of Betty, Betsy, Bess or Elisa. She might have been 'braw', had her face not been marked with the ravages of smallpox. From letters written by Burns, it is evident she was the object of his affection during the latter half of 1786 – sometime following the death of Mary Campbell in May and his departure for Edinburgh in the same year. It does not appear to have been a very serious affair. In a hurried note to John Richmond in Edinburgh, written on 27th September, 1786, Burns concludes, 'Bettsy Miller awaits me'. On his return to Mauchline from Edinburgh, after a period of six months, he reported to James Smith, then in Linlithgow, in a letter dated 11th June 1787, 'I slept at John Dow's, and called for my daughter, Mr. Hamilton and family, your mother, sister and brother my quondam Eliza etc., all, all well'. *(CL 118)*

Both Helen and Elizabeth Miller figure in an unfinished poem by Burns, which came to be known as 'The Mauchline Wedding', probably written in 1786, although the wedding took place in July, 1785, as indicated in the first line of the poem. It was not until 1788, however, that Burns enclosed the verses in a letter to Mrs. Dunlop. He wrote:

'You would know an Ayrshire lad, Sandy Bell, who made a Jamaica fortune, and died some time ago. A William Miller, formerly a Mason, now a Merchant in this place, married a sister germain of Bell's for the sake of £500 her brother had left her. A sister of Miller's who was then Tenant of my heart for the time being, huffed my Bardship in the pride of her new Connections, and I, in the heat of my resentment resolved to burlesque the whole business. . .' *(CL 154)*

Burns then sets down five verses of 'The Mauchline Wedding'. The fragment is mainly devoted to Helen and Elizabeth's preparation for their brother's wedding. Two verses, the second and fourth, serve to illustrate the sister's preoccupation with dress.

> The rising sun o'er Blacksideen
> Was just appearing fairly,
> When Nell and Bess got up to dress
> Seven lang half-hours o'er early!
> Now presses clink and drawers jink,
> For linens and for laces;
> But modest Muses only *think*
> What ladies under dress is
> On sic a day

> But now the gown wi' rustling sound
> Its silken pomp displays;
> Sure there's nae sin in being vain
> O' siccan bonie claes !
> Sae jimp the waist, the tail sae vast–
> Trouth, they were bonie birdies !
> O Mither Eve, ye wad been grieve
> To see their ample hurdies
> Sae large that day !!! *(CW 157)*

Burns continues the letter, 'Against my muse had come thus far, Miss Bess and I were once more in Unison, so I thought no more of the piece. Tho' the folks are rather uppish, they are such as I did not choose to expose, so I think this is about the second time I ever scrawled it.' It is a great pity that Burns never finished the poem. What heights it may have attained had he gone on to describe the wedding itself.

It is generally agreed that the Elizabeth Miller was the Eliza of Burns's song 'From Eliza I must go', written sometime during the period when the poet intended emigrating to Jamaica, and when he and Elizabeth were in 'unison'. The song was included in the Kilmarnock Edition.

The song has two verses; here is the first:

> From thee, ELIZA, I must go,
> And from my native shore:
> The cruel fates between us throw
> A boundless ocean's roar;
> But boundless oceans roaring wide,
> Between my love and me,
> They never, never can divide
> My heart and soul from thee. *(CW 50)*

On 8th September, 1794, Elizabeth married William Templeton, [14] who had come from Auchinleck and taken over James Smith's drapery business in the village. Sadly, Elizabeth died the following year giving birth to her first child.

CHRISTINA MORTON was the most attractive of the Mauchline belles. When Burns wrote, 'There's beauty and fortune to get with Miss Morton,' he was doing her no more than poetic justice. According to contemporary reports, she was 'a remarkably handsome person – her beauty was of the full, ripe, rosy cast, and a young woman of great propriety of demeanour and sweetness of manner.' [15] In addition to her beauty she had inherited a fortune of £500.

Christina was the daughter of Hugh Morton, who owned the Black Horse Inn, [16] the top flat of which was used for dancing and singing purposes. It has been claimed that it was in this hall that Burns met Jean Armour on Mauchline Race Night. It has also been claimed that it was here that Robert and Jean were married,[17] but there are so many doubts surrounding Burn's marriage, that this claim must be treated with a certain amount of scepticism.

Blackie's edition of *Burns* states that Christina had a secret passion for the poet and was disappointed when he showed a preference for Jean Armour. It is said that because of this she went to New Cumnock and worked with a farmer at the harvest, giving as the reason, 'that there were so many clashes going on about Robert Burns and her, that she wished to be out of the way.'[18] On 27th December, 1788, Christina married Robert Paterson, a draper and general merchant in Mauchline. Of the marriage there were four sons and two daughters.[19]

Robert Paterson figures prominently in a letter which Burns sent to John Tennant Jr. on 13th September, 1784. It is evident from the first part of the letter that the poet had intended being present at a social evening, but was prevented from doing so because of a sudden and unexpected illness. The lasses being present suggests that the occasion was a dance or a rocking, held somewhere outwith Mauchline, as Burns tells Tennant that he had recovered sufficiently the following morning 'to be able to ride home.' Burns, however, was given an account of the evening, as he explains in the letter:

> 'I have been informed by Mr. Robert Paterson how affairs went among you on Friday night, tho' by the bye I am apt to suspect his information in some particulars. He tells me you used all the powers of your eloquence, first on my friend Miss R. (Ronald?) and next on Miss C --, to have the liberty of escorting them home, but all to no purpose, and I assure you Mr. Paterson plumes himself not a little that he has been able to foil so formidable an antagonist. – In short, as Mr. Robt. is very sanguine in all his projects, he seems fully assured of carrying his point; and I declare I never saw a man more intoxicated with success in my life. – However to do the gentleman justice his passion is but the raptures of a Lover in Romance, not the rant of a dramatic Hero. – Her sweet, sonsy face, which I have so often admir'd, he knows no more about it but only as it helps him to distinguish her from another person; and tho' he talks of her as being "a grand cracker" to speak in Mr. Paterson's own style, yet he seems to have little idea of her engaging frank, honest-hearted manner; and for good sense and education they are rather against him, as being so much superior to his own, they entangle him in a thousand difficulties; but like a true Merchant he has stated it in the Ledgers of his fancy thus; Stock Dr. to cash by Mrs. Paterson's portion £300. We talk of air and manner, of beauty and wit, and lord knows what unmeaning nonsense, but – there – is solid charms for you – who would not be in raptures with a woman that will make him £300 richer ?'

Jean Armour in later life, the 'jewel o' them a'.

If one of the young ladies referred to in the letter was either Jean or

Anna Ronald of the Bennals, as De Lancey Ferguson suggests, they were both very attractive marriage prospects. In addition to their beauty and personal charms, which Burns has put on record, [20] they were assured of a handsome dowry. Burns is in no doubt that Paterson was preoccupied with money and success, and it comes as no surprise that he finally won a lass with a fortune of £500. Christina lived to a ripe old age and died sometime in the early 1850s.

The sixth belle was of course, JEAN ARMOUR. She is undoubtedly the most celebrated of the belles. Although regarded as the plainest, in Burns's eyes she was the 'jewel o' them a'. The fact that her life was interwoven with his, gives her pre-eminence over all the others. As Scott Douglas so rightly recorded, 'Of Armour's history, immortality has taken charge.'

JEAN ARMOUR
1765 – 1834
WIFE OF ROBERT BURNS
ERECTED BY
BURNS HOWFF CLUB
SEPTEMBER 2004

Jean Armour
is recognised at last in sculpture. Two Burns Clubs have the distinction
of providing two statues, one in Mauchline and one in Dumfries.

JOHN RICHMOND

Poosie Nancie's, c 1876.
An ill-famed drinking house owned by Poosie Nancie. It was within this drinking den that Burns,
Richmond and Smith encountered a gang of singing and carousing vagrants, one evening, which
inspired Burns to write 'The Jolly Beggars' Painting by Munro S Orr.

Some months before the death of William Burnes at Lochlie Farm on 13th
February, 1784, Robert and brother Gilbert had secretly negotiated a sub
let of Mossgiel Farm from Gavin Hamilton, the Mauchline lawyer and fellow
Mason. It proved a wise move and provided a safe haven for the family, following
the sequestration at Lochlie. Mossgiel lay within the Parish of Mauchline, and
about one mile from the village.

Poosie Nancie's to-day.

Following their first meeting, it appears that Gavin Hamilton took a friendly interest in the poet. In addition to granting a sub let of the farm, he gave Robert and Gilbert the opportunity to purchase cattle and dairy utensils at a private sale. It was also probably due to his advice that the members of the family were able to salvage something from their father's estate, as preferred creditors for unpaid wages.

It is almost certain that it was through Burns's business dealings with Hamilton that he became acquainted with John Richmond, who was employed as a clerk in Hamilton's office. Six years younger than Burns, he was in some respects a kindred spirit; a rebel against the narrow conventions of Mauchline society, and a willing participant in any ploy that would shock the 'unco guid' and raise the hackles of the orthodox. He and Burns soon became boon companions.

Richmond was born in 1765, the younger son of Henry Richmond, Laird of Little Montgarswood in the Parish of Sorn. He was probably descended from another John Richmond, who, in the middle of the 17th century, occupied Mossgavil (old spelling of

Baxter's Close, Edinburgh.
It was here that Burns shared lodgings with Richmond[1] on his first visit
to Edinburgh in 1787. From the painting by Henry G. Duguid.
National Gallery of Scotland

Mossgiel) and was a servant of Lord Loudon, and a bailie in the burgh of the barony of Mauchline.[1] Nothing is known of Richmond's early childhood, except that he attended a school in Newmilns, some ten miles distant from Little Montgarswood, where he boarded with some friends. We next hear of him at the age of seventeen, when he entered the legal firm of John and Gavin Hamilton, which suggests that he had received a fairly liberal education.

A contemporary described him as 'a great crony of Burns, but a rough chap, and reported wild on account of his fun, energy, and free ways, though all they could say against him was he was fond o'company.'[2] He was Burns's frequent companion, and together with James Smith and William Hunter, an intelligent shoemaker, they formed the notorious Court of Equity. They met frequently in John Dow's Whitefoord Arms, and tried those members of the community, especially the rigidly righteous, who denied their sexual sins. As has already been mentioned in the sketch on James Smith, Burns was 'judge', Smith assumed the mantle of 'procurator fiscal' and –

> Richmond, the third, or trusty clerk,
> Our minutes regular to mark,
> And sit dispenser of the law
> In absence of the former twa. *(CW 227)*

Hunter, 'weel skill'd in dead and living leather' was 'messenger at arms.'

While it had been necessary for each member of the Tarbolton Bachelors' Club 'to be a professed lover of one or more of the female sex', for membership of the Court a man must have given proof of his virility. This the four 'officials' had certainly done, as all were 'fornicators by profession.'

On three consecutive Sundays in January, 1785, Richmond mounted the cutty stool in Mauchline Parish Kirk to receive a lengthy harangue on the sins of the flesh from the Rev. 'Daddy' Auld, for his fornication with local lass, Jenny Surgeoner, who as a result, bore him a daughter.[3] Perhaps it was as a consequence of this indiscretion, that he went to Edinburgh in November of the same year, where he joined William Wilson, W.S. as a clerk. A more likely explanation may have been his desire to pursue his legal studies in the wider ambience of the Capital. Whatever the reason, it is evident he had no thought of marrying Jenny Surgeoner at that stage.

At the foot of the Cowgate in Mauchline, on the opposite corner from John Dow's Whitefoord Arms, stood the house owned by the ill-famed Poosie Nancie. Her real name was Agnes Gibson, and along with her half-witted daughter, Racer Jess, she kept an ale shop come lodging house, where beggars and gangrel bodies foregathered. At that time the countryside swarmed with beggars. William Aiton in his *Agricultural Report for Ayrshire*, published in 1811, wrote, 'In the daytime they prowl through the towns, or roam the country, begging, stealing or swindling, as opportunity may offer. At night they return to their miserable haunts to consume their spoils, in feasting, drinking, swearing, and carousing.'

It was such a gang of beggars who were singing and carousing in Poosie Nancie's howff, one night in the Autumn of 1785, that attracted the attention of Burns, Richmond and Smith, who happened to be in the vicinity. The trio ventured in to witness the scene, but they did not wait long. Long enough, however, to provide Burns with the material for his immortal; 'Jolly beggars,' *(CW 182)* which Henley described as 'this irresistible presentation of humanity caught in the act and summarised forever in terms of art' A few days after the visit, Burns recited part of the cantata to Richmond, who later claimed that originally, it included songs for a sailor, a sweep, and Racer Jess.

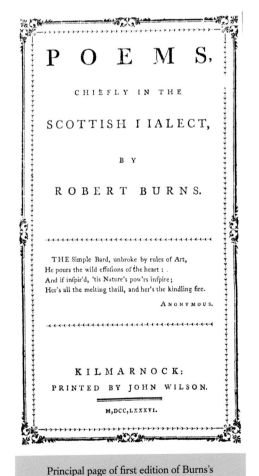

POEMS,

CHIEFLY IN THE

SCOTTISH IIALECT,

BY

ROBERT BURNS.

THE Simple Bard, unbroke by rules of Art,
He pours the wild effusions of the heart : .
And if inspir'd, 'tis Nature's pow'rs inspire;
Her's all the melting thrill, and her's the kindling fire.
ANONYMOUS.

KILMARNOCK:
PRINTED BY JOHN WILSON.

M,DCC,LXXXVI.

Principal page of first edition of Burns's poems, which has become known as the Kilmarnock Edition

The cantata was never published during Burns's lifetime as it was considered too licentious. It appeared first, in an imperfect form, in a chapbook by Stewart and Meikle in 1799, as 'The Jolly Beggars', although the title 'Love and Liberty' is generally agreed as being more descriptive of the sentiments and theme of the piece. Stewart was a nephew of John Richmond, and in 1802 he published the complete work. In a marginal note he stated that 'the original manuscript was long in the hands of John Richmond . . . . and he, (Richmond) remembers taking the song (of Merry Andrew) with him to Edinburgh in 1786.'[4] James C.Dick suggested that when George Thomson wrote to Burns in September, 1793, enquiring about the cantata, 'he had heard of it casually, perhaps through Richmond, who was then resident in Edinburgh.'[5]

This was extremely unlikely as Richmond left Edinburgh and returned to Mauchline, long before 1793, and before Burns agreed to collaborate with Thomson in the work of the Select Scottish Airs.

Following Richmond's arrival in Edinburgh, nothing was heard of him for three months. This was revealed in a letter which Burns sent to him on 17th February, 1786, replying to one he had received from Richmond the previous day. The poet commenced by reproaching his friend for his silence and neglect. Burns was obviously most displeased, as he concluded the letter, 'I can scarcely forgive your long neglect of me, and I beg you will let me hear from your regularly by Connel. If you would act your part as a friend, I am sure neither good or bad fortune should estrange or alter me.' *(CL 76)*

Before Burns's next letter to Richmond, his affair with Jean Armour had reached a climax. Jean had returned to Mauchline from Paisley, where she had been sent to live with an Aunt and so escape, temporarily, the inevitable scandal and gossip. She had written to the Kirk Session admitting she was pregnant and named Burns as the father. Robert's offer of marriage had been rejected, and Jean's father, acting on advice, had mutilated the 'marriage lines', which Burns had given her. His spirits were at a very low ebb; he had tried to put her out of his mind by indulging in 'all kinds of dissipation and riot, mason meetings, drinking matches and other mischief, but all in vain' *(CL 111)* The ship, however, was on its way home that was to take him to Jamaica and out of her life forever.

On 9th July, Burns sent another letter to Richmond. Apparently he had become more reconciled to his situation, although it is evident from the letter that he still retained a love for Jean, however he tried to disguise it. He wrote:

> 'I have waited on Armour since her return home, not by – from any the least view of reconciliation, but merely to ask for her health; and to you I will confess it, from a foolish hankering fondness – very ill-plac'd indeed. The mother forbade me the house; nor did Jean shew that penitence that might have been expected. – However, the Priest, I am inform'd will give me a Certificate as a single man, if I comply with the rules of the Church, which for that very reason I intend to do. Sunday morn: I am just going to put on Sackcloth and ashes this day. I am indulged so far as to appear in my own seat . . . my book will be ready in a fortnight. If you have any Subscribers, return me them by Connel.' *(CL 77)*

The 'Kilmarnock Edition' of Burns's poems was published on 31st July 1786, Six hundred and twelve copies were printed and the edition was sold out in just over a month. Anticipating that Burns would derive some profit from the publication, James Armour had obtained a warrant to secure a sum of money from him, for the support of the child that Jean was expecting. Burns went into hiding to escape service of the warrant, and it was from one of those hiding places, Old Rome Foord, that he sent his next letter to Richmond. His refuge was the home of his mother's half sister, Jean Broun and her husband, James Allan.[6] The letter gives an up-to-date account of his plans for emigration, and also shows how distraught his state of mind was at that particular time.

'My hour is now come – you and I will never meet in Britain more.- I have orders within three weeks at farthest to repair aboard the Nancy, Capn. Smith, from Clyde to Jamaica, and to call at Antigua. This, except to our friend Smith, whom God long preserve, is a secret about Mauchline. – Would you believe it ? Armour has got a warrant to throw me in jail till I find security for an enormous sum. This they keep an entire secret, but I got it by a channel they little dream of; I am wandering from one friend's house to another, and like a true son of the Gospel, "I have nowhere to lay my head." I know you will pour an execration on her head, but spare the poor ill-advised girl for my sake; tho' may all the Furies that rend the injured enrage Lover's bosom, await the old harridan, her Mother, until her latest hour.. . . .I write, it in a moment of rage, reflecting on my miserable situation – exiled, abandoned, forlorn.

I can write no more – let me hear from you by the return of Connel – I will write you ere I go.' *(CL 77)*

The publication of his poems brought fame to Burns and spread his name beyond the boundaries of his native Ayrshire. It stayed Armour's hand, who, no doubt, had second thoughts about pursuing someone who had become something of a celebrity overnight. It was with a great sense of relief that Burns wrote again to Richmond on 1st September, 1786. The opening passage gives details of the poet's change of plans for his impending passage to Jamaica. The letter continues:

Dr. John Moore, to whom Burns wrote his famous autobiographical letter in 1787, the original of which is now in the British Museum. Engraving from *The Land of Burns*.

'The warrant is still in existence, but some of the first Gentlemen in the county have offered to befriend me; and besides, Jean will not take any step against me without letting me know, as nothing but the most violent menaces could have forced her to sign the petition. I have called on her once and again of late. As she, at this moment, is threatened with the pangs of approaching travail; and I assure you, my dear Friend, I cannot help being anxious, very anxious, for her situation. She would gladly now embrace that offer she once rejected, but it shall never be more in her power. I saw Jenny Surgeoner of late, and she complains bitterly against you – you are acting very wrong, my friend; her happiness or misery is bound up in your affection or unkindness. Poor girl! She told me with tears in her eyes that she had been at great pains since she went to Paisley, learning to write better; just on purpose to be able to correspond with you; and had promised herself great pleasure in your letters Richmond, I know you to be a man of honour, but this conduct of yours to a poor girl who distractedly loves you and whom you have ruined – forgive me, my friend, when I say it is highly inconsistent with that manly integrity that I know your bosom glows with. Your little sweet innocent too – but I beg your pardon; 'tis taking an improper liberty. "He would not have done a shameful thing, but once, Tho' hid from all the world and none had known it. He could not have forgiven it to himself" - Otway. I do not know if Smith wrote you along with my book; but I tell you now, I present you with that Copy, as a momento of an old friend, on these conditions – you must bind it in the neatest manner, and never lend it, but keep it for my sake.' *(CL 77)*

Burns certainly took a liberty in reproaching Richmond for his unmanly conduct toward Jenny Surgeoner. It savours very much of hypocrisy on his part, when it is recalled that he had behaved no better towards Betty Paton, the previous year. Indeed, it was only six weeks before writing this letter that he had assigned to Gilbert the profits of the Kilmarnock Edition, and his share in Mossgiel, in consideration of Gilbert undertaking to provide for Betty Paton's child. "Dear bought Bess" had been born some fifteen months before, and in view of the lapse of time, it may be questioned if Burns's action was taken in the interest of the child, or to prevent any monies from the publication falling into the hands of James Armour.

Two more letters were written by Burns to Richmond during September, 1786. Both were brief, one on the 3rd gave the news that Jean Armour had given birth to twins, and on the 27th he informed his friend that he was going to try for a second edition of his poems. In his autobiographical letter to Dr. Moore, Burns wrote, 'I had taken the last farewell of my few friends; my chest was on the road to Greenock; I had composed a song "The gloomy night is gathering fast" *(CW 250)* which was to be the last effort of my muse in Caledonia, when a letter from Dr. Blacklock to a friend of mine, overthrew all my schemes by rousing my poetic ambition." Dr. Thomas Blacklock, a blind Edinburgh poet and man of letters, had received a copy of the 'Kilmarnock Edition' from the Rev. Dr. George Lawrie of Loudon. He was so impressed with the poems, that in his letter of thanks to Lawrie, he suggested that the poet should consider publishing a second and more numerous edition. He prophesied 'a more universal circulation than anything of the kind that had been published within my memory.' [7] Lawrie passed the letter to Gavin Hamilton, who in turn showed it to Burns. The result was that Burns abandoned all thoughts of emigrating to Jamaica. He borrowed a pony and set off for Edinburgh on 27th November, 1786, arriving the following morning, somewhat under the weather, due to the lavish hospitality he had received en route.

The only intimate friend Burns had in the Capital was Richmond, who occupied a humble room in Baxter's Close on the north side of the Lawnmarket. It appears that he offered to share his room and bed with Burns. Whether some prior

Dr. Thomas Blacklock, the blind Edinburgh poet who was largely instrumental in Burns abandoning his plan to go to Jamaica, and instead to proceed to Edinburgh to try for a second publication of his poems. Engraving by W & F Holl from *The Land of Burns*

arrangement had been made is not known, but Burns readily accepted his friend's offer. The room was rented from a Mrs. Carfrae, who charged Richmond 2/6 per week, which was increased to 3/- when Burns joined him. The Rev. Archibald Lawrie, son of the Rev. George Lawrie, already mentioned, who was then a student at Ediinburgh University, visited Burns and described the lodging as:

'. . .down a long dark nesty closs, his room (up a flight of dark stairs) lighted by one window, which, whatever light it might throw on the sheet of white paper then before him, could contribute but little to enliven his mind. At this time he was much engaged in company; on the mantelpiece above his chimney he had a small bit of white paper pasted up. On my observing on it the names of Earl Glencairn, Sir John Whitefoord, etc, etc, I asked him what it meant. He told me it was invitations to dinner and supper for weeks to come, that his old rhyming jade of a muse had introduced him to such a train and tribe of strangers that he had nothing to do but visit the great; as he had a strong aversion at making promises without fulfilling them, he had pasted up the names of his friends with the dates of their invitations, lest he should make any mistake. – In this dark retreat our Poet lived for the first six months he remained in Edinburgh, and as his finances were at that time low, he could not afford an apartment for himself, he was therefore obliged to put up with half a small room and half a small bed.' [8]

In one of his letters Burns gives a lively description of Mrs. Carfrae and the characters who occupied the rooms directly above:

> 'I have just now had a visit from, my Landlady who is a staid, sober, piously-disposed, sculduddery – abhorring, widow, coming on her grand climacterick. She is at present in sore tribulation respecting some "Daughters of Belial" who are on the floor immediately above – and as our floors are low and ill-plaistered we can easily distinguish our laughter-loving, night-rejoicing neighbours – when they are eating, when they are drinking, when they are singing, when they are etc., my worthy Landlady tosses sleepless and unquiet, "looking for rest but finding none" the whole night.'

Burns spent almost six months in Edinburgh. On 22nd April, 1787, he had the satisfaction of seeing the purpose of his visit fulfilled, when the second of his poems was published. During his stay he had been accepted by the highest level of Edinburgh society – the aristocracy, landed gentry, judges, professors, historians, and other men of letters. On a lower level he became a member of the Crochallan Fencibles, a convivial club of wits and bon vivants that met in Dawney Douglas's tavern in Anchor Close. Richmond, it seems, remained very much in the background. Knowing how much he enjoyed the convivial evening in Mauchline, one wonders if he was ever invited to join in the frolics of the Fencibles, or did Burns treat him strictly as a fellow lodger ?

At the beginning of July, 1787, following a tour of the West Highlands, Burns returned to Mossgiel and it was from there that he wrote to Richmond on 7th July, making reference to his friend's employer, William Wilson, who died on 18th June. In the opening paragraph the poet wishes to know about Richmond's future and reveals in scathing fashion, his opinion of Wilson:

> 'I am all impatience to hear your fate since the old confounder of right and wrong has turned you out of place, by his journey to answer his indictment at the bar of the other world. He will find the practice of the court so different from the practice in which he has for so many years been thoroughly hackneyed, that his friends, if he had any connections truly of that kind, which I rather doubt, may well tremble for his sake. His chicane, his left-handed wisdom, which stood so firmly by him, to such good purposes, here, like other accomplices in robbery and plunder, will, now the piratical business is blown, in all probability turn king's evidence, and then the devil's bagpiper will touch him off "bundle and go" If he has left you any legacy, I beg your pardon for all this; if not, I know you will swear to every word I said about him.' *(CL 80)*

Within three months of Wilson's death, Richmond returned to Mauchline, possibly toward the end of August, 1787, and established himself there as a writer, having spent under two years in Edinburgh. Dr. Charles Rogers in his Book of Robert Burns states that Richmond spent four years in the Capital. All the factual evidence tends to show that Rogers was incorrect. The existence of a letter dated 7th September, 1787, from Gavin Hamilton to 'Mr. John Richmont, (sic) writer in Mauchline,[9] suggests that Richmond had set up practice in Mauchline sometime before the date of Hamilton's letter. In a letter of 20th October, which Burns sent to Richmond at Mauchline, he stated, 'It will be a fortnight at least before I leave Edinburgh, and if you come for the winter session when it sits down, perhaps we shall have the pleasure of meeting once more in auld Reekie. – I lodge at Mr. Cruickshank's, No 2d, St. James's Square, Newtown.' It seems to indicate that when Richmond left Edinburgh in August he was undecided as to his future – whether to return to the Capital or remain in Mauchline. That he decided to remain in Mauchline is borne out by another letter of 7th February, 1788, from Burns, addressed to 'Mr. John Richmond, Writer, Mauchline' In it he wrote, 'As I hope to see you soon, I shall not trouble you with a long letter of Edinburgh news.' *(CL 81)*

It is generally believed that when Burns returned to Edinburgh on 8th August, he found that Richmond had taken in another fellow lodger, and he was obliged to look elsewhere. Reference to three letters which Burns wrote at that period, help to clarify the position. On 31st July, in a letter to William Nicol, sent from Mossgiel, he said, 'I had promised to lodge with our common friend, Mr. Cruickshank, but I know it will be quite inconvenient as he will be leaving town.' *(CL 81)* This would indicate that Richmond had informed Burns sometime preciously, that the room would not be available to him on his return. Two reasons could have been given – firstly, Richmond's intention to return to Mauchline sometime in August, when he would give up the let of the room, and secondly, notice to Burns that he had taken in a fellow lodger.

Highland Mary's birthplace was a cottage to the left of this picture to the rear of Auchamore Farm, Dunoon.

The Pier and Highland Mary Statue, Dunoon.

Statue of Highland Mary at Dunoon Pier, erected in 1859.

The second letter written by Burns to William Tytler *(CL 291)* and dated 'Lawnmarket, Monday, noon, August, 1787' would seem to contradict the claim that Burns had to find a room elsewhere. On this point two theories are possible ; either Richmond managed somehow to accommodate Burns temporarily, for one or two nights, or the poet used Baxter's Close as an accommodation address. The third letter was written by Burns on 14th August, 1787 and addressed to Archibald Lawrie, *(CL 128)* who had been his visitor at Baxter's Close. He wrote it in an 'attic storey, alias the garret,' believed to have been the flat of Latin Master, William Nicol, who had offered Burns temporary accommodation until their departure on 25th August, for a tour of the Highlands. The flat was over Buccleuch Pend (since demolished) in Buccleuch Street.

Some writers have claimed that the friendship was strained following six months together as fellow lodgers. Others have asserted that the two friends quarrelled at that time, but no documentary proof has been produced to substantiate these claims. Indeed the last two letters which Burns sent to Richmond are sufficiently cordial in tone to dispel any suggestion of strained relations or disagreement at this time. In his letter of 25th October, Burns gives a brief account of his tour of the Highlands, and informs Richmond that he is busy 'assisting with a collection of Scotch Songs set to music by an engraver in the town.' The concluding paragraph displays no lack of warmth on Burns's part. It reads:

'I long much to hear from you, how you are, what are your views, and how your little girl comes on. By the way, I hear I am girl out of pocket and by careless murdering mischance too which has provoked me and vexed me a good deal. I beg you will write me by post immediately on receipt, of this, and let me know the news of Armour's family, if the world begin to talk of Jean's appearance any way.' *(CL 81)*

Burns's very casual reference to being 'a girl out of pocket' was occasioned by the death of his daughter Jean, one of the first set of twins, who had been cared for by the Armours since here birth. The letter shows that Jean Armour was still very much in his thoughts, perhaps more so as she was again pregnant by him.

The last communication Richmond received from Burns was a very brief note, written from Edinburgh on 7th February, 1788. Its brevity was due to the fact that Burns was returning to Mauchline a fortnight later, and would bring Richmond up to date with all the Edinburgh news when they met. At this point the correspondence ceased.

Round about 1817 – the date is uncertain – Richmond gave information about Burns to James Grierson of Dalgoner, who was an antiquarian and avid collector of every scrap of information concerning the poet. Grierson passed his notes to Joseph Train, who subsequently supplied John Lockhart with the following stories when he was engaged in writing his biography of Burns.[10]

'**HIGHLAND MARY** – Truth deprives her history of much of its charm. Her character was loose in the extreme. She was kept for some time by a brother of Lord Eglinton's, and even while a servant with Gavin Hamilton, and during the period of Burns' attachment it was well known that her meetings with Montgomerie were open and frequent. The friends of Burns represented to him the impropriety of his devotedness to her, but without producing any change in his sentiments. Richmond told Mr. Grierson that Montgomerie and Highland Mary frequently met in a small alehouse called the Elbow – and upon one occasion, he and some of Burns's friends, knowing they were actually together in the Elbow, - and having often in vain tried to convince Robert of her infidelity, upon this occasion they promised to give ocular proof of their assertions. The party retired to the Elbow – Richmond (Mr. Grierson's informant) was one, and they took their seats in the kitchin (sic) from which two rooms branched off to the right and left – being all the accommodation the house contained. They had taken their position in the kitchin (sic) to be sure that no one could leave the other room without being observed. After waiting long, and when Burns was beginning to ridicule their suspicions, at last Mary Campbell appeared from one of the rooms – was jeered by the party, in a general way – blushed and retired. Another long interval elapsed and Burns began to rally his spirits, which were very much sunk – and Montgomerie (Colonel or Capt.) walked out of the same room. – Burns coloured deeply – compressed his lip – and muttered, 'damn it.' After enduring considerable banter from his friends, he soon gave way to the general hilarity of the evening, and his friends thought he had seen enough of Highland Mary but in a few days after, he returned 'like the dog to its vomit.'

'CLARINDA – Richmond informed Mr. Grierson that one day this personage called at their lodgings for Burns who had gone out. – Richmond knew her well, and also the nature of the intimacy that existed between her and the poet – and he instantly volunteered his services to find Burns – but so affraid (sic) were both he and Clarinda (Mrs. Maclehose) that she should be discovered, he locked her into their appartment (sic) and took the key with him. – Being unsuccessful in his search to find Burns, he at last returned and liberated the Prisoner.'

Painting of 'Clarinda'
by an unknown artist.
(not from life)

If Richmond's story about Highland Mary is true, it means that Burns was so besotted that he was prepared to marry someone who was known to be a mistress of another, and that Gavin Hamilton employed a woman of easy virtue as a servant in his household. The story is extremely difficult to believe when it is remembered that three years after her death, Burns was inspired to write 'To Mary in Heaven' *(CW 372)* and describe her in one of his letters as 'my ever dear Mary, whose bosom was fraught with Truth, Honor, Constancy and Love'... *(CL 182)*. In the absence of additional evidence it is impossible to state with absolute conviction that Richmond's story is true or false. Not so with his fanciful tale of Clarinda. By reference to dates and Burns's movements in Edinburgh, it is possible to prove conclusively that the story is undoubtedly false. Richmond stated that Clarinda called at 'their lodgings' and that he locked her into 'their apartment.' The only lodgings which he and Burns shared was at Baxter's Close, which Richmond vacated toward the end of August, 1787, when he returned permanently to Mauchline. Burns did not meet Clarinda until 4th December, 1787, and he was then living with William Cruickshank at 2 St James Square. How Richmond concocted this fabrication it is difficult to imagine, but having proved the falseness of the Clarinda story, how is it possible to trust in the veracity of the other? It is

John Richmond's house,
in Mauchline today.

rather significant that Lockhart very wisely did not include either story in his biography of Burns, published in 1828. It may be relevant at this point to quote Richmond's nephew, Henry Richmond, who became laird of Montgarswood. Apparently he had a poor opinion of his uncle, as he is reported to have 'frequently and without scruple characterised him as one of the greatest liars.' [11]

On 5th August, 1791, Richmond made amends for his previous indiscretion when he married Jenny Surgeoner, who was six years his senior. There were no children of the marriage, other than Janet, who had been born out of wedlock six years previously. He is reported to have been 'expert in business and attentive to its concerns.' He became a respectable member of Mauchline society, and in later years when he was questioned by visitors about Burns, he evaded their questions, apparently not wishing to recall some of the wild escapades of his youth. It is claimed, however, that he would not allow a word to be uttered in his presence to Burns's disadvantage, and he was adamant that when they lodged together the poet kept regular hours and was always sober.

Richmond's wife died in 1836, aged 76, and he died ten years later in his eighty first year. Both were buried in Mauchline Kirkyard. Janet, their daughter, married William Alexander, a Mauchline merchant, and there were four sons and three daughters of the marriage. Two sons and two daughters emigrated to Australia and it is possible that some of their descendants are still living there. [12]

Mauchline

To all intents and purposes the friendship between Burns and Richmond ended sometime after Burns returned to Mauchline in February, 1788, and possibly before he took up residence in Dumfries. For the last eight years of the poet's life no letters were exchanged, or if there were, none has survived. It could be argued that some of the information that Richmond supplied to Grierson did nothing to enhance Burns's memory, and there is a hint here that there could have been an estrangement. The little that is known of Richmond's life, following his return to Mauchline, gives rise to the suspicion that, having opted for Mauchline respectability, he wished to distance himself from Burns. His reluctance to answer questions about the Bard seems to confirm this. Prof. De Lancey Ferguson has stated that the friendship 'was spent and empty before the correspondence closed.' [13] The last three letters from Burns to Richmond do not support this statement, as they show no lack of warmth or cordiality. It is possible that the friendship may have become 'spent' shortly thereafter. The reason for the final break in the correspondence is never likely to be known.

JOHN LAPRAIK

Anyone reading a life of Burns and coming across the name of John Lapraik would no doubt wonder where such an unusual name originated. It is perhaps French in origin and has gone through various forms of spelling before finally emerging as Lapraik. According to one source, the name derives from the old castle of Leprevik, now in ruins, about a mile and a half south of East Kilbride in Lanarkshire.[1] The family of Leprevik or Leprevick is said to have had a grant of the heritable office of sergeant and coroner of the Lordship of Kilbride in the reign of Robert III, and confirmed to them by several charters of the James's.[2] Robert Chambers cites Wood's Peerage, which states that in 1364, avid II a charter of William de Cunningham, Lord of Carrick, to James de Leprevik, of half of the lands of Polkairne, in the parish of Ochiltree, King's Kyle, which shows that there were persons of that name in the district at that early period.[3] A legend has it that a Frenchman called La Privick was one of Queen Mary's retinue, when the Queen returned to Scotland from France in August, 1561. Following the defeat of Mary and her forces at Langside in 1568, the Queen fled to England, 'and La Privick found himself Laird of Dalfram - about three miles west of Muirkirk.'[4] The story is just too plausible to be acceptable.

John Lapraik, the subject of this sketch, is more likely to be descended from James de Leprevick, who was granted half the lands of Polkairne, in the parish of Ochiltree in 1364. This seems to be supported by records which show that there was a John Leprevik in Dalquhram, in the parish of Ochiltree, in 1575, and in the same year there was another John Lekpreuik in Grenoktoun, in the parish of Muirkirk.[5]

On 11th June, 1661 the session minutes of Muirkirk Parish Kirk record that John Leckpryke presented a bill of complaint against William Broune, his wife and daughter, for the sclandering of him with thift. One witness declared:

> 'that William Broune said to her that John Leckpryke had taken in ane yew of his, and had eaten the haggis of his in his house.' The subsequent minutes are silent on the outcome.[6] This John Leckpryke was probably the great grandfather of John Lapraik.

The Lapraik form of spelling seems to have been adopted round about 1679. An entry in the session records for that year, reads, 'James Lapraik received thirteen shillings and fourpence for mending the back kirk style.'[7]

John Lapraik was born in 1727 in Laigh Dalquhram (now spelt Dalfram) in the parish of Muirkirk, the eldest son of John Lapraik, laird of Dalfram. The property had been in the possession of the family for several generations. Nothing is known of the nature and extent of his education, but considering the schooling that was then available, it must have been fairly elementary. On the death of his father, he inherited the property at an early age. Not only did he become laird of Upper and Nether Dalfram, but he also held the lease of the mill and property at Muirshill, about half a mile distant.

In March, 1754 he married Margaret Rankine, eldest daughter of William Rankine of Lochhead and sister of John Rankine of Adamhill (see page 66). A contract of marriage was drawn up and from it we learn that Margaret brought with her a dowry of £100. In the event of his death, his wife was to receive, subject to certain contingencies, an annuity of 200 merks Scots. In addition to the signatures of the contracting parties, i.e. John Lapraik, William Rankine and Margaret Rankine, the document was also signed by John Rankine, which seems to suggest that he may have put up some of the money for the dowry. Lapraik's property, detailed in the document, consisted of:

> 'All and haill that eight shilling ninepenny land of old extent of Dalquhram, alias Nether Dalquhram, and all and haill the eight shilling ninepenny land of old extent of Upper Dalquhram, commonly called Laigh Hall; as also, all and haill the eight shilling ninepenny land of old extent of Dalquhram, called Douglas Dalquhram, with the respective houses, biggins, yeards, parts, and pendicles, and haill pertinents of the said several lands and teinds, parsonage and vinerage of the same, all lying within the parish of Muirkirk, lordship and late regality, now barony of Kylesmuir, and sheriffdom of Ayr, together with the fishing and salmond and other fishing in the water of Ayr.' [8]

It is interesting to note that the 'eight shilling ninepenny lands of old extent', as mentioned in the contract, relate to a system of land valuation from the earliest times, when a twofold division of land operated:

> 'first by magnitute into ox-gate or ox-gang, husband-land, and plough-land, extending in the Lowlands at least, to 1,326 and 104 acres respectively; and next by value, as pound, merk, shilling or penny land, with multiples of each.' [9]

It would appear that the lands of Dalfram were about 68 acres in total and not too highly valued.

Lapraik and his wife appear to have lived in happy wedded bliss until 1763 or 1764 when Mrs. Lapraik died shortly after the birth of her fifth child. Undoubtedly this was a bitter blow to Lapraik who was left with five young children. After a decent interval he met and wooed Janet Anderson of the neighbouring farm of Lightshaw, who was fourteen years his junior. The marriage, which took place in 1766, appears to have been a happy one. In verses written at this time, he expresses something of the pain and sorrow occasioned by his first wife's death and the joy he now shared with Janet:

> Ye gods! Who reside in the regions above,
> Deprive me of life, or inspire her with love!
> Make Jenny's fond bosom to feel for my pain,
> That I may sweet peace and contentment regain.
>
> She smiled sweetly on me, and gave me her hand,
> And with blushes did own she was at my command:
> Transported with joy, while she lean'd on my breast,
> I thanked the kind gods who had heard my request
> So I to all sorrows and cares bid farewell -
> While Jenny does love me no care I can feel.

Life seems to have gone on happily in the Lapraik household until 1773, when the failure of the Douglas and Heron Bank placed Lapraik in serious financial difficulties. Although he was not a shareholder, he had borrowed heavily and had also acted as guarantor for others.

Because of the difficult situation in which he now found himself, he let the lands of Dalfram but continued to work the smaller property of Muirshill, of which he was the tacksman. A few years later he also leased the sheep farm of Netherwood on the water of Greenoak. He continued in this situation for nine years, struggling to clear his feet. About 1784 he sold all the lands of Dalfram and returned to Muirshill, but the money he received from the sale was insufficient to clear his debts. He was still harassed by legal prosecution and finally he suffered the indignity of being imprisoned in Ayr jail. His period in prison appears to have been very temporary, as some of his friends came to his rescue as guarantors. In the preface to his book of poems, published in Kilmarnock in 1788, he refers to this unfortunate event:

> 'In consequence of misfortune and disappointments, he (the author) was, some years ago, torn from his ordinary life and shut up in retirement. Imagining, however, that he had a kind of turn for rhyming, in order to support his solitude, he set himself to compose the following pieces.'

He also claims in his preface that he 'was denied that share of education which is necessary to form the gentleman and poet and, what is more against him still, he has never had leisure to read.' Despite this self denigration, the preface reads well and shows that he had made good use of whatever education he had received.

While I can either sing or whistle,

Your friend

and Servant,

Mossgiel near Machline

April 1785

Robert Burness

Conclusion of Burns's 'First Epistle to John Lapraik'
At this time the poet was still using the old form of spelling his surname.
He dropped the 'e' in 1786.

His poems touch on many of the subjects which Burns himself covered - the Seasons, Hogmanay, back-biting and falsehood. Verses on melancholy and solitude no doubt reflect the state of his mind, following the death of his first wife, and were evidently composed before his imprisonment. He found inspiration too in unpoetic subjects, eg 'Lines put upon a post leading to the Tar-work at Muirkirk, 1786.'

> Halt passengers, come here and see,
> What fortune has bestowed on me,
> A field run over with moss and glaur,
> Yet in its bowels is coal-pit tar;
> Not only Tar, but Paint and Oil,
> And salts to make one spout a mile,
> Magnesia, and God knows what,
> Are all extracts from my coal-pit.

While imprisoned in Ayr, he is said to have written the tender love lyric, addressed to his wife:

> When I upon thy bosom lean
> 	Enraptured I do call thee mine;
> I glory in those sacred ties
> 	That made us one who once were twain.
> A mutual flame inspires us both -
> 	The tender look, the melting kiss;
> Even years shall ne'er destroy our love,
> 	Some sweet sensation new will rise.
> Have I a wish? 'tis all for thee;
> 	I know thy wish is me to please;

Our moments pass so smooth away
    That numbers on us look and gaze.
Well pleased to see our happy days,
    They bid us live and still love on;
And if some cares shall chance to rise,
    Thy bosum still shall be my home.

I'll lull me there and take my rest;
    And if that aught disturb my fair,
I'll bid her laugh her cares all out,
    And beg her not to drop a tear.
Have I a joy? tis all her own;
    Her heart and mine are all the same;
They're like the woodbine round the tree,
    That's twined till death shall us disjoin.

It was this song that brought Burns and Lapaik together, the poet having heard it sung at a rocking (social evening). Gilbert Burns describes the occasion:

> 'It was at one of these rockings at our house, when we had twelve or fifteen young people with their rocks, that Lapraik's song, beginning 'When I upon thy bosom lean', was sung, and we were informed who was the author. Upon this, Robert wrote his first epistle to Lapraik, and the second in reply to his answer.' [10]

Lady with rock or distaff.
This was the method used for spinning thread before the introduction of the spinning wheel.

Burns, in his epistle, expresses his appreciation of the song and hopes that he may become acquainted with the author:

On fasten-e'en we had a rockin,
To ca' the crack and weave our stockin;
And there was muckle fun and jokin
    Ye need na doubt;
At length we had a hearty yokin,
    At 'sang about.'

> There was ae sang, amang the rest,
> Aboon them a' it pleas'd me best,
> That some kind husband had addrest
>   To some sweet wife;
> It thirl'd the heart-strings thro' the breast,
>   A' to the life.
>
> I've scarce heard ought describ'd sae weel,
> What gen'rous, manly bosoms feel;
> Thought I, 'Can this be Pope, or Steele,
>   Or Beattie's work?'
> They tauld me 'twas an odd kind chiel
>   About Muirkirk. *(CW 101)*.

Scott Douglas observed that 'Burns was never a fastidious critic; but it is not very easy to understand his admiration of Lapraik's poetry.'[11] Although he praised the song, Burns must have thought that it required improving, before submitting it to James Johnson for inclusion in *The Scots Musical Museum*.[12] When it appeared in that publication, in 1790 it had been improved, obviously by Burns, and given a more 'hamely attire.' In an interleaved copy of *The Scots Musical Museum* which Burns presented to Captain Robert Riddell of Glenriddell, he wrote:

> 'This song ('When I upon thy bosom lean') was the work of a very worthy, facetious old fellow, John Lapraik, late of Dalfram, near Muirkirk; which little property he was obliged to sell in consequence of some connexion as security for some persons concerned in that villainous bubble, THE AYR BANK. He has often told me that he composed this song one day when his wife had been fretting o'er their misfortunes.'[13]

It is interesting to speculate what Burns's reaction would have been had he known that Lapraik was guilty of plagiarism. About 1828, a song, very similar to Lapraik's lyric, was discovered in an old magazine, which led to the belief that Lapraik was an imposter, who had passed off the song as his own. Henley and Henderson, however, were inclined to give Lapraik the benefit of the doubt. They stated that 'Lapraik's song ... closely resembles one in Ruddimans Weekly Magazine, 11th. October, 1773, 'When on thy bosom I recline', dated Edinburgh, 11th. October, and signed 'Happy Husband.' It has been too rashly inferred that Lapraik plagiarised from this lyric; he may have written it himself.'[14] Thomas Crawford, writing as recently as 1960, is of the same opinion and contends that there is no evidence to brand Lapraik as a plagiarist and suggest that Lapraik may have been 'Happy Husband.'[15]

In an excellent article, entitled 'Imposing on Burns', which appeared in the Burns Chronicle, Davidson Cook furnishes evidence to prove that Lapraik could not have written 'When I upon thy bosom lean.' He points out that following the failure of the Douglas and Heron Bank in June, 1772, Lapraik was imprisoned in Ayr jail, which must have been subsequent to June 1772, and it was while he was in jail that he is said to have written the lyric. Davidson Cook reveals that he found the magazine version of the song in *The Scots Magazine* for April, 1772, (p 207), printed anonymously and headed 'Sonnet by a Husband.' He also uncovered what he assumed to be the original version in *The Universal Magazine of Knowledge and Pleasure* for October, 1771, (p 209). It is printed below:[16]

SONNET
By a Husband, but not a modern one.

When on thy bosom I recline
Enraptur'd still to call theee mine -
   To call thee mine for life,
I glory in the sacred ties
(Which modern wits and fools despise)
   Of husband and of wife.

One mutual flame inspires our bliss,
The tender look - the melting kiss
   Ev'n years have not destroy'd;
Some sweet sensation every new
Springs up - and proves the maxim true,
   That love can ne'er be cloy'd.

Have I a wish, 'tis all for thee;
Hast thou a wish, 'tis all for me,
   So soft our moments move,
That angels look with ardent gaze,
Well pleas'd to see our happy days,
   And bid us live - and love.

If cares arise (and cares will come)
Thy bosom is my softest home,
   I lull me there to rest;
And is there aught disturbs my fair,
I bid her sigh out all her care,
   And lose it in my breast.

> Have I a joy, 'tis all her own,
> Or her's and mine are all but one;
>   Our hearts are so intwin'd,
> That, like the ivy round the tree,
> Bound up in closest amity,
>   Tis death to be disjoin'd. 'CL10'

There seems little doubt that Lapraik altered the song by the unknown poet, which had appeared in print at least eight months before Lapraik was imprisoned in Ayr jail. If he had written the lyric under the pseudonym 'Happy Husband', as suggested by Henley and Henderson and Thomas Crawford, why did he find it necessary to alter it when he published his book of poems in 1788?

Burns's first epistle appears to have been warmly welcomed by Lapraik and it is believed that he responded in rhyme. Allan Cunningham states that 'The reply of Lapraik has been recorded; it was in its nature pleasing, and drew from the Bard of Mossgiel a second epistle, on which he says much of his toils and his musings.' Unfortunately 'Honest' Allan did not state where the reply is recorded.[17] It appears that a correspondence was carried on for some time, as Burns addressed a further two epistles to Lapraik. It is unfortunate that Lapraik's replies - if they were in rhyme - have not survived, but from what we know of his poetry, it is reasonable to assume that they would not have possessed any great intrinsic merit.

In a verse in his first epistle, Burns proposes a meeting in Mauchline:

> But Mauchline race, or Mauchline fair.
> I should be proud to meet you there;
> We'se gie ae nicht's discharge to care
>   If we forgather
> An' hae a swap o'rhymin' - ware
>   Wi ane anither. *(CW 103)*

No doubt Burns and Lapraik met as proposed, and although there is no record of the meeting, it must have been an enjoyable one. This may be inferred from Burns's third epistle, which he sent to Lapraik on 13th September, 1785. In it he promises to visit Lapraik at Muirsmill:

> But if the beast and branks be spar'd
> Till kye be gaun without the herd,
> An a' the vittel in the yard,
>   An' theekit right,

> I mean your ingle-side to guard
> > Ae winter night.
> Then muse-inspirin' aqua-vitae
> Shall make us baith sae blythe an' witty
> Till ye forget ye're auld an' gatty,
> > An be as canty
> As ye were nine years less than thretty,
> > Sweet ane an' twenty! *(CW 128)*

It is generally supposed that during the course of the winter, Burns did pay a visit to Muirsmill, where he spent a happy evening with Lapraik and returned to Mossgiel the following day.

Encouraged by the success of Burns's Kilmarnock Volume of poems, and no doubt flattered by the attention paid to him by Burns, Lapraik decided to put his own verses into print. An octavo volume, running to 240 pages, entitled *Poems on Several Occasions* was issued from the press of John Wilson of Kilmarnock in 1788. Few of the pieces, however, were of sufficient poetic merit to attract much attention from the public, and the book met with little or no success. It is rather surprising that he did not include any of the epistles which he is supposed to have written to Burns. This suggests that his replies to Burns may have been written in prose. One epistle to the poet, written sometime after their first correspondence, is included and is chiefly an apology for his venturing to court the muse in his old age:

> I liked the lasses onco weel,
> > Langsyne when I was young,
> Which sometimes kittled up my muse,
> > To write a kind love song.

He confirms that it never occurred to him to trouble the world with his 'dull, insipid, thowless rhyme' -

> Till your kind muse, wi' friendly blast,
> > First tooted up my fame,
> And sounded loud thro' a' the wast,
> > My lang-forgotten name.

The following extracts are from a poem called 'Poet's Apology for Rhyming'. While the verses do not display the genius of poetry, they are characterised by common sense and keen observation. They also breathe that spirit of independence so dear to Burns:

Mauchline

No satire keen shall make me rage,
    Ev'n tho' my fate were worse;
My head's grown empty by old age,
    But not so toom's my purse!

My means and credit, fickle things,
    They both are fled and gone;
And I my weary days maun pass
    Unheeded and unknown!

* * * * * * * * *

I for a feast will never fawn,
    Nor pour out my complaint:
If welcome's hand is now withdrawn,
    I'll stay at home content.

I'll make my pottage, boil my kail,
    Remote and little known;
With ink I'll black the other sheet,
    Regardless of man's frown.

* * * * * * * * *

I'm not so vain as to pretend
    To teach men to behave;
Yet still am of a nobler mind
    Than ever be their slave.

I love a friend that's frank and free
    Who tells to me his mind;
I hate to hing upon a hank,
    With hums and ha's confined.

It would appear that shortly before Lapraik published his book of poems he entertained the notion of emigrating to America. With this prospect in mind, he wrote a poem entitled 'Farewell to his Native Country':

> Farewell, ye deal delightful fields,
>   Where first my breath I drew!
> Farewell, my much respected friends,
>   I bid you all adieu!
> For other fields and other plains,
>   And other clouds and skies;
> For other distant, unknown scenes,
>   I must now sail the seas!

* * * * * * * * * *

> In ease I spent my youthful days;
>   My friends they me carest;
> Quite free of care, in sports and plays,
>   I was supremely blest!
> I ne'er envied the rich and great,
>   Nor did I wealth pursue;
> Yet now I leave my native seat,
>   And bid a long adieu!
>
> You friends who graced my little book,
>   And share my joy and woe,
> May health and peace still be your lot,
>   And wealth still on you flow!
> Your friendship I shall ne'er forget
>   I'll to your memory kneel!
> To every friend, with aching heart
>   I bid a sad farewell!

Of the subsequent history of Lapraik there is little to relate. About 1796, when he was well advanced in years, he surrendered the lease of Muirsmill and lived for a short period in a cottage at Nether Wellwood, which had originally been built as an inn. He removed from this house to Muirkirk, where he opened a small public house in

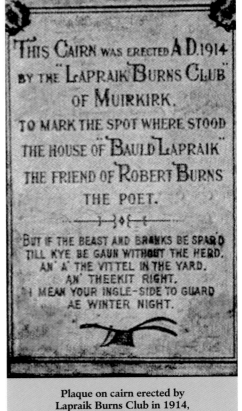

Plaque on cairn erected by Lapraik Burns Club in 1914, marking the spot where John Lapraik's house once stood in Muirkirk.

Kirkgreen. It also served as the village post office and it was there that Lapraik lived until his death on 7th May, 1807, having reached the grand old age of eighty. He is buried in Muirkirk Kirkyard.

Burns was too well versed in the art of poetry not to recognise Lapraik's limitations as a poet, but at that particular period the 'bard' of Muirkirk was an essential part of Burns's literary environment, and he provided the stimulus which Burns needed. The poet could afford to be generous in praising Lapraik, secure in the knowledge that his own verses were so much superior. We can forgive Lapraik's plagiarism when we remember that it was through it that Burns inspired to write two of his best verse epistles.

WILLIAM FISHER ('HOLY WILLIE')

William Fisher was related to a family whose connection with Mauchline Parish went back several generations. A tombstone in Mauchline churchyard commemorates one, John Fisher, who was a merchant and died on 21st October 1706. William's parents are also buried in the churchyard and the inscription on the tombstone indicates that Andrew Fisher, farmer at Montgarswood, died on 17th April, 1781, in his eighty-ninth year, and his wife, Jean Fisher, in March, 1782, at the age of seventy-five.

It is claimed that an ancestor of William Fisher was involved in the execution of five Covenanters at the Cross of Mauchline in 1685. The story goes that General Drummond, following a mock trial, was unable to procure ropes for the execution, and the villagers refused to render him any assistance. However, a man by the name of Fisher said that he would 'mak a shift' to provide the ropes, and actually furnished Drummond with the necessary materials to enable him to carry out the execution. Thereafter, Fisher was known by the name of 'mak a shift', and it is said that the stigma continued in the family down to William Fisher's time. [1]

The five Covenanters were buried at the Low Green, where an obelisk (third memorial) outside the present primary school commemorates their martyrdom. A stone from the original memorial was set into the school wall in 1885, and bears the following inscription –

> Bloody Dumbarton, Douglas, and Dundee
> Moved by the devil, and the Laird of Lee,
> Dragg'd these five men to death with gun and sword,
> Not suffering them to pray, nor read God's word:
> Owning the work of God was all their crime;
> The eighty-five was a saint-killing time.

The hole where the gibbet was fixed is now marked with a stone cap or cup.[2] If, as suggested, Fisher was involved it is more than likely that he was related in some way to William Fisher. He may have been John Fisher, the merchant who died n 1706

William Fisher owes his humiliating immortality to Robert Burns, who lampooned him in one of the most brilliant satires of all time – 'Holy Willie's Prayer'. *(CW 93)* Indeed it was Burns who bestowed on Fisher the appellation of 'Holy Willie'. The poem is a devastating broadside on the hypocrisy of 'Holy Willie' and all those of the 'Auld Licht' persuasion. Willie is shown at prayer and throughout the poem he gives the impression that he enjoys a special relationship with God, and addresses Him almost as an equal.

He is confident that God has chosen him to be one of the elect, and he is, therefore, destined for salvation. In the last verse he reminds God to continue to bless him and his kin with material prosperity and spiritual superiority, so that he may be exalted above all others, and in the last two lines he concedes, almost as an afterthought, that all the glory shall be God's:-

But Lord, remember me and mine
Wi' mercies temporal and divine !
That I for grace and gear may shine,
    Excell'd by nane !
And all the glory shall be thine !
    AMEN ! AMEN !

Burns had an intimate knowledge of the Bible, and it is hardly surprising that 'Holy Willie's Prayer' has a remarkable similarity to the parable of the Pharisee and the tax collector, as given by St. Luke (New International Version, chap.XV III, verses 9-14)

To some who were confident of their own righteousness and looked down on everybody else, Jesus told this parable, 'Two men went up to the temple to pray, one a Pharisee and the other a tax collector. The Pharisee stood up and prayed about himself, "God, I thank you that I am not like all other men – robbers, evildoers, adulterers – or even like this tax collector. I fast twice a week and give a tenth of all I get." But the tax collector stood at a distance. He would not even look up to heaven, but beat his breast and said, "God have mercy on me a sinner."

'I tell you that this man, rather than the other, went home justified before God.

Obelisk outside school gates; third memorial to same martyrs, erected in 1885.It also shows the stone cap, being the spot where the gibbet was erected.

For everyone who exalts himself will be humbled, and he, who humbles himself will be exalted.'

A note on the poem which Burns wrote for the Glenriddell M.S. explains:

'Holy Willie was a rather oldish bachelor, elder in the Parish of Mauchline, and much and justly famed for that polemical chattering which ends in tippling orthodoxy, and for that spiritualised bawdry which refines to liquorish devotion. In a sessional process with a gentleman in Mauchline – a Mr. Gavin Hamilton – Holy Willie and his priest Father Auld, after full hearing in the Presbytery of Ayr, came off but second best, owing partly to the oratorical powers of Mr. Robert Aitken, Mr. Hamilton's counsel, but chiefly to Mr. Hamilton's being one of the most irreproachable and truly respectable characters in the country. On losing his process the Muse overhead him at his devotions.'

Inscription on base of obelisk.

Burns's note is not strictly accurate. When the poem was written in 1785, William Fisher was then forty-eight years of age and married to Jean Hewatson. He was born, presumably at Montgarswood Farm and baptised at Mauchline on 24th February, 1737.

He was a regular worshiper at Mauchline Parish Kirk under the Rev. William ('Daddy') Auld, a rigid Auld Licht, and he was ordained an elder on 26th July, 1772. He appears to have applied himself most diligently to his duties in visiting the sick and aged. He offered up prayers for them in a very powerful and pious manner, but it is said that he lacked a sense of Christian forbearance and held very narrow views on the administration of Church discipline. [3]

In his note Burns refers to the dispute between Mauchline Kirk Session and Gavin Hamilton, the Mauchline lawyer and friend of the poet. Some writers, possibly influenced by Burns's poem, have claimed that it was Fisher who instigated the process against Hamilton, but an examination of the Session Records shows that, while Fisher's name appears regularly in the minutes, so do the names of other elders, particularly James Lamie, who seems to have played a major role in the proceedings. Fisher's involvement appears to have been only as a member of the Committee deputed to act on behalf of the Session.

Kirk Session records show that between 1777 and 1788, Gavin Hamilton was three times in dispute with the Session. The first, which some biographers have tended to ignore, was concerned with Hamilton's failure to account for monies collected by him in his capacity as collector of stents for the years, 1776, 1777 and 1778. The stents, which were for the relief of the poor, were set by Heritors in 1771 at a penny for each pound of their rental value and were calculated to bring in about £20 per annum. The records also reveal that Hamilton had 'delayed for five or six years to make out a disposition to John Mitchell of Friendlesshead of the lands of Braefoot, sold to the said Mitchell by the Session on behalf of the poor, whereby the poor shall want the principal and interest of said purchase amounting to £8 stg.' One writer has stated that Burns's 'description of Gavin Hamilton as "the poor man's friend in deed" may well be challenged.' [4] Indeed there is no record in the minutes that Hamilton ever passed over any monies to the Session. The dispute rumbled on until 1785 when the Session decided to broaden the complaint against Hamilton, and charged him with unnecessary absence from church on two Sundays in December, 1784, and three Sundays in January, 1785: breaking the Sabbath by setting out on a journey to Carrick, 'tho advised and admonished against it by the Minister 'and that he 'habitually if not totally neglects the worship of God in his family'. The result of this unedifying dispute was that it went to the Presbytery of Ayr and thereafter to the Synod of Glasgow, who both found in Hamilton's favour. An uneasy peace followed but it did not last long. In 1787 the 'Holy Beagles' were again in pursuit and Hamilton was accused of profaning the Lord's Day by ordering his servant to dig potatoes in his garden.

This third dispute lasted for over five months and illustrates very clearly the rigid Sabbatarianism of 'Daddy' Auld and the Kirk Session. It found its way again to the Synod of Glasgow where it was dismissed in March, 1788. [5]

'Holy Willie's Prayer' was written following the judgement on the second dispute, given by the Presbytery of Ayr in January, 1785. Manuscript copies of the poem were passed among Burns's friends and how they must have laughed. Not only is the prayer a scathing indictment of the Calvinist doctrine of predestination, but it is also irresistibly funny. The poem set the countryside in a roar and Burns must have been inundated with requests for copies. One such request came from the Rev. John McMath, New Licht assistant to the

Rev. Dr. Patrick Woodrow at Tarbolton. Burns duly obliged and accompanied it with a verse epistle. He may have had some misgivings that the poem was too daring when he wrote:

My musie, tir'd wi' monie a sonnet
    On gown, an ban', an douse black- bonnet,
Is grown right eerie now she's done it,
    Lest they should blame her,
An rouse their holy thunder on it
    An anathem her.

I own 'twas rash, an rather hardy,
That I, a simple, countra Bardie,
Should meddle wi' a pack sae sturdy,
    Wha, if they ken me,
Can easy wi' a single wordie
    Louse Hell upon me.

But I gae mad at their grimaces,
Their sighin, cantin, grace-proud faces,
Their three-mile prayers, an hauf-mile graces,
    Their raxin conscience,
Whase greed, revenge, an pride disgraces
    Waur nor their nonsense. *(CW 129)*

Painting of 'Holy Willie',
from a Burns series cigarette
card set of 28, issued by Scottish
Co-operative Wholesale Society
in 1924.

Holy Willie's Prayer was not included in the Kilmarnock or Edinburgh editions of the poems, for obvious reasons. Sir Walter Scott, writing in the *Quarterly Review* in 1809, said that it was 'unfortunately cast in a form too daringly profane to be received into Dr. Currie's Collection' (1800), although it first appeared in a tract, issued by Stewart and Meikle of Glasgow in 1799.

In his autobiographical letter to Dr. Moore of 2nd August, 1787, *(CL 246)* Burns wrote:

'Holy Willie's Prayer .... alarmed the Kirk Session so much that they held three several meetings to look over their holy artillery, if any of it was pointed against profane Rhymers.- Unluckily for me, my idle wanderings led me, on another side, point blank within reach of their heaviest metal.'

The first shot was fired on 2nd April, 1786, a year after the poem was written. An extract from the Session minute of that date, reads:

'The Kirk Session being informed that Jean Armour, an unmarried woman is with child, and that she has gone off from the place of late, to reside elsewhere, the Session think it is their duty to enquire . . . But appoint James Lamie and William Fisher to speak to the parents.'

This is an example of the inquisitorial methods used by the Kirk Session at that time. If the minister or an elder heard of any indiscretion concerning a member of the congregation it was his duty to bring it before the Session, who then had to enquire if the report was true or false, and deal with it as circumstances required. Enquiring into the lapses of the parishioners seems to have been one of the Session's main functions. This is borne out by a minute of Galston Kirk Session in 1647, which stated that 'the Session did consider that they have need of some more elders for watching over the manners of the Congregation.' [6]

The result of Lamie's and Fisher's enquiries led inevitably to Burns and Jean acknowledging the sin of fornication, and being rebuked by 'Daddy' Auld, before the whole congregation, on three penitential Sundays in July/August, 1786.

Fisher also features in 'The Kirk's Alarm'. Although Burns wrote it at Ellisland in the Autumn of 1789, it is a satire on a theological controversy which had arisen in the Presbytery of Ayr. In 1786, Dr. William McGill, one of the two ministers at Ayr, published *A Practical Essay on the Death of Jesus Christ*, for which he was ultimately charged with heresy before the Synod of Glasgow who ordered the Presbytery of Ayr to investigate the charge. In May, 1789, the General Assembly quashed the decision of the Synod, but instructed the Presbytery to maintain purity of doctrine. A committee was set up to consider McGill's teaching. It was composed of fifteen ministers and ten elders. Fisher was one of the elders chosen and he was included in Burns's satire, along with those ministers who were against McGill. [7] The stanza on Fisher is more libellous than satirical:

> Holy Will, Holy Will, there was wit i' your skull,
> When ye pilfer'd the alms o' the poor,
> The timmer is scant when ye're taen for a saunt,
> Wha should swing in a rape for an hour,
> Holy Will! Ye should swing on a rape for an hour.

What grounds Burns had for writing such an accusation is not known, but there is certainly no evidence in the Mauchline Kirk Session records that Fisher was ever charged with the appropriation of poor funds. The libel was siezed on by nineteenth century biographers, who accepted Burns's imputation without question. First to latch on to it was Allan Cunningham, who embroidered it with his own touch of mendacity when he wrote, 'He (Fisher) permitted himself to be filled fou, and in a moment when "self got in" made free, it is said, with the money of the poor of the parish.' [8] In another wild flight of fancy he declared that Burns's satire 'made Holy Willie think of suicide,' [9] but his assertion has no foundation in fact and it would appear to be just another instance of one of 'Honest' Allan's embellishments.

It is of interest that about five years before Burns wrote 'The Kirk's Alarm', a theft of the poor funds did occur in Mauchline. The offender was Robert Gibb, who had acted as temporary Church officer, and he was charged with the theft before the Kirk Session on 20th July, 1784. He was appointed to distribute the funds to the poor, and he had deducted out of each payment he made a halfpenny to recompense him for his services. His misdemeanour was not considered as very flagrant, but he was, nevertheless, seriously reprimanded by the Session. The case serves to illustrate that the Session was not prepared to overlook any tampering with the poor funds. No other charge of this nature came before the Session during the entire period of William Fisher's service as an elder. [10]

The Rev. Dr. Andrew Edgar, who as minister of Mauchline Old Church from 1874 to 1890, offers a most credible explanation as to how this scurrilous tag may have been attached to Fisher. He writes:

> 'It is well enough known that cock and bull stories of elders appropriating the poor's funds have always formed part of rural gossip. The records of this parish tell of a man that was called to account by the Session in 1735 for saying that some of the elders drank the poor's money. That is just a sample of the idle fables that senseless and ill-conditioned people would make themselves and others believe. And William Fisher was the kind of man that people were apt to raise stories about. To a certain class of people he must accordingly have been obnoxious, and they would naturally enjoy the pleasure of finding some little rent in his garments. Stories to his discredit would be eagerly received, not examined very carefully, industriously circulated, and adorned with exaggerations. Myths would eventually assume the form of historical facts.' [11]

On 7th August, 1789, Burns sent a copy of 'The Kirk's Alarm' to John Logan of Knockshinnoch. In the accompanying letter he gave strict instructions:

> 'I have as you will see finished 'The Kirk's Alarm', but now that it is done, and I have laughed once or twice at the conceits in some of the Stanzas, I am determined not to let it get into the Publick ; so I send you this copy, the first I have sent to Ayr-shire, except some few Stanzas which I wrote off in embrio for Gavin Hamilton, under the express provision and request – that you will only read it to a few of us, and do not on any account, give, or permit to be taken, any copy of the Ballad.' *(CL 123)*

Despite Burns's plea to John Logan not to give or allow copies to be taken, there are numerous manuscripts of the satire in existence. In several of them the stanza on 'Holy Willie' is omitted, which seems to suggest that it was only included in those copies sent to amuse friends like Gavin Hamilton. When Burns wrote out the poem for the Glenriddell volume in 1791, the libellous stanza was not inserted.[12] Was it a lapse of memory on Burns's part, or was it the version of 'The Kirk's Alarm' for which he wished to be remembered ? On the other hand Burns may have had second thoughts about the stanza on 'Holy Will', especially if he suspected that it was based on nothing more than idle gossip.

In 1790, the year after 'The Kirk's Alarm' was written, William Fisher fell from grace. On 14th October, he stood before the eighty-one year old 'Daddy 'Auld, and in the presence of the Kirk Session, and was rebuked for drunkenness. The harangue which the minister delivered has been preserved in his Book of Rebukes:

> 'I am sorry that I have occasion to rebuke any member of the session for the sin of drunkenness. Drunkenness is a sin highly aggravated in a Christian, and provoking in the sight of God. God has denounced many woes against the drunkard, and has declared that they shall not inherit the Kingdom of God. He forbids all rioting and drunkenness, and commands us to be sober and temperate in all things. Drunkenness is a sin against a man's soul; it stupefies the understanding, robs him of his reason, and renders him worse than a beast. It is a sin against the body, for it occasions disease, and exposes to danger and death . It is not only a vicious and sorry, but a very expensive sin . It has ruined many families and clothed many drunkards in rags. Solomon sets forth the natural tendency of this vice, as well as the punishment appointed for it, in these words, Prov.xxiii, 21: "The drunkard and the glutton shall come to poverty" and ver. 29 of the same chapter, "Who hath woe? who hath sorrow? who hath contentions ? who hath babbling? who hath wounds without cause? who hath redness of eyes?" The answer is easy "They that tarry in taverns and drink strong drink." Besides, drunkenness is a great reproach to the Christian, for it is a disgrace to human nature, and was so abominable to some heathen nations that they were wont to fill their slaves drunk and present them in that condition to their children, so that their children might learn from their early days to abhor the vice of drunkenness. We may conclude this rebuke with an advice or two. Be upon your guard in all time coming against this bewitching sin, shun bad company, avoid taverns as much as possible, and abhor the character of a tippler. Abstain carefully from strong drink, and from everything that may intoxicate and injure you, and withal seek wisdom from Heaven to guide you, and grace to enable you to walk steadfastly in the ways of sobriety and Holiness all your days.' [13]

'Daddy' Auld was a stern unbending character and a strict upholder of church discipline. It is evident from his solemn rebuke to Fisher that he was not prepared to overlook any transgression from a member of the Session. Apparently Fisher's 'aggravation' (a favourite expression of Auld's) did not affect his position as he continued to serve as an elder for another nine years. In 1799 Fisher's tack of Montgarswood expired and he leased the farm of Tongue-in- Auchterless, in the Parish of Sorn. From that date his connection with Mauchline Old Church ceased. [14]

Throughout his life Burns was fond of writing epitaphs, some of them not very complimentary, like the one he wrote on 'Holy Willie':

> Here Holy Willie's sair worn clay
>   Taks up its last abode;
> His saul has ta'en some other way,
>   I fear the left-hand road..
>
> Stop! There he is as sure's a gun,
>   Poor silly body see him;
> Nae wonder he's as black's the grun,
>   Observe who's standing wi' him.
>
> Your brunstane Devilship, I see
>   Has got him there before ye!
> But haud your nine-tail cat a wee,
>   Till ance you've heard my story.
>
> Your pity I will not implore,
>   For pity ye have nane.
> Justice, alas! has gi'en him o'er,
>   And mercy's day is gane.
>
> But hear me, Sir, Deil as ye are,
>   Look something to your credit:
> A cuif like him wad stain your name,
>   If it were kent ye did it! (CW 95)

It is generally considered a rather poor performance compared with 'Holy Willie's Prayer' and Burns must have been conscious of this as he did not include it in the Glenriddell volume along with the 'Prayer'. Although written in 1785, it was not published during Burns's lifetime and no holograph in Burns's hand is known to exist. It first appeared in a tract issued by Stewart in 1801.

On 13th February, 1809, Fisher came to a sad end. The generally accepted story is that he had gone to Mauchlne, a distance of some four miles, for a meeting with his landlord. Going home, intoxicated, in a great storm of wind and rain, he had got about halfway

Old Mauchline Parish Church
demolished in 1827, the present Church built on the same site and opened for worship in 1829.
It is of interest that two communion cups, presented by the Heritors to the Church in 1777 and
used in 'The Holy Fair', are still in use to-day.

when he lost his way. At a point on the road, near South Auchenbrain Farm, he fell into a ditch and was drowned. A. B. Todd, who was editor of the *Cumnock Advertiser* for over thirty years, left this pertinent observation:

> 'It is a curious fact that in the 'Epitaph on Holy Willie', Burns said of him: 'His saul has tae'n some other way, I fear the left-hand road', and that Fisher, on his way home that night, took the left hand side of a fence and ditch near the farm of Meikle Auchenbrain, and so was drowned, for had he taken the right hand and the proper side he would have been safe.' [15]

The nearest we can get to an on-the-spot report also comes from the pen of A.B.Todd:

> 'Most people know that this canting, tippling creature was drowned in a ditch when going home intoxicated from a Mauchline Fair in the year, 1809, but few are likely to know that my own father was one of those who got his body entangled among the thorns in a raging torrent about two o'clock on the following morning, his head down and his feet up and only seen, with the water gushing over him, for there had been a great storm of wind and rain during the night. My father's farm was less than a mile from the place, and some of Fisher's family had come seeking him after midnight and had roused my father to go in search of him.... My father sent his man with a horse and cart home with the body to the Tongue, 'Holy Willie's' farm in the north-east part of the parish of Mauchline, he himself going on before to break the sad tidings to the new-made widow.' [16]

It is not surprising that several stories about Fisher have survived. They may be apocryphal but they tend, nevertheless, to show the reputation he had earned as a tippling, canting, sycophantic character was not misrepresented. It would appear that he was always eager to cultivate the good graces of the Rev. 'Daddy' Auld. When a subject was under discussion in the Session, he always endeavoured to find out the minister's thoughts before committing himself. His constant expression on such occasions was, 'And what say you Mr. Auld ? I'll say wi' you Mr. Auld !'

That he was a tippler there can be little doubt. It seems that the Mauchline Fair, which was held twelve times a year, was an occasion for him to indulge, and when in drink his foremost thought was the castigation of his wife and family. Staggering home one night someone saw him gesticulating fiercely and shaking his fist at some imaginary object. Curious to know the

Gavin Hamilton's House, still standing and occupied.

cause of those wild actions, the onlooker crept a little closer and overheard Fisher say, 'If the door's barred I'll mak it a faut, and if it's no' barred I'll mak it a faut, and if there's nae faut I'll hae a faut !' An incident which illustrates another side of his character was often told in Mauchline family circles. On one occasion he was called, in his capacity as an elder, to offer up a prayer for a sick member of the congregation. If there was one thing in which he prided himself, it was his superior gift of prayer, and perhaps this is the reason why Burns couched his satire in this particular form. Having rendered a powerful and lengthy prayer for the sick person, he turned with the greatest insensitivity to the guidman of the house and asked, 'Did you ever hear the parallel o' that ?'[17]

'Holy Willie's Prayer' conveys Burns's extreme dislike of William Fisher and all that he represented. Some of it, no doubt, stemmed from the poet's intense hatred of hypocrisy and hypocrites, and Fisher was certainly one. The case of Mauchline Kirk Session against Gavin Hamilton gave Burns an opportunity, not only to rally to Hamilton's support, but also to lampoon the Session and the doctrine of predestination.

On the face of it, it would appear that Burns was rather severe on him, but A.B.Todd recalls that Fisher was well known to his father and mother, and his father – 'good Cameronian that he was – used to laugh immoderately at the 'Holy Willie's Prayer' of Burns, and would say that, though it was "gey rough", it was as true a picture of the man as any given in the Chronicles of Judah and Israel.' [18]

Fisher fell into the error, prevalent at that time, of mistaking cant for religion, and thought 'three mile prayers an' hauf-mile graces' as the infallible signs of godliness. He also had a reputation of being over inquisitive when females were being examined for the sin of fornication, but whether he lifted 'a lawless leg on Meg' or 'three times wi' Leezie's lass', we have only Burns's word on that.

'Holy Willie'
by unknown artist.

Professor Snyder summed it all up very neatly when he wrote:

> 'But had he (Fisher) been ten times the rascal that his worst enemies represented, he would still be remembered with gratitude by all readers of Burns, for he it was who was the hero of 'Holy Willie's Prayer' – as caustic and mordant piece of satire as was ever penned in the British Isles.' [19]

THOMAS WALKER

The person to whom Burns addressed his 'Reply to a Trimming Epistle,' was Thomas Walker, a tailor who lived at Poole on the river Lugar, a few miles from Ochiltree. He has been described as a 'respectable character for sobriety, honesty and glee.' [1] He courted the Muse and was on very friendly terms with William Simpson, schoolmaster at Ochiltree, who was a man of education and no mean versifier, although he steadfastly refused to allow his poems to be published. Tradition has it that Simpson received a copy of Burns's 'Twa Herds' and was immediately prompted to send a complimentary poetical epistle to the poet. [2] This was quickly answered by Burns in May, 1786, who sent Simpson a rhyming epistle in return. In it the poet expresses his great love of nature and his desire to celebrate Ayrshire in his works. Included is his famous comment on the secret of composition.

> The Muse, nae poet ever fand her,
> Till by himself he learn'd to wander,
> Adown some trottin burn's meander,
>   An no think lang:
> O sweet to stray, an pensive ponder
>   A heart-felt sang!
>
> The warly race may drudge an drive,
> Hog-shouther, jundie, stretch, an strive,
> Let me fair Nature's face descrive,
>   And I, wi' pleasure,
> Shall let the busy, grumbling hive
>   Bum owre their treasure.   *(CW 109)*

Simpson was no doubt delighted to have drawn an epistle from Burns, and showed it to Walker, who thought he might be equally fortunate if he sent the poet a brotherly epistle. Accordingly he strung together a dreary performance of twenty- six stanzas in 'Standard Habbie', Burns's favourite measure, and sent it to Mossgiel. Several weeks passed and still there was no answer from Burns. With the publication of the Kilmarnock Edition, Walker thought that it might be opportune to renew his attempt to extract a reply from Burns. He changed his approach, however, and to try and rouse the poet, he adopted the role of moral censor. Fortunately he showed it to Simpson before despatching it, on whose advice the epistle was reduced from twenty-one to ten stanzas. This required considerable rearrangement and alteration, which the schoolmaster managed with so much skill that one writer has suggested that Burns himself may have been the author of the 'Trimming Epistle' as well as the 'Reply'.[3] It is generally believed, however, that

Simpson had as much to do with its composition as had Walker. Since the text of the 'Trimming Epistle' is not easily accessible, it is printed here for the benefit of readers:

What waefu' news is this I hear,
Frae greeting I can scarce forbear,
Folks tell me ye're gaun aff this year
    Out owre the sea,
And lasses, wham ye lo'e sae dear,
    Will greet for thee.

Weel wad I like war ye to stay,
But, Robin, since ye will away,
I hae a word yet mair to say
    And maybe twa:
May He protect us night an' day,
    That made us a'

Where art thou guan, keep mind frae me,
Seek Him to bear thee companie,
And, Robin, when ye come to die,
    Ye'll win aboon,
An' live at peace an' unity
    Ayont the moon.

Some tell me, Rab, ye dinna fear
To get a wean, an' curse an' swear,
I'm unco wae, my lad, to hear
    O sic a trade:
Could I forswear ye to forbear,
    I wad be glad.

Fu' weel ye ken ye'll gang to Hell
Gin ye persist in doing ill -
Wae's me! Ye're hurlin' down the hill
    Withouten dread.
An' ye'll get leave to swear your fill
    After ye're dead.

There, walth o' women ye'll get near,
But gettin' weans ye will forbear,
Ye'll never say, my bonnie dear
    Come, gie's a kiss-
Nae kissing there – ye'll girn an' sneer,
    An'ither hiss.

O Rab! Lay by thy foolish tricks,
An' steer nae mair the female sex,
Or some day ye'll come through the pricks,
    An' that ye'll see:
Ye'll find hard living wi' Auld Nicks,
    I'm wae for thee.

But what's this comes wi' sic a knell,
Amaist as loud as ony bell,
While it does mak' my conscience tell!
    Me what is true,
I'm but a ragget cowt mysel'
    Owre sib to you!

We're owre like those wha think it fit
To stuff their noddles fu' o' wit,
An' yet content in darkness sit,
    Wha shun the light.
To let them see down to the pit,
    That lang dark night.

But fareweel, Rab, I maun awa',
May He that made us keep us a',
For that wad be a dreadful' fa'
    And hurt us sair;
Lad, we wad never mend ava,
    Sae, Rab, tak care.

Burns's 'Reply' can be found in all the standard editions of his works.

It has been argued by a number of writers that the 'Reply' was not the work of Burns, but of Simpson, who imitated the poet's handwriting and despatched to Walker by a circuitous route. It has also been suggested that Walker fell for the hoax but was so horrified by the blasphemy and bawdry that he consigned it to the flames. This may well be true as no original manuscript has survived. The case for Simpson as the author is based mainly on a report that not long after the 'Reply' was written, Simpson met Burns and informed him of the liberty he had taken with his name. 'You did well,' said the poet, 'You have thrashed the tailor much better than I could have done.' [4]

Against that story, however, is the fact that the 'Reply' was first published by Thomas Stewart of Glasgow in 1801 as the work of Burns. This was fourteen years before Simpson died and he did not challenge the authorship. It is also argued that Simpson could not have known in such detail of Burns's appearance before the Session. It should be noted that Stewart was a cousin of John Richmond, and it is thought that Burns passed copies of the tailor's 'Rhyming Epistle' and his 'Reply' to Richmond, and it was from this source that they came into the possession of Stewart. [5]

Old village of Ochiltree c.1895,
where William Simpson was schoolmaster.

Most biographers are of the opinion that the work is unmistakably Burns, as the quality of the verses are up to the poet's high standard. Scott Douglas stated that the 'Reply' was by Burns, 'a fact as proclaimed by the verses themselves'. Another source attests that they were written by the same hand as wrote the 'Epistle to John Rankine'. [6]

Apparently Simpson and Walker were in the habit of exchanging verses. In one of the poems addressed to Walker, who had been complaining of the absence of the Muses, the dominie, who obviously had the measure of the tailor, mentions Burns in the last verse:

> I send up these lines by J.W. from school,
> To you, Mr.Walker, head tailor in Poole,
> Who makes on the Muses this mournful complaint,
> Because they look on your productions asquint;
> While off to Mossgiel from Parnassus they canter
> Whenever Rab Burns but plays cheep on his chanter.

It seems that Walker had a squint in his eyes. He is reported as saying that he could fix one eye on the seam and look about him with the other. [7] Simpson makes reference to this in the fourth line of the above verse, and also in the following lines taken from a longer poem, addressed to the tailor, entitled 'To Tom Walker in Affliction':

> Ye're nae sae very scant o' grace,
> Whate'er's the dispensation,
> As ere set up your squinting face
> An' fret at tribulation.

Walker was rather sensitive to his affliction and replied to Simpson in the following quatrain:

> For a' the Kirklands e'er were born,
> Had but my case been yours,
> I wadna planted sic a thorn
> Amang sic bonnie flowers.

Another local poet with whom Walker was on very friendly terms was James Fisher, (no relation to 'Holy Willie'), who came to Ochiltree about 1788. He was blind almost from birth, but was a fairly accomplished musician which was his chief means of earning a living.[8] In the verses of Fisher and Walker there is evidence that they both embraced the truly orthodox doctrines of the period, and looked with disfavour on the irreligious and immoral tendency of Burns's writings. [9] In his first set of verses to Walker, the blind poet makes reference in one verse to the 'Rhyming Epistle':

Wow man! Ye hae some unco turns;
I heard some things ye sent to Burns,
In whilk ye gae him gay ill purns
        To red, I think;
But what they were, my muse adjourns
        To tell distinct.

In his reply Walker wrote:

Saints now-a-days may weep and mourn,
To think how ages yet unborn,
Will see religion turned to scorn
        By Robin's books;
An' a' the Bible reft an' torn
        By clergy fouks.

Not much is known about Walker other than he was a tailor, who lived in Poole and dabbled in verse. He was born about 1751 and died at Sorn Bridgend in 1833 at the advanced age of 82, and is buried in Sorn Kirkyard. He published a religious pamphlet entitled *A Picture of the World*, which later gained him some fame and was widely distributed. [10]

'The Holy Fair'
from the painting by Alexander Carse.

EDINBURGH

'Edina! Scotia's darling seat!
All hail thy palaces and tow'rs.'

THE CROCHALLAN FENCIBLES

In November, 1786, Burns arrived in Edinburgh to try for a second edition of his poems. The enthusiasm with which he was received in the Capital showed the wisdom of his mission. Within a very short time he had a publisher – William Creech, whose shop in the High Street was the meeting place for all the literary men in the city. Creech had a business association with the printer, William Smellie, and very soon Burns found himself seated on a stool in Smellie's untidy printing office at the foot of Anchor Close, correcting proof sheets of his poems and engaging in lively conversation with the printer. It seems that Smellie's outward appearance was as untidy as his printing shop. Burns has left us this picture of the man, in lines that were intended to be part of a long poem, but never completed.

> Crochallan came :
> The old cock'd hat, the brown surtout the same,
> His grisly beard just bristling in its might
> ('Twas four long nights and days to shaving-night) ;
> His uncomb'd, hairy locks, wild-staring, thatch'd
> A head for thought profound and clear unmatch'd ;
> Yet, tho' his caustic wit was biting rude,
> His heart was warm, benevolent and good. *(CW 433)*

William Smellie.
Engraving by H.E. Holl from *The Land of Burns.*

Smellie was a remarkable character. He had edited the first *Encyclopaedia Britannica* and had written much of it himself. He was also the author of a *Philosophy of Natural History*. In Burns's view he was 'a man positively of the first abilities and greatest strength of mind, as well as one of the best hearts and keenest wits that I have ever met with.' (CL 319) He and the poet became 'unco pack an' thick thegither', as was expected in men whose interests in so many respects were similar. Both had a propensity for bawdry. In one of his letters Burns referred to Smellie as, 'that old Veteran in Genius, Wit and Bawdry', (CL 315) and it was inevitable that the printer should introduce the poet to the Crochallan Fencibles, a convivial club of wits and bon vivants, which met in Dawney Douglas's tavern, also in Anchor Close and a short distance from the printing shop.

The club appears to have originated with Smellie about the year 1778. It took its name from a mournful Gaelic air and song, *Cro Chalein*– the Cattle of Colin. According to tradition, Colin's wife died at an early age, but her spirit returned soon afterwards and was seen on summer evenings tending her husband's cattle. The song seems to have been Dawney Douglas's favourite, and it was easily adapted by the club to Crochallan.

The Fencible part of the title was in mock imitation of the regiments then being raised, as a consequence of the alarm caused by the American War of Independence.

Each member bore some pretended military rank. 'Colonel' of the Corps was William Dunbar, Writer to the Signet, and said to have introduced Burns to the works of Spenser. Obviously a hearty blade, he is remembered in a song by the bard, written 'out of compliment to one of the worthiest fellows in the world.'

Johnnie Dowie, who owned a tavern in Anchor Close. It was here that Burns spent many a jovial hour. Portrait by Kay.

> As I cam by Crochallan,
>   I cannily keekit ben;
> Rattlin, roaring Willie,
>   Was sitting at yon boord-en',
> Sitting at yon boord -en',
>   And amang guid companie ;
> Rattlin, roarin Willie,
>   Ye're welcome hame to me. *(CW 320)*

Next in rank was 'Major' Charles Hay, afterwards Lord Newton, who is credited with the saying, 'Drinking is my occupation – law is my amusement.' Smellie was 'Recorder'. William Craig, cousin and generous friend of 'Clarinda', and later as Lord Craig, was 'Provost' Other members included Robert Cleghorn, farmer of Saughton Mills; Captain Matthew

Henderson, subject of an elegy by Burns; Alexander Cunningham, Writer; Hon. Henry Erskine, Dean of the Faculty of Advocates; Lord Gillies, Judge of the Court of Session; James Johnson, Engraver; William Nicol, Latin Master of the High School; Allan Masterton, Writing Master at the High School; 'Auld Tennant' of Glenconner, friend of William Burnes; Dr. Gilbert Stuart; Hon. Alexander Gordon, Advocate; Peter Hill, Clerk to William Creech; Robert Ainslie, lawyer's apprentice; John Dundas, Edward Bruce, Alexander Wight and William Dallas, Writers to the Signet; and one Williamson of Cardrona in Peeblesshire.

Smellie also held the commission of 'Hangman', and in this capacity it was his duty to drill the new recruits. This he did by subjecting them to a severe test of badinage in order to try their temper. Although he introduced Burns to the Crochallans, he apparently did

'Burns' Tavern' it was situated in Anchor Close and Burns spent many an evening here. It was owned by Johnnie Dowie who died in 1817, the new owner renamed it the Burns Tavern.

not spare his protégé, the bard declared at the conclusion of his initiation, that he had 'never been so abominably thrashed in his life.' However, he must have acquitted himself well in the battle of wits, as it afterwards became a favourite amusement of the members to pit the poet against the 'Hangman' and enjoy the verbal contest which followed. Another custom of the club was, that those individuals who committed a fault, were subjected to a mock trial, when the barrister members were able to display their forensic talents.

Dawney Douglas's tavern was one of the most famous in the old town at that time, and it still lives vividly in our imagination, thanks to the wonderful description of it by Robert Chambers in the *Traditions of Edinburgh*. It was situated a few yards down Anchor Close, but before reaching it a client passed an entry on the left-hand side leading to a stair, decorated with the inscription, 'THE LORD IS ONLY MY SVPORT.' Another door bore the equally devoted declaration, O LORD IN THE IS AL MY TRAIST', while

Smellie's Printing Office at the foot of Anchor Close.
From the painting by Henry G. Duguid. National Gallery of Scotland.

immediately beyond was the entrance to Dawney's tavern. Considering the high jinks and mad pranks that took place within its walls, the architrave on the doorway bore the not inappropriate supplication, 'BE MERCIFVL TO ME'. [1] Chambers writes:

'The frequenter of Douglas's, after ascending a few steps, found himself in a pretty large kitchen -- a dark fiery Pandemonium, through which numerous ineffable ministers of flame were continually flying about, while beside the door sat the landlady, a large, fat woman, in a towering head-dress and large-flowered silk gown, who bowed to everyone passing. Most likely on emerging from this igneous region, the party would fall into the hands of Dawney himself, and so be conducted to an apartment. A perfect contrast was he to his wife ; a thin, weak, submissive man, who spoke in a whisper, never but in the way of monosyllables. He had the habit of using the word 'quietly' very frequently, without much regard to its being appropriate to the sense; and it is told that he, one day, made the remark that 'the Castle had been firing to-day, *quietly*', which, it may well be believed, was not soon forgotten by his customers. Another trait of Dawney was that some one had lent him a volume of Clarendon's history to read, and daily frequenting the room where it lay, used regularly, for some time, to put back the reader's mark to the same place; whereupon, being by-and-by asked how he liked the book, Dawney answered, 'Oh, very weel; but dinna ye think it's gay mickle the same thing o'er again?' The house was noted for suppers of tripe, rizzared haddocks, mince collops, and hashes which never cost more than sixpence a head. On charges of this moderate kind the honest couple grew extremely rich before they died.' [2]

The principal room in the tavern, and the one in which the Crochallan's met, was called the 'Crown Room'. It was handsomely panelled, with a decorated fireplace, and two tall windows towards the alley. It was a good size, with a separate access, and was reserved only for large companies and important persons. It was claimed that Mary, Queen of Scots had used it as a Council Chamber, and the crown had been placed in a niche in the wall while the council was in session. The Crochallan Fencibles dated their documents from 'Queen Mary's Council Room',[3] but as one writer has observed, 'We shrewdly suspect that the whole tradition has its origin in the *Crochallan Mint*.'[4]

One or two anecdotes of the Crochallans' mad escapades have survived and serve to illustrate what 'characters' the club had within its ranks Robert Chambers quotes from a privately printed memoir that Williamson of Cardrona –

'– got rather tipsy one evening after a severe field-day. When he came to head of Anchor Close, it occurred to him that it was necessary for him to take possession of the castle (some half mile up the hill). He accordingly set off for this purpose. When he got to the outer gate, he demanded immediate possession of the garrison, to which he said he was entitled. The sentinel, for a considerable time, laughed at him; he, however, became so extremely clamorous, that the man found it necessary to apprise the commanding officer, who immediately came down to inquire into the meaning of such impertinent conduct. He at once recognised his friend Cardrona, whom he had left at the festive board of the Crochallan-Corps only a few hours before. Accordingly, humouring him in the conceit, he said, 'Certainly you have every right to the command of this garrison; if you please, I will conduct you to your proper apartment.' He accordingly conveyed him to a bedroom in his house. Cardrona took formal possession of the place, and immediately afterward went to bed. His feelings were indescribable

Kay's portrait of **Lord Newton**.

when he looked out of his bedroom window next morning, and found himself surrounded with soldiers and great guns. Some time afterwards, this story came to the ears of the Crochallans; and Cardrona said he never afterward had the life of a dog, so much did they tease and harass him about his strange adventure.' [5]

Another humorous story concerns Dr. Gilbert Stuart, who had been closely associated with Smellie in the publication of the *Edinburgh Magazine and Review*. He died the August before Burns came to Edinburgh.

> 'Dr. Stuart came one evening to the house of Mr. Smellie in a state of complete intoxication, and was immediately put to bed. Awakening in the course of the night, he conceived himself in a brothel, and alarmed the family by repeatedly vociferating *house*! house! Mr. Smellie came as soon as possible to the bedside of his friend, to learn what he wanted and endeavoured to persuade him to go quietly again to sleep. On seeing Mr. Smellie almost naked, and still impressed with the idea of being in a house of bad fame, he addressed Mr. Smellie with great emphasis in nearly the following words: 'Smellie! I never expected to find you in such a house. Get on your clothes, and return immediately to your wife and family; and be assured I shall never mention this affair to anyone.' [6]

Reference has already been made to 'Major' Charles Hay. On one occasion when he was an advocate, he appeared before the notorious Lord Braxfield after a night of hard drinking. The opposing counsel had also indulged the previous evening and the condition of both was obvious. 'Gentlemen,' said Braxfield, 'Ye may just pack up your papers and gang hame. The tane o' ye's rifting punch, and the other's belching claret – and there'll be nae gude got out o' ye the day!' [7]

Burns formed many lasting friendships among the Crochallans. Cunningham proved a faithful friend, and following the poet's death, busied himself raising funds for the benefit of the widow and children. Nicol was the poet's travelling companion on the Highland Tour and Burns kept up a lively correspondence with Cleghorn, who

Lord Glencairn, who became Burns's great patron when he went to Edinburgh. Engraving by H. Robinson, from *The Land of Burns*

was the poet's medium for conveying his bawdy verses – original; and collected – to the Fencibles. With James Johnson the poet collaborated in the publication of the *Scots Musical Museum*, and 'it was Johnson who opened the gates through which Burns poured the lyric flood at which the world still wonders.'[8] Unfortunately, all the letters except one, which passed between Burns and Smellie were destroyed by Smellie's biographer, Robert Kerr, who piously explained, 'Many letters of Burns to Mr. Smellie which remained, being totally unfit for publication, and several of them containing severe reflections on many respectable people still in life, have been burnt.'[9]

'Recorder' Smellie's chronicles of the Crochallan Fencible's high jinks have never come to light – if, in fact, they ever existed in the first place. Some of the Fescennine verses, originally penned for Crochallan ears only, are to be found in *The Merry Muses*, but the group's frolics have, for the most part, been consigned to discreet oblivion, and perhaps it is better so. As Burns once wrote to Mrs. Dunlop, 'You may guess that the convivial hours of men have their mysteries of wit and mirth, and I hold it a piece of contemptible baseness to detail the sallies of thoughtless merriment, or the orgies of accidental intoxication to the ear of cool sobriety or female delicacy.' And who would disagree with that?

Village of Ecclefechan,
showing house on left where Thomas Carlyle was born and brought up.

WILLIAM NICOL M.A.

William Nicol, like Robert Burns, was born in very humble circumstances. His father was a poor but respectable tailor, who earned a meagre living in the village of Ecclefechan in the Parish of Hoddam. He later moved to Dunbretton, and it was there that William was born in 1744, being the only child of the marriage. When he was still very young his father died, without being able to make any provision for his widow and son. Nothing is known of his mother but she must have been a woman of strong character; not only was she able to maintain herself and William, but she gave him every encouragement to make something of his life, no doubt recognising his aptitude for learning. It was her desire that he should study for the ministry.

High School,
Edinburgh c1786.

Nicol received his early education from an itinerant teacher named John Orr, whose unsettled life was attributed to his once having laid a ghost, and his services were in demand as an exorcist. Nicol attained his first knowledge of Latin from Orr, and, when a young lad, felt sufficiently qualified to open a school in his mother's house. He often recalled this period of his life, when it required all the tact of his mother to keep the young teacher and his pupils in order, for whenever she had occasion to leave the house, lessons were abandoned and they proceeded to plunder the good woman's cupboards.

Later Nicol attended classes in the Grammar School of Annan, and having saved a little money by tutoring private pupils, he was able to enrol as a student at Edinburgh University. When he completed the Arts Curriculum he commenced the study of theology, perhaps in deference to his mother. From what we know of his later life it would appear that he was totally unsuited for the ministry, and, no doubt realising this himself he gave up theology and took up the study of medicine, which was also abandoned after a brief spell. He then concentrated on classical studies, in which he excelled.

While at university he supported himself by a tutorial practice and translating theses for medical students. This seems to have been his main source of income until 1774, when he won an open competition conducted by the Town Council of Edinburgh to fill a vacancy for a classics master in the High School.' [1]

Nicol was a man of considerable intellect and was regarded as one of the finest Latin scholars of his day. Unfortunately his talents were diminished by a fierce irascible temper, boorish manners, and a coarse contempt for custom and the establishment. On the other side of the coin, a friend who knew him intimately, testified that 'Nicols heart was warm and full of friendship... He would go to any length to serve and promote the views and wishes of a friend, but whenever low jealousy, trick, or selfish cunning appeared, his mind kindled to something like fury and madness. For a time he was one of the most popular teachers in the High School, but as the years passed his popularity waned, because of his ungovernable temper and his frequent resort to flogging,' [2] Numerous biographers have quoted the following passage by Lord Cockburn from *Memorials of his Time*, as referring to Nicol:

> 'The person to whose uncontrolled discipline I was now subjected, though a good man, an intense student, and filled, but rather in the memory than in the head, with knowledge, was as bad a schoolmaster as it was possible to fancy. Unacquainted with the nature of youth, ignorant even of the characters of his own boys, and with not a conception of the art or the duty of alluring them, he had nothing for it but to drive them, and this he did by constant and indiscriminate harshness.'

In the first edition of the *Memorials*, published in 1856, the identity of the person is not disclosed. In 1910 an illustrated edition was published, with a footnote on page 3 which states that the person to whom the passage refers, was Alexander, afterwards Professor Christison, who was elected to the Chair of Humanity at Edinburgh University in 1806. A similar footnote appeared in an edition published in 1945. No doubt the description fitted Nicol, but it also applied to other masters of the High School at that time. Although the school had a reputation for learning, it was also notorious for flogging and harshness.

Burns and Nicol met during the poet's first winter in Edinburgh, possibly through the Crochallan Fencibles as Nicol was a member of that club of wits and practical jokers. That they had met and become close friends is evident from a letter dated 1 June, 1787, which Burns sent to Nicol during his Border tour, and addressed, 'Kind, honest hearted Willie'. It is the only extant letter which Burns wrote in the 'mither tongue'. In the following extract he deals with his travels and with two young ladies he met:

'I hae dander'd owre a' the kintra frae Dunbar to Selcraig, and hae forgather'd wi' monie a guid fallow, and monie a weel far'd hizzie. - I met wi' twa dink quines in particular, ane o' them a sonsie, fine fodgel lass, baith braw and bonie; the tither was a clean-shankit, straught, tight, weel-far'd winch, as blythe's a lintwhite on a flowerie thorn, and as sweet and modest's a new blawn plumrose in a hazle-shaw.- They were baith bred to mainers by the beuk, and onie ane o' them has as muckle smeddum and rumblegumption as the half o' some Pesbytries that you and I baith ken- They play'd me sik a deevil o' a shavie that I daur say if my harigals were turn'd out, ye wad see twa nicks i' the heart o' 'me like the mark o' a kail-whittle in a castock.'

I was gaun to write you a lang epistle, but, Gude forgie me, I gat myself sae notoriously bitchify'd the day after kail-time that I can hardly stoiter but and ben.' *(CL 342)*

On numerous occasions Burns boasted in his letters that he was intoxicated when he certainly was not, and this letter is a prime example. No drunk man could have composed such a masterpiece, and the assertion that he was 'notoriously bitchify'd' is nothing more than harmless bravado.

On his return to Mauchline, following his Border tour with Robert Ainslie, Burns wrote to Nicol on 18th June. Always one to observe 'men, their manners, and their ways' he reflects in the letter on the Edinburgh nobility and the Mauchline folk:

'I never, my friend, thought Mankind very capable of any thing generous, but the stateliness of the Patricians in Edinburgh, and the servility of my plebeian brethren, who perhaps eyed me askance, since I returned home, have nearly put me out of conceit altogether with my species.' *(CL 345)*

No sooner had he despatched his letter to Nicol than he was off again on a tour of the West Highlands, visiting Inveraray and Dumbarton, where he was made an Honorary Burgess. Back later in Mauchline at the end of June, he wrote again to Nicol on 29th July informing him that:

'A letter from Creech's I just now received oblidges (sic) me to be in Edinburgh against this day or tomorrow se'enight, though my stay will be but a few days.- If you do not leave town immediately at the commencement of the vacation, I hope to have the heart-felt pleasure of once more meeting a friend to whom I owe so much, and for whom I have so high an esteem.' *(CL 345)*

It is obvious from the letters quoted that Burns and Nicol enjoyed a very warm friendship, which had been forged during the poet's first visit to Edinburgh. The high regard Burns had for his friend was expressed in an epitaph, which he penned about this time:

> Ye maggots, feed on Nicols brain,
> For few sic feasts ye've gotten;
> An' fix your claws on Nicol's heart,
> For deil a bit o't's rotten. *(CW 299)*

When Burns returned to Edinburgh on 8th August, he knew that the room in Baxter's Close, which he shared with Richmond on his first visit, was no longer available. It is possible, however, that he spent one or two nights there before moving into an attic room, in Nicol's house above Buccleuch Pend near St. Patrick's Square.

His intention to spend only a few days in the Capital, was overset by Creech's delay in settling accounts for the 1787 edition. Indeed, it was to be many weeks before he was able to return to Mauchline, and even then, he had still not received a final settlement from his publisher. In the meantime, he and Nicol arranged to undertake a tour of the Highlands. In a letter to his friend, Ainslie, Burns wrote, 'Tomorrow I leave Edinburgh in a chaise: Nicol thinks it more comfortable than horse-back, to which I say, Amen.' *(CL 330)*

To hire a chaise, horses and driver for three weeks would no doubt be costly. It has been suggested that Burns probably bore the full cost as Nicol had to eke out his schoolmaster's salary by translating into Latin the theses of University students. [3] - He was poorly paid for this work and often had to wait lengthy periods for settlement. Many of the difficult cases were passed to Alexander Young, W.S. for collection, who left the following account of Nicol:

> 'At this time I looked upon Nicol as a far greater Poet and genius than Burns. He had considerable, indeed constant employment in translating the Medical and Law Theses of the graduates at the University, for which he made liberal charges, but was very little paid. I was employed by him to recover many of the claims from English students, concerning which I corresponded with the late Mr. Roscoe (then an Attorney in Liverpool) ; and on communicating to Mr. Nicol some of Mr. Roscoe's letters signifying that several of his claims were considered to be doubtful, if not desperate, he fell into an extravagant rage, swore, the most unseemly oaths and uttered the grossest blasphemies, that ' if our Saviour were again on Earth and had employed him to transfer a Thesis without paying him for it, he would crucify him over again.' [4]

After reading Young's memoranda, his friend, the Rt. Hon. Charles Hope, who later became Lord Granton, added his own comments:

> 'I met Burns several times at dinner in different Houses, when he first came to Edinr. but I was not at all intimate with him, That visit of his to Edinr. was a great

misfortune to him, and led to all his after follies and misconduct, and ultimately to his ruin and ultimate death — to all of which his intimacy with Nicol mainly contributed - Nicol, as you say, was a good Scholar; but I did not consider him as a better Scholar than Adam or Fraser - His passions were quite ungovernable, and he was altogether a most unprincipled Savage.' [5]

It is interesting to read what Lord Cockburn had to say about Hope - 'His great defect was a want of tact. Declamation was his weapon, and it is one that is seldom sheathed in correct wisdom. The result was that, though possessed of superior abilities, he was often felt to be unsafe.' [6]

Mrs. Dunlop of Dunlop,
She received more letters from Burns than any of his other correspondents, despite a period of estrangement. From an engraving by H. Robinson in *The Land of Burns.*

Fortunately, twentieth century research has disproved much of Hope's comments, but it was typical of the way the polite society of Edinburgh judged Burns, especially after his death. Burns's association with Nicol, however, did not exactly enhance his reputation. Mrs. Dunlop and Clarinda did not approve. Obviously Mrs. Dunlop had heard something of the Edinburgh gossip; in a letter to Burns she referred to his 'recounter with the Schoolmaster, who, the world says, has already damned you as an author, and now well-nigh killed you as a man,' [7] Clarinda wrote, '(Miss Nimmo) has almost wept to me at mentioning your intimacy with a certain famous, or infamous man in town.' [8] Dugald Stewart also recorded that he had 'heard of Burns's predilection for convivial, and not very polite society.' [9]

Burns and Nicol left Edinburgh on 28th August, and the same day the poet noted in his journal, 'I set out for the north with my good friend Mr. N.' Their journey took them by way of Linlithgow, Falkirk, Stirling, Crieff, Aberfeldy, Blair Atholl, then through Srathspey to Aviemore and Inverness. From there they headed east through Nairn, Forres and Fochabers to the coast of the Moray Firth at Cullen and Banff. They then cut across country to Peterhead and down the coast to Aberdeen, Stonehaven and Montrose. Their journey back to Edinburgh was by way of Dundee, Perth and Kinross to Queensferry, where they crossed the Forth, reaching the capital on Sunday, 16th September.

The brief notes in Burns's journal reflect the hurried nature of the tour, which was due to the irascibility and impatience of Nicol. One writer has stated that Burns described his companionship as being like 'travelling with a loaded blunderbuss at full cock.' [10] There is ample evidence that Burns was hurried away from certain places that he visited during the tour, where it may have been to his advantage to prolong his stay. Such a visit was at Blair Castle, where he spent two delightful days with the Duke and Duchess of Atholl and their family. Here he met Robert Graham of Fintry, who had just been appointed a Commissioner of the Scottish Board of the Excise, and who, later, was to play a very influential role in Burns's appointment and subsequent career in the Excise. Had Burns been able to remain another day at Blair Castle, however, he would have met

Blair Castle, where Burns spent two days with the Duke and Duchess of Atholl.

Henry Dundas, who was then Treasurer of the Navy, and the most powerful government minister in Scotland. At that time Dundas controlled all government appointments, which were subject to patronage, and may have been able to place Burns in a well paid sinecure. It appears that no invitation to stay at the castle was extended to Nicol, who was placed in the care of Josiah Walker, tutor to the Duke's son. Walker kept him happy, giving him a fishing rod and introducing him to some good stretches of river, 'This quite absorbed his attention wrote Walker, 'and allayed his jealousy while the poet was made a pet of in the mansion.'[11] Other evidence that Burns was hurried away is contained in a letter which Walker sent to the poet on 13th September, 1787, in reply to one he had received from Burns, dated, 5th September. In it Walker wrote:

'I hope your disappointment on being forced to leave us as great as appeared from your expression.... You know how anxious the Duke was to have another day of you, and to let Mr. Dundas have the pleasure of your conversation as the first dainty with which he would entertain an honoured guest. You know likewise the eagerness the ladies showed to detain you, but perhaps you do not know the scheme which they devised, with their usual fertility of resources. One of the servants was sent to your driver to bribe him to loose or pull off a shoe from one of the horses, but the ambush failed. *Proh imirum* The driver was *incorruptible.*' [12]

Even worse embarrassment befell Burns at Fochabers, ancestral seat of the Duke and Duchess of Gordon. Burns had met the Duchess in Edinburgh during the preceding winter, and presuming on this acquaintance, he left Nicol at the local inn and proceeded to Gordon Castle to call on the Duke and Duchess. Dr. Robert Coupar of Fochabers, subsequently furnished Dr. James Currie with an account of Burns's visit:

'At the castle, our poet was received with the utmost hospitality and kindness; and the family being about to sit down to dinner, he was invited to take his place at table as a matter of course. This invitation he accepted, and after drinking a few glasses of wine, he rose up and proposed to withdraw. On being pressed to stay, he mentioned, for the first time, his engagement with his fellow- traveller, and his noble host offering to send a servant to conduct Mr. Nicol to the castle, Burns insisted on undertaking that office himself. He was, however, accompanied by gentleman, a particular acquaintance of the Duke, by whom the invitation was delivered in all the forms of politeness. The invitation came too late, the pride of Nicol was inflamed into a high degree of passion by the neglect which he had already suffered. He had ordered the horses to be put to the carriage, being determined to proceed on his journey alone; and they found him parading the streets of Fochabers, before the door of the inn, venting his anger on the postillion for the slowness with which he obeyed his commands, As no explanation nor entreaty could change the purpose of his fellow-traveller, our poet was reduced to the necessity of separating from him entirely, or of instantly proceeding with him on their journey. He chose the last of these alternatives, and seating himself beside Nicol in the post-chaise, with mortification and regret he turned his back on Gordon Castle, where he had promised some happy days.' [13]

No mention is made of this unfortunate incident in Burns's journal, but on 20th October he wrote to James Hoy, the Duke's librarian, who probably was the gentleman who accompanied the poet back to Fochabers to try and persuade Nicol to come to the castle. Burns enclosed the verses 'On Castle Gordon',[1] *(CW 293)* and promised to leave a curse among his legacies to:

'. . . that unlucky predicament which hurried me, tore me away from Castle Gordon - May that obstinate Son of Latin Prose be curst to Scotch-mile periods, and damn'd to seven- league paragraphs, while Declension and Conjugation, Gender, Number and Time, under the ragged banners of Dissonance and Disarrangement eternally rank against him in hostile array. !!!!!!' *(CL 361)*

The Duchess of Gordon.
Burns met her during his stay in Edinburgh. He was invited to several of her drawing-room parties and Burns listed her as one of his "avowed Patrons and Patronesses"
From a painting by George Romney, Scottish National Portrait Gallery.

It says much for Burns's patience and forbearance that he got back into the chaise with Nicol. He must have been extremely embarrassed and we can easily imagine the angry silence which followed, as the two travellers continued their journey to Cullen. By the time they reached Banff, however, Burns's good humour had apparently been restored, but Nicol's chagrin still smouldered. Here they breakfasted with Dr. George Chapman. Headmaster of the local Academy, who had invited his star pupil, George Imlach, then a boy of thirteen, to join the party. Many years later Imlach recalled the meeting:

'During breakfast, Burns played off some sporting jests at his touchy *compagnon de voyage*, about some misunderstanding which took place between them at Fochabers, in consequence of Burns having visited the castle without him; and the good old doctor seemed much amused with the way the poet chose to smooth down the yet lurking ire of the dominie.' [14]

When the two travellers reached Aberdeen, Burns had the great pleasure of meeting Bishop Skinner, son of the Rev. John Skinner (1721-1807) author of the song, 'Tullochgorum', which Burns described as 'the best Scotch song ever Scotland saw.' The Bishop gave his father a very full account of his meeting with the poet. The opening passage again confirms the intolerance of Nicol and the restriction it imposed on Burns:

'Our time was short, as he was just setting off for the south and his companion hurrying him, but we had fifty 'auld sangs' through hand, and spent an hour or so most agreeably.' [15]

At Montrose he met his cousin, James Burness and would have prolonged his stay, but, as he explained in a letter to him, written from 'Townfield', (probably the local inn) at six o'clock in the morning:

'Mr. Nicol and Mr. Carnegie (driver of the chaise) have taken some freak in their head and have wakened me just now with the rattling of the chaise to carry me to meet them at Craigie to go on our journey some other road and breakfast on the way. I must go, which makes me very sorry.' *(CL 61)*

In the same letter he asked that any mail should be sent to him care of Creech, an indication that he had made up his mind not to lodge with Nicol again on his return to Edinburgh, It may also suggest that he had had enough of his travelling companion, at least for a spell.

Back in the capital Burns tried again for a settlement with Creech, but without success. In a postscript to a letter dated 28th September, to Patrick Miller, he stated, 'I am determined not to leave Edinburgh till I wind up my matters with Creech, which I am afraid will be a tedious business.' *(CL 241)* To relieve the tedium and ostensibly to pay a visit to Sir William Murray of Auchtertyre, near Crieff, whom he had met at Blair Castle, he set off about 4th October, in company with Dr. James Adair, who was the son of an Ayrshire doctor, and a kinsman of Mrs. Frances Dunlop. Many years later Adair furnished Dr. Currie with an account of their jaunt, which included a more moderate picture of Nicol than those recounted by Alexander Young and Lord Granton:

'At Stirling we met with a company of travellers from Edinburgh, among whom was a character in many respects congenial with that of Burns. This was Nicol, one of the teachers of the High Grammar School of Edinburgh - the same wit and power of conversation, the same fondness for convivial society, and thoughtlessness of tomorrow, characterised them both; Jacobitical principles in politics were common to both of them, and these have been suspected, since the revolution in France, to have given place in each to opinions apparently opposite. I regret that I have preserved no memorabilia of their conversation either on this or other occasions, when I happened to meet them together.' [16]

From Auchtetyre Burns wrote to Nicol on 8th October. In the opening passage he said, 'I find myself very comfortable here, neither oppressed by economy nor mortified by neglect,' *(CL 345)* Was he having a sly dig at Nicol, remembering the dominie's tantrums at Fochabers?

When Burns returned to Edinburgh, following his short tour with Adair, he lodged with William Cruickshank until he left in February of the following year. Cruickshank was also a Classical Master at the High School. Unlike Nicol he was very popular with his pupils. Lord Brougham, who attended the High School in 1790/91 remembered him as 'a very able and successful teacher, as well as a worthy man.' [17] It can well be imagined that Burns lodging with Cruickshank would not go down very well with Nicol, who was very jealous of anyone who became more friendly with the poet than himself. This is borne out in a letter of 3rd March, 1788, which Burns sent to Cruickshank from Mauchline. Mindful of Nicol's innate jealousy, he wrote, 'I would send my compliments to Mr. Nicol, but he would be hurt if he knew I wrote to any body, and no to him.' *(CL 359)*

In the autumn of the same year Cruickshank became involved in a matter which must have tested Burns's patience and placed a strain on his friendship with Nicol. Mrs. McLehose (Clarinda), heartedly disliked Nicol and never approved of Burns's association with him. She passed on any malicious gossip she heard about him to Burns, who suspected that most of the stories originated from Dr. Adam, Rector of the High School, with whom Nicol was constantly warring. Burns, perhaps imprudently, related one of those stories to Cruickshank, saying he had heard it from a lady of his acquaintance. Cruickshank repeated it to Nicol, and there the matter might have rested, but for a litigation that arose out of a fresh quarrel between Nicol and Adam. Nicol repeatedly pressed Burns to give him the name of the lady, which the poet refused to divulge; he even threatened to have a summons served on Burns if he persisted in withholding the information.

In a letter dated 23rd August, 1788, written from Mauchline, Burns enlisted the aid of a mutual friend, Robert Ainslie:

> 'Heaven knows how I should proceed! I have this moment wrote to Mrs. Mc—se, telling her that I have informed you of the affair; and I shall write to Mr. Nicol by Tuesday's post that I will not give up my female friend till farther consideration; but that I have acquainted you with the business and the name; and that I have desired you to wait on him, which I entreat, my dear Sir, you will do; and give up the name or not, as Your and Mrs.Mc—se's prudence shall suggest.' *(CL 335)*

The letters to Mrs. McLehose and Nicol have not survived, but as Burns heard nothing more of the matter, it must be assumed that Ainslie was able to placate Nicol and free Burns of any involvement

Robert Ainslie.
He accompanied Burns in his order tour, but in later life he became very pious and was averse to discussing Burns.

in the quarrel. It has been suggested that, arising from this unpleasant business Burns and Nicol became estranged, but there is no evidence to suggest that the friendship was affected in any way.

During the autumn vacation of the High School in 1789, Nicol and his family relaxed at Willie's Mill, near Craigieburn, on the outskirts of Moffat. He was visited by Burns, who had commenced farming at Ellisland, six miles north of Dumfries, and by Allan Masterton, who had been on a visit to Dalswinton. Masterton was then writing master at a private school in Stevenslaw's Close, and in 1795 became joint writing master in the High School. He was also a gifted musician and something of a composer. The meeting of the three friends appears to have been a joyful one which Burns celebrated with a matchless drinking song, 'Willie Brew'd a Peck o' Maut', to which Masterton composed the air.

> O Willie brew'd a peck o' maut,
> And Rob and Allan cam to pree;
> Three blyther hearts, that lee-lang night,
> Ye wad na found in Christendie.

Chorus
> We are na fou, we're nae that fou,
> But just a drappie in our e'e;
> The cock may craw, the day may daw,
> And ay we'll taste the barley bree. *(CW 364)*

Nicol's wife was Janet Cairns, sister of Edward Cairns, laird of Torr; whose estate and mansion lay in the parish of Rerrick in the Stewartry of Kircudbright, about a mile north of Auchencairn. Their father had made a fortune as a button manufacturer in the Midlands, and was at one time Lord Mayor of Birmingham.[18] Tradition has it that Nicol proposed marriage to Janet while she was attending a boarding school, presumably in Edinburgh, It was money that she had inherited that enabled Nicol to purchase on 26th March, 1790, the remote hill farm of Meikle and Little Laggan. It extended to 384 acres and was situated on the southern flank of the Keir Hills in Glencairn parish, Nithsdale, about six miles distant from Ellisland. Nicol paid £1700 for the property, which he regarded as a long-term investment and a possible place to settle when he retired.

It was probably at the meeting in Moffat that Nicol arranged for Burns to look over the lands at Meikle and Little Laggan and give him a report. It appears it was also at Moffat that Burns agreed to accept into his care, a mare belonging to Nicol. The beast was in poor condition, and the arrangement was for Burns to revive her sufficiently, and then offer her for sale at some neighbouring fair. Burns, however, was unable to inspect the lands at Laggan, as he explained in a melancholy letter to his friend on 13th December, 1789.

'I have been so ill, my ever dear Friend, that I have not been able to go over the threshold of my door since I saw you. As I could not see and inspect Laggan farm personally, I have sent for two friends of mine that know it well, and on whose judgement of land I could depend very far, and from what they inform me, I think you have every reason to proceed with your purchase..... Now for your unfortunate old mare. I have tried many dealers for her and I am ashamed to say that the highest offer I have got for her, is fifty shillings. However, I tried her yesterday in the Plough, and I find that the poor creature is extremely willing to do what she can, so I hope to make her worth her meat to me, until I can try her at some fair.' *(CL346)*

By the time Burns wrote again to Nicol on 9th February, 1790, his health had improved, but he had bad news to impart:

'That d-mned mare of yours is dead. I would freely have given her price to have saved her: she has vexed me beyond description..... While she was with me. She done for her that could be done; and the accident has vexed me to the heart. In fact, I could not pluck up spirits to write to you on account of the unfortunate business.' *(CL 346)*

In the same letter he tells Nicol of George Sutherland's theatrical company, playing to packed houses in the Assembly Rooms and of people having to be turned away for lack of room, although 'some of our clergy have slipt in by stealth now and then..... A new theatre (Theatre Royal) is to be built by subscription, the first stone to be laid on Friday first to come.' At the close of the letter he writes, 'I have strung four or five barbarous stanzas, to the tune of Chevy Chase, by way of Elegy on your poor unfortunate mare, beginning (the name she got here was Peg Nicholson).' No doubt the verses were meant to soothe his irate friend on his loss:

> Peg Nicholson was a good bay mare
>   As ever trod on airn;
> But now she's floating down the Nith,
>   And past the mouth o' Cairn
>
> Peg Nicholson was a good bay mare,
>   And rode thro' thick and thin;
> But now she's floating down the Nith,
>   And wanting even the skin.
>
> Peg Nicholson was a good bay mare,
>   And ance she bore a priest;

> But now she's floating down the Nith,
>   For Solway fish a feast.
>
> Peg Nicholson was a good bay mare,
>   An' the priest he rode her sair;
> And much oppress'd and bruis'd she was,
>   As priest-rid cattle are. *(CW 380)*

As the letter indicates, the name of Peg Nicholson was given to the mare by Burns, after the mad woman, Margaret Nicholson, who had attempted to assassinate King George III in 1786. Scott Douglas suggests that the expressions 'priest- rid' and 'the priest he rode her sair', refers to Nicol's original intention to enter the ministry. It was not until May that Burns was able to inspect the property at Laggan himself. In a letter to his friend, dated 28th May, he reported on the rich deposits of limestone that he found there. He concluded that 'the farm itself is a most beautiful one, and in my opinion as with the whole neighbourhood's opinion, is an exceedingly cheap purchase.'

On 27th January,1791 the Commissioners of Excise formally agreed that Burns's name should be placed on the Register of Persons recommended for Examiner and Supervisor. In August of the previous year, however, Nicol wrote an amusing letter to their mutual friend, Robert Ainslie, in the belief that Burns had been promoted to the rank of Examiner:

> 'As to Burns, poor folks like you and I must resign all thoughts of future correspondence with him. To the pride of applauded genius is now superadded the pride of office. He was lately raised to the dignity of an Examiner of Excise, which is a step preparative to attaining that of *supervisor*. Therefore we can expect no less than that his language will become perfectly *Horatian -' odiprqfaman vulgus el arceo'*. However, I will see him in a fortnight hence, and if I find that Beelzebub has inflated his heart like a bladder with pride, and given it the fullest distension that vanity can effect, you and I will burn him in effigy, and write a satire, as bitter as gall and wormwood, against government for employing its *enemies* like Lord North, to effect its purposes. This will be taking all the revenge in our power.' [19]

Nicol knew better than accuse Burns of being 'inflated like a bladder with pride.' His letter to Ainslie is nothing more than a piece of mock solicitude. In ranking Burns as an enemy of the government, he no doubt had in mind the poet's Jacobitical leanings.

At the end of 1792, someone denounced Burns to the Board of Excise as a person disloyal to the government, and an enquiry was ordered into his conduct and principles. Burns certainly had expressed his radical opinions indiscreetly on several occasions, but the incident which apparently sparked off the denouncement occurred in the Dumfries

Theatre on the evening of 28th October, when it was alleged that Burns had remained seated with his hat on during the playing of the national anthem. It was also alleged that he had joined the clamour from the pit for Ca ira, the French republican song; the only outcome of the enquiry was that Burns received a private caution and told to be more circumspect in future.

News of the affair quickly reached Edinburgh and in some quarters it was whispered that Burns had been dismissed from the service. Nicol responded with a letter on 10th February, 1793, which Hilton Brown described as 'one of the most sensible letters Burns ever received.' [20] It has not survived, but fortunately Burns made a copy of it for the Glenriddel MS. The following is an extract, preceded by Burns's headnote:

> 'FROM MY WORTHY FRIEND Mr. NICOL OF THE HIGH SCHOOL, EDINBURGH: ALLUDING TO SOME TEMERAIRE CONDUCT OF MINE IN THE POLITICAL OPINIONS OF THE DAY DEAR CHRISTLESS BOBBIE - What is become of thee?? Has the Devil flown off with thee, as the gled (kite) does with a bird?. If he should do so there is little matter, if the reports concerning thy *imprudence* are true. What concerns it thee whether the lousy Dumfriesian fiddlers play 'Ca ira' or 'God save the King?' Suppose you had an aversion to the King, you could not, as a gentleman, wish God to use him worse than He has done. The infliction of idiocy is no sign of Friendship or; Love; and I am sure damnation is a matter far beyond your wishes modest of political conduct who flourished in the victorious reign of Queen Anne, viz, the Vicar of Bray, who during the convulsions of Great Britain which were without any former example, saw eight reigns, in perfect security; because he remembered that precept of the *sensible, shrewd, temporising* Apostle,' We ought not to resist the Higher Powers.' [21]

Burns replied on 20th February with a humorous screed of mock contrition, but, underlying all the playful satire there is a sense of resentment that Nicol, of all people, should have the temerity to preach to him, Burns's head note to his letter seems to bear this out:

> 'AS MY FRIEND NICOL, THOUGH ONE OF THE WORTHIEST, AND POSITIVELY THE CLEVEREST FELLOW I EVER KNEW, YET NO MAN, IN HIS HUMOURS, HAVING GONE GREATER LENGTHS IN IMPRUDENCE, UNHOLINESS, etc., THAN HE; I WROTE HIM AS FOLLOWS:

> O thou, wisest among the Wise, meridian blaze of Prudence, full moon of Discretion, & Chief of many Counsellors! - How infinitely is thy puddle- headed, rattle-headed, wrong-headed, round-headed slave indebted to thy supereminent goodness, that from the luminous path of thy own right-lined rectitude, thou

lookest benignly down on an erring Wretch, of whom the zig-zag wanderings defy all the powers of Calculation, from the simple copulation of Units up to the hidden mystery of Fluxions! May one feeble ray of that light of wisdom which darts from thy sensoriurn, straight as the arrow of Heaven against the head of the Unrighteous,& bright as the meteor of inspiration descending on the holy and undefiled Priesthood - may be my portion; so that I may be less unworthy of the face and favour of that father of Proverbs and master of Maxims, that antipode of folly and magnet among the Sages, the wise and witty Willie Nicol! Amen! Amen! Yea, so be it!'

Another lengthy paragraph in similar vein follows, and Burns then rounds off the letter, with continued mock contrition:

> 'May thy pity and thy prayers be exercised for,-
> O thou lamp of Wisdom & mirror of Morality!
> Thy devoted Slave -
> RB' *(CL 349)*

Nicol and Masterton spent a week in Dumfries during the summer of 1793. Apparently, Burns attended to his excise duties during the day, and met his two friends for a meal in the Globe Inn in the evening, There is a story, perhaps apocryphal, that one evening Nicol and Masterton arrived at the Globe to find that Burns had forgotten to order the meal -Mrs. Hyslop, the innkeeper's wife, said she had a tup's head prepared for the family and they were welcome to share it. When the three friends sat down to the meal, Nicol suggested, that Burns should be fined for his neglect and asked to produce a grace. Whereupon Burns repeated the following grace extempore:

> O Lord when hunger pinches sore
>   Do Thou stand us in stead,
> And send us from Thy bounteous store,
>   A tup or wether head! *(CW 409)*

At the end of the meal another fine was imposed on the poet, when he again rose to the occasion and produced a grace after meal:

> O Lord, since we have feasted thus,
>   Which we so little merit,
> Let Meg now take away the flesh,
>   And Jock bring in the spirit! [22]   *(CW 409)*

Mention has already been made of the quarrel between Nicol and Dr. Adam, Rector of the High School. In December, 1782. Nicol, having experienced what he considered a public affront from Dr. Adam, waylaid him one night in the High School Wynd and inflicted serious injuries upon him. He subsequently confessed to the assault, and apologised to the Rector and town council, as patrons of the school. The quarrel, however, seems to have dragged on until 1790, when it became so serious that the town council found it necessary to intervene, in order to avoid further scandal. The following extract from the town council minutes indicates the action taken:

Dr. Alexander Adam.
Rector of the High School, Edinburgh, from
1764 to 1819 The portrait by Sir Henry Raeburn,
was commissioned by fourteen of his pupils and
painted shortly before his death.
Scottish National Portrait Gallery.

'25th January 1791 —
The Lord Provost informed that the reason of calling this meeting of council was to take into consideration an interlocutor and report by the magistrates relative to the long dispute between the Rector and one of the subordinate masters of the High School, which had been laid before His Majestie's Advocate, Solicitor General, and Extraordinary Assessor for the city. Then the said interlocutor and report was read, and is of the following tenor:-'Edinburgh, *19th January, 1791,* - The magistrates having considered the different petitions of Doctor Alexander Adam, Rector of the High School of Edinburgh, answers for Mr. William Nicol, one of the masters of the said school,... find it proven that Mr. Nicol, as one of the subordinate masters of the said school, has been guilty of a verbal injury of a contumelious nature to Dr. Adam, as Rector, for which he ought to receive a severe reproof, with a proper certification, and report their opinion that the whole masters of the school shall be convened before the council assembled at a full meeting....Which report before engrossed, being considered by the council they unanimously approved, and in addition thereto, were of opinion that the Lord Provost should intimate to the Rector that his conduct was not altogether free from blame.'

The minute goes on to refer to some general regulations relating to the better administration of the High School, and then proceeds:

'Thereafter Doctor Adam and Mr. Nicol being called for, they appeared along with the other masters... The Lord Provost, from the chair, reprimanded Mr. Nicol in very severe terms, and intimated to him that immediate dismission from his office would be the consequence of a future transgression of a similar nature.' [23]

It will be observed from the minute that Dr. Adam was found to be not entirely blameless. He held the *appointment* of Rector of the High School for over forty years and was regarded as an excellent teacher and scholar. Sir Walter Scott wrote that 'it was from this respectable man that I first learned the value of that knowledge I had hitherto considered only a burdensome task'. Such eminent men as Lord Brougham and Lord Cockburn have left high testimonies to his worth. [24] It is interesting to note, however, that William Cruickshank had also been involved in a quarrel with Dr. Adam. We learn this from a letter which Burns sent to Cruickshank in December, 1788:

Lord Cockburn.
Published posthumously
Memorial of his Times
which contained vivid
descriptions of some of
the characters in Edinburgh
at the time.

'It gives me a very heavy heart to read such accounts of the consequences of your quarrel with that puritanic, rotten-hearted, hell-commissioned scoundrel, Adam. If, not withstanding your unprecedented industry in public, and your irreproachable conduct in private life, he still has you so much in his power, what ruin may he not bring on some others I could name.' *(CL 360)*

While Burns's sympathy and understanding would be on the side of Cruickshank, there must have been some serious cause for him to vent his spleen on Adam in such a way.

Heron in his *Memoirs* made reference to Nicol's dispute with Adam. He said that Nicol's 'latter years were vexatiously embittered by a contest with a creature, that, although accidentally exalted into competition with him, was unworthy to *unloose* his *shoe-latchet.*' [25]

Nicol and Adam fell foul of each other again in 1795. The town council minute of 18th March refers to another complaint brought against Nicol by the Rector.

A sub-committee recalled that 'a gross assault had been made on Dr. Adam on the street, in December, 1782, which by the intervention of two honourable gentlemen was made up, Mr. Nicol having acknowledged his fault in a letter publickly (sic) read in the High School. . . After so heinous a fault, Mr. Nicol being forgiven, it was to have been expected that his future would have been circumspect'. In 1790, however, ' he had used contumacious language to Dr. Adam', for which he was severely reprimanded and warned. Dr. Adam now complained that Nicol had refused him admission to his classroom and had announced that he intended opening a class for private teaching, the object of which, Dr. Adam contended, was to deprive him of a portion of his fees. By this time the town council, no doubt heartily sick of the squabble, resolved that 'if Mr. Nicol continue his private school,- which he took up after the last examination, apparently with the view of hurting the Rector's class, - after the 1st April next, he shall be dismissed from his office'. [26]

Nicol refused to give way and resigned his post as master. In September, 1785, he gave notice, by public advertisement, of his intention to open a private school in Jackson's Land, for the purpose of 'instructing young gentlemen in the LATIN LANGUAGE'. [27]

When Burns died on 21st July, 1796, John Lewars, his fellow exciseman, undertook the task of writing to Burns's relatives and friends informing them of the poet's death. Nicol responded to Lewar's intimation with a letter, dated 30th August, which reveals his heartfelt loss on the death of his friend.

> 'Dear Sir,
> I beg leave to offer you my sincerest acknowledgements for the early intelligence though of the most disagreeable and shocking Nature, which you communicated to me, on occasion of the premature death of my dearly beloved Burns. I would have made them long before this time, if I had been capable of writing. But I have been, ever since that time, confined, in a great measure to my bed, and highly distressed by a jaundice combined with some other complaints; but thanks to God, I have now every mark of convalescence. I was obliged to retire from the town to country Quarters at Stockbridge, where, except on an occasional visit to the town, I am determined to reside, for some time.
>
> Since the death of our friend I can no longer view the face of Nature, with the same rapture; and social joy is blighted to me, for ever. It gives me great pain to see, that the encomiums, passed upon him, both in the Scotch and English newspapers, are mingled with reproaches, of the most indelicate and cruel Nature. But stupidity and idiocy rejoice, when a great man and an immortal genius falls; and they pour forth their invidious reflections, without reserve, well knowing, that the dead Lion, from whose presence, they formerly scudded away, with terror, and, at whose voice they trembled through every nerve, can devour no more.'

He then goes on to enquire about Burns's money. Obviously the poet had informed Nicol of the sums he had received from Creech for the publication of the Edinburgh Edition and the Copyright of his poems. He was also privy to the fact that Burns had given £250 to Gilbert to help him out of difficulties at Mossgiel. He expresses concern that Gilbert may be tempted to 'press his own interest to that of the large and unprovided family of his brother.' (With hindsight we know that Gilbert squared the debt in 1820 from the £250 he received from Cadell and Davies for editing the unsuccessful eighth edition of Currie's works). Nicol continues the letter by requesting Lewars:

> 'Give my most respectful compliments to Mr. Syme, and tell him, as the subscriptions are going on very slowly here, to write Dr. Moore, Physician at London, who was a great admirer of Burns, to institute one there. A considerable sum perhaps might be procured.

> The fanatics have now got it into their heads, that dreadful bursts of penitential sorrow issued from the breast of our friend, before he expired. But if I am not much mistaken in relation to his firmness, he would disdain to have his dying moments disturbed with the sacerdotal gloom, and the sacerdotal howls. I knew he would negotiate with God alone concerning his immortal interests.

> Give my best compliments to Mrs. Burns, and tell her I shall never [be] [w]anting to the interests of her. In a word we [sh]all never see the likes of Burns again. His poems, constructed on a slender, nay almost aerial basis, [one word] the most expansive vigour of genius. Where material [one word] would have been wanting perhaps to almost every other Mortal [one word] like an electrical kite soars aloft, and draws down ethereal [one word] from heaven.
>   I am [one or two words],
>   yours Will Nicol' [28]

When Nicol wrote this letter he was a sick man. The 'jaundice combined with some other complaints' proved to be cirrhosis of the liver, which brought about his death on 21st April, 1797, some nine months after the death of Burns. He was buried in the Old Calton Cemetery in an unmarked grave.

Had he been spared he would have been well qualified to undertake a biography of Burns. He had an intimate knowledge of the poet, and a command of language that was second to none. Speculating on this, Prof. Thornton said, 'Nobody would have more furiously followed the whole truth than Nicol, and incidentally, broken more heads..' [29]

When Burns went to Edinburgh he measured himself against the literati and 'met no real intellectual challenge'. [30] It is not surprising that when he met Nicol, probably in the convivial company of the Crochallan Fencibles, he was attracted by the dominie's wit and intellectual vigour, which must have been a refreshing change from the studied gentility he often had to endure in the Edinburgh drawing rooms. Both Nicol and Burns were complex characters and resembled each other in many ways. Both possessed a lively intellect, were very well read and excelled in stimulating conversation. They also shared a hatred of cant and hypocrisy and were keenly critical of the establishment of the day. When they met, it was not just a convivial get-together, but a meeting of two great minds, and it was this, more than anything else which held the friendship together.

There is ample evidence that Burns was very much aware of Nicol's faults and failings, and was willing to put up with them. The way he bore Nicol's tantrums during the Highland Tour is ample testimony to his patience and understanding. Despite all his shortcomings, it is generally agreed that Nicol's heart was in the right place, and once he had given his hand in friendship he proved a loyal and generous friend. In one of his letters to Nicol, the poet commented on the frailty and uncertainty of many of his friendships. *(CL 343)* It is certainly true that very few lasted to the end of his life, but his friendship with Nicol endured 'through good report and bad report' right to the end.

The following 'conclusion', first collected from a facsimile in an auction catalogue, (MS not traced) possibly written shortly before his death, shows the depth of Burns's feelings for his schoolmaster friend.

> 'O Mr. Nicol, can time ever extinguish the gloomy remembrance of you in my bosom! The idea of your uncommon abilities may dissipate a little in comparison, but where, except surrounding the Fountain of Goodness, shall I find a heart to equal yours.
>
> Adieu!
> Robt Burns' *(CL 350)*

'LANG SANDY' WOOD

During the second winter Burns spent in Edinburgh he met with an accident. Returning home one evening he was thrown from a coach, driven by a drunken coachman, and sustained 'a good, serious, agonizing, damn'd hard knock on the knee'. *(CL 417)* **It was so badly wrenched that he was confined to his room at No 2 St. James's Square for four weeks. The accident prevented him from keeping a tea-drinking appointment with Mrs. Nancy McLehose and led to the start of the celebrated Clarinda/Sylvander correspondence.**

Doctor 'Lang Sandy' Wood.
From a painting by David Alison,
Scottish National Portrait Gallery.

The surgeon who attended him was Alexander Wood, affectionately known as 'Lang Sandy' because of his lanky figure. He was a subscriber to the 1787 Edinburgh Edition, and seems to have been an ardent admirer of the poet and his works. A warm friendship developed during the four weeks he ministered to Burns, and although there is no documentary evidence to prove the point, he is said to have used his influence to secure an appointment for Burns in the Excise. First mention of this was made by Robert Heron in *A Memoir of the Life of the Late Robert Burns*, published in 1797.

'Mr. Alexander Wood, the surgeon who attended him during the illness occasioned by his hurt, no sooner understood his patient's wish, to seek resource in the service of the Excise, than he, with the usual activity of his benevolence, effectually recommended the poet to the Commissioners of the Excise and the name of Burns was enrolled in the list of their *expectant-officers*.' [1]

A few days after the poet's unlucky fall, Lord President Dundas died, and it would appear that Burns was persuaded by the surgeon to write some suitable verses by way of tribute to his Lordship's memory. There may have been some reason in Wood's mind, apart from the merits of the Lord President, for making the suggestion. Perhaps he imagined that it would be in the poet's interests, since the late Lord President's brother was the powerful Henry Dundas ('King Harry the Ninth'), while his son was Solicitor General. The idea misfired, however, and some years later, in a letter to his friend, Alexander Cunningham, Burns expressed his feelings on the subject:

'Twas on the death of the late Lord President Dundas. My very worthy and most respected friend, Mr. Alexr. Wood, Surgeon, urged me to pay a compliment in the way of my trade, to his Lordship's memory. Well, to work I went, and produced a copy of Elegiac verses, some of them, I vow, rather commonplace, and others rather hide-bound, but on the whole, though they were far from being in

Rev. Alexander "Jupiter" Carlyle.
His diary was most revealing on many contemporaries, especially Lang Sandy Wood. He was nicknamed *Jupiter* because of his noble profile and bearing. He was a minister of Inveresk Church for 57 years. His autobiography was only published in 1860 which gives a flavour of his time. From a Portrait by Sir Henry Raeburn, Scottish National Portrait Gallery.

my best manner, they were tolerable; and had they been the production of a Lord or a Baronet, they would have been thought very clever. I wrote a letter which, however, was in my very best manner, and enclosing my Poem, Mr. Wood carried altogether to Mr. Solicitor Dundas that then was, and not finding him at home, left the parcel for him. His Solicitorship never took the smallest notice of the Letter, the Poem or the Poet. From that time, highly as I respect the talents of their family, I never see the name, Dundas, in the column of a newspaper, but my heart seems straitened for room in my bosom, and if I am obliged to read aloud a paragraph relating to one of them, I feel my forehead flush, and my nether lip quivers. Had I been an obscure Scribbler, as I was then in the hey-day of my fame; or had I been a dependent Hanger-on for favour or pay; or had the bearer of the letter been any other than a gentleman who has done honour to the city in which he lives, to the Country that produced him, and to the God that created him, Mr. Solicitor might have had some apology.' *(CL 461)*

Alexander Wood was the son of a well-to-do farmer, who farmed an area of ground lying between Canonmills and the present Queen Street. It was popularly known as Wood's Farm and the farmhouse stood on the western extremity, near what is now Wemyss Place. It was there that he was born in 1725. [2] It is difficult to visualise that this area, which is now so much a part of modern Edinburgh, was then open countryside.

Wood studied medicine at Edinburgh University, and first entered into practice in Musselburgh. It was about this time that he met Dr. Alexander 'Jupiter' Carlyle, Minister of Inveresh, who, in his *Autobiography*, left his impressions of the young doctor:

> '. . . Sandie Wood was very young, not above twenty-one or twenty-two, but there being an opening here by means of the illness of the senior practitioner, Wood was invited out by a few of the principal people, and got immediately into some business . . . Sandie Wood was a handsome stout fellow, with fine black eyes, and altogether of an agreeable and engaging appearance, Some scrapes he got into with women drove him from this place in two or three years for his good. One gentlewoman he got with child, and did not marry. When he got over this difficulty, another fell with child to him, whom he married. She died of her child; and Sanders was soon after called to a berth in Edinburgh.' [3]

Lord Byron.
Although an Englishman he spent his early years
in Scotland and had a great admiration for Burns.

Following his return he became a Fellow of the Royal College of Surgeons in 1756, and entered into partnership with Messrs. Rattray and Congleton, eminent men of their day, ultimately succeeding to the practice. He appears to have been gifted with great natural talents and possessed an uncanny ability to diagnose complaints.

He attained great professional celebrity in Edinburgh, where his philanthropy and kindness were proverbial. It is recorded that he was one of those consulted by Sir Walter Scott's parents on their son's lameness.[4] His unfailing attention to the indigent sick whom he visited, often in the most wretched conditions, after he had given up general practice, is proof of his complete dedication to his profession. He was held in very high esteem by his medical colleagues, and his dexterity and skill in operating did much to raise the standard and reputation of the surgical department of the Royal Infirmary.

Sir Walter Scott.
He met Burns during the poet's visit to Edinburgh in 1787. Although still a boy, he was greatly impressed. In the Journal entry 1826 Scott wrote "Long life to thy fame and peace to thy soul, Rob Burns."
From a painting by Sir Henry Raeburn,
Scottish National Portrait Gallery.

In a fragment of the fifth Canto of 'Child Harold', which appeared in *Blackwood's Magazine* in 1818, Lord Byron wrote:

'Oh! for an hour of him who knew no feud ---
The octogenarian chief, the kind old Sandy Wood;'

And in a note to the stanza, he spoke of him as:

'Sandy Wood – one of the delightful reminiscences of old Edinburgh – who was at least eighty years of age, when in high repute as a medical man, he could yet direct himself in his walks with the 'High Schuil laddies', or bestow the relics of his benevolence in feeding a sheep or a raven.'[5]

The sheep and the raven mentioned by Byron were well-known to the people of Edinburgh at that time. They appear to have been particular pets of 'Lang Sandy', who was also noted for his love of animals. The story goes that 'Willy', a sheep pastured on ground which now forms part of St Andrew's Square, was to be seen daily, standing at the railings, watching for the surgeon going to or coming from his home in York Place. His coat-pocket always contained a tit-bit for 'Willy', and invariably, the sheep would trot after him as he visited his patients throughout the town.

A domesticated raven at an ale-and-porter shop in North Castle Street also kept a daily vigil for him. It could recognise him at a distance when he passed along George Street and, swooping low, would accompany him on one of his forenoon walks--- he never used a carriage when he could walk, declaring that no vehicle could be found that would take him through the narrow closes and up the turnpike stairs.

He was a familiar figure in the streets of Edinburgh and became extremely popular with the poorer classes, no doubt because of the good work he did among them. Proof of this is to be found in the following story. Sir James Stirling, Lord Provost at the time, was unpopular on account of his opposition to a scheme for the reform of the Royal Burghs of Scotland. He and 'Lang Sandy' were so alike in appearance that one was often mistaken for the other. One evening an angry mob, under the impression that they had the Provost, were dragging the kind Doctor to the edge of the North Bridge with the intention of throwing him over, when he managed to yell above the din, 'I'm "Lang Sandy" Wood—Tak' me to a lamp an' ye'll see' The crowd, when they realised their mistake, instantly released him and dispersed with shouts of laughter.

Although Sir James and Sandy were held in such different respect by the townspeople, they were intimate friends. The story goes that on one occasion they met in the High Street, when the Provost put a guinea in the Doctor's hand, at the same time complaining of indigestion and stomach trouble and asking for his advice. Without speaking, Sandy retreated from Sir James, who continued to follow him for some considerable distance, finally reproaching him for having taken his guinea without offering any advice in return. It was probably one of the easiest guineas that he had ever earned as his simple reply shows – 'You're quite wrong, Sir James, I hae been

Dr. James Currie.
Burns first biographer, he started the legend that Burns was an alcoholic.

167

gi'en ye the best possible advice a' this while. If ye'll tak' haud o' my coat - tail and follow me for a week, as ye've been daein' for the last ten minutes, ye'll hae nae mair trouble wi' your stomach.'

Another humorous story has survived of his confrontation with his prospective father-in-law. It took place shortly after his return to Edinburgh, following his amorous indiscretions in Musselburgh. He sought the hand of Vera, second daughter of George Chalmers, W.S., and when asked how he proposed to support a wife and family, he took out his lancet case and said, 'I have nothing but this and a determination to succeed in my profession'. His future father-in-law was so impressed by his direct and honest reply that he readily gave his consent.

He was a great admirer of the great Mrs. Siddons, and when she was appearing at the theatre in Edinburgh, he was usually to be found in the pit, which was a favourite spot of the theatrical critics of the day. According to reports it was a point of fashion with the ladies to faint during the performance, and Sandy's services were very much in demand on such occasions, much to his disgust. One evening, when the house had been disrupted by repeated scenes of this kind, and when he was making his way out of the pit to attend some silly females, a friend remarked as he struggled past, 'This is glorious acting, Sandy', referring to Mrs. Siddons, to which Sandy retorted, 'Yes, and a damned deal o't too.' [6]

The Edinburgh of his day was a city of clubs and taverns, and many a song was generated over a bottle of claret. 'Lang Sandy' seems to have enjoyed this side of life as he was a member of many clubs. He could sing a good song and indulge in, what he called 'a bit of sensible nonsense.' A book of songs, bearing the quaint title of *Cantilenae Gymnasticae*, was dedicated to him and a fellow surgeon.

He was a keen golfer and continued to play until the very last years of his life. Although his calling kept him busily occupied, he could always find time for healthful relaxation and social pleasures.

In 1792, he appeared with an umbrella, the first person in Edinburgh to do so – a huge gingham apparatus that caused something of a sensation. It is appropriate that one of Kay's portraits shows him as a venerable octogenarian, with umbrella under his arm, making his way over the North Bridge. A second portrait by Kay, represents him at the height of his powers, with a cane thrown smartly over his shoulder and his tricorne hat set at a jaunty angle.

He died on 12th May, 1807, and was buried in the churchyard at Restalrig. A large number of books have been written on old Edinburgh --- its annals, romance,

Kay's portrait of Wood as an octogenarian.
Wood was the first person in Edinburgh to carry an umbrella.

characters, streets and clubs. In many of them is to be found some anecdote or reminiscence associated with 'Lang Sandy' Wood.

Like Robert Burns, he possessed 'the pitying heart that felt for human woe', and his character was nobly expressed in the following lines, part of an epitaph, written by Sir Alexander Boswell:

> But cold the heart that feels no genial glow,
> Pondering on him whose ashes sleep below;
> Whose vivid mind, with grasping power, could reach
> Truths that the plodding schools can never teach,
> Who scorned, in honesty, the specious wiles
> Of dull importance, or of fawning smiles ;
> Who scouted feelings frittered and refined,
> But had an ample heart for all mankind. [7]

PETER HILL

On 29th November, 1786, Robert Burns rode into Edinburgh. The main purpose of his visit was to try and secure a second edition of his poems. Within two weeks he had been introduced to the publisher, William Creech, whose bookshop was at the east end of the Luckenbooths,[1] and immediately below the flat where Allan Ramsay had opened the first circulating library in Scotland. Both in his shop and in his house in Craig's Close, which was nearby, Creech entertained all the literary figures and Edinburgh personalities of the day. These meetings, which came to be known as Creech's levees, were usually held in his house in the morning and in his shop in the afternoon. Lord Cockburn described Creech's shop as:

Peter Hill.
Portrait by Samuel Edmonston,
National Gallery of Scotland.

'The natural resort of lawyers, authors and all sorts of literary idlers, who were always buzzing about the convenient hive.'[2]

Creech seems to have spent most of his time presiding over those gatherings, with the result that the day-to-day running of the business was entrusted to his chief clerk, Peter Hill. An Edinburgh bookseller, who, for a time was in Creech's employment, supplied Robert Chambers with notes on the publisher's business habits:

'My friend, Mr. Creech, was rather a tardy man of business, and paid little attention to it. Previous to my becoming his clerk, he had my friend, Mr. Miller, and several other respectable young men, to take care of his business. Being so much occupied with literary people, he seldom handled his own money. His clerk balanced the cash every night, and carried on that to next day. He had a levee in his house till twelve every day, attended by literary men and printers. Between twelve and one he came to the shop, where the same flow of company lasted till four, and then he left us, and we saw no more of him till next day.' [3]

After reaching agreement with Creech to publish his poems, it would appear that Burns dealt mainly with Peter Hill, who handled much of the business matters relating to the Edinburgh edition. A warm friendship developed, which continued until shortly before the poet's death.

Peter Hill was the eldest son of James Hill and his wife Margaret Russell and was born at Dysart, Fife, on 20th November, 1755. [4] James Hill was collector of shore dues at Dysart, and is said to have been able to carry a 4 gallon barrel of gin in each hand. He accidentally drowned in 1770, no doubt in the course of his duties. His widow was left with three sons and three daughters, and shortly after her husband's death, she removed to Leith with her family. Young Peter Hill's first job was in the nursery and seed shop of a Mrs. Eagle, situated in modern-day Paisley Close, off the High Street. [5]

According to Edward Topham, writing in 1774, 'The most profitable trade in Edinburgh appears to be that of a Bookseller'. With this in mind, it perhaps influenced Hill to work for William Creech, becoming his principal clerk in1784. He was in charge of the business when Creech was in London in the summer of 1787, and it was during this period that Burns started corresponding with him. Indeed, as the friendship developed, Hill acted as Burns's business agent in Edinburgh, carrying out all sorts of financial transactions on his behalf. One writer has suggested that there was no love lost between Hill and Creech, [6] and it was probably the principal reason why Hill left Creech in 1788 and set up business on his own account. His first shop was in Parliament Close (Square), with a distinctive signboard bearing a representation of the head of James Thomson, the poet of *The Seasons*.[7] Lockhart described it as 'a long and dreary shop, where it is impossible to imagine any group of fine ladies or gentlemen could assemble.' [8] On the other hand, Archibald Constable, who served his apprenticeship with Hill, stated that 'the most respectable persons in Edinburgh', and ' the most remarkable strangers' foregathered in Hill's shop. One of the most remarkable strangers was Captain Grose, the antiquary, who inspired Burns to write 'Tam o' Shanter'. It is interesting to note that Constable lodged with Hill and was responsible for arranging the stock, studying the catalogues and attending book sales.[9] In 1795 he began business on his own account and went on to become the foremost publisher in Scotland, but in 1826 he was brought down in the financial crash, which involved Sir Walter Scott and the printer, James Ballantyne.

Nineteen letters of Burns to Hill have survived covering a period from May, 1787 to the end of January, 1796. Fifteen letters from Hill to Burns were included among

Captain Grose.
The celebrated antiquarian, who made a deal with
Burns that if he provided a witch tale of Alloway
Kirk, he would include the old kirk in his *Antquities of
Scotland*, which he ultimately did. Burns' response was
the immortal tale of 'Tam o'Shanter'. We are greatly
indebted to Captain Grose for having inspired this
wonderful tale.

three hundred letters addressed to the poet and found among his papers at the time of his death. These were passed to Dr. James Currie, the poet's first biographer. Their ultimate fate is unknown, but Currie prepared a summary of each letter in a manuscript running to 56 pages. Unfortunately the document has been so badly damaged by damp, that what is left of the summary relating to Hill's letters, adds little of interest to the correspondence. [10]

The poet's earlier letters to Hill are mainly concerned with business and orders for books. As the friendship ripened, however, his letters became more intimate and were interspersed with broad humour and 'hearty blasts of execration' on his pet subjects of frugality, poverty and selfishness.

It is rather significant that when Hill established his own business, Burns passed all his orders for books to him. Chambers states that 'having no similar affection for Creech, Burns resolved to send to Hill for any books he might henceforth have occasion for.' [11] The poet and his friend, Robert Riddell of Friar's Carse, had been instrumental in forming the Monkland Friendly Society, which had for its chief object the establishment of a circulating library. Exactly when it was founded is uncertain but Burns mentions it in a letter to Hill, dated 2 April, 1789. *(CL 313)*

At the beginning of the letter, Burns apologises for writing on Excise Notepaper, and with a rich touch of humour concludes; 'When I grow richer I will write to you on gilt-post, to that make amends for this sheet. At present every guinea has a five-guinea errand with my dear sir, your faithful, poor, but honest friend.'

About the end of 1789 and the beginning of 1790, Burns had become interested in the dramatic plays being performed by George Sutherland's company in the Assembly Rooms, Dumfries, (the Theatre Royal had not then been built). Undoubtedly, it was because of this interest that he ordered the following books from Hill on 2 March, 1790:

'I want likewise for myself, as you can pick them up, second-handed, or anyway cheap copies of Otway's dramatic works, Ben Johson's, Dryden's, Congreve's, Wycherly's, Vanbrugh's, Cibber's, or any Dramatic works of the more Moderns, Macklin, Garrick, Foote, Colman or Sheridan's – A good Copy of Moliere in French I much want – any other good Dramatic Authors, in their native language I want them, I mean Comic Authors chiefly, tho' I should wish Racine, Corneille and Voltaire too –' *(CL 316)*

Burns's request for 'comic authors chiefly' suggests that he may have contemplated another tale similar to 'Tam o' Shamter', or was a study of the playwrights a preparation for his declared intention to write 'something in the rural way of the Drama-kind'? We shall never know, but what is certain that he was intent on becoming familiar with the works of the leading dramatists of the seventeenth century, and in the process adding to his own very considerable knowledge of literature. The last paragraph of the letter is given over to some observations on the sin of selfishness:

'I am out of all patience with this vile world for one thing, mankind are by nature benevolent creatures, except in a few scoundrelly instances I do not think that avarice of the good things we chance to have is born with us, but we are placed here amid so much Nakedness, and Hunger, and Poverty and Want, that we are under a damning necessity of studying Selfishness, in order that we may exist! Still there are, in every age, a few souls, that all the Wants and Woes of life cannot debase to Selfishness, or even given the necessary alloy of Caution and Prudence. If ever I am in danger of vanity, it is when I contemplate myself on this side of my disposition and character.- God knows I am no Saint; I have a whole host of Follies and Sins to answer for, but if I could, and I believe I do it as far as I can, I would wipe away all tears from all eyes.[12] Even the knaves who have injured me, I would oblige, tho' to tell the truth, it would be more out of vengeance to shew them that I was independent of, and above them, than out of the overflowings of my benevolence.'

Sometime in 1790, Hill had rendered his account to Burns, which amounted to £6. 7s. 5d. On 17 January, 1791, the poet sent £3 as partial payment, and his inability to discharge the whole amount produced a hearty blast on the curse of poverty. *(CL 317)*

'Poverty! Thou half-sister of Death, thou cousin- german of Hell, where shall I find force of execration equal to thy demerits! – By thee, the venerable

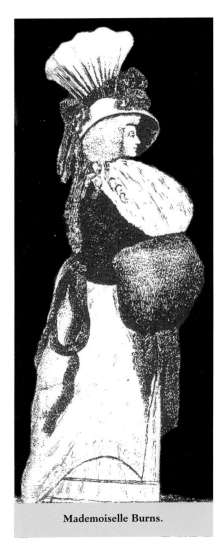

Mademoiselle Burns.

Ancient, though in thy invidious obscurity, grown hoary in the practice of every virtue under Heaven, now laden with years and wretchedness, implores from a stony-hearted son of Mammon whose sun of prosperity never knew a cloud, a little, little aid to support his very existence, and is by him denied and insulted.'

The poet continues in the same lengthy vein until, one feels, he has run out of breath, before finally vindicating his invective in the following passage:

'Well, divines may say what they please, but I maintain that a hearty blast of execration is to the mind, what breathing a vein is to the body; the overloaded sluices of both are wonderfully relieved by their respective evacuations. – I feel myself vastly easier than when I began my letter and I can now go on to business.'

During his West Highland Tour in June, 1787, Burns rode down Loch Lomondside and spent a day sailing on the Loch. He was, therefore, familiar with its beauty and it must have come as a pleasant surprise when he received Hill's letter of 1 October, 1788, enclosing a copy of the 'Address to Loch Lomond'. In his reply sent from Mauchline, Burns wrote: *(CL 311)*

'I have been here in this country, about three days, and all that time, my chief reading has been the Address to Loch Lomond you were so obliging as to send me. Were I impanelled one of the Author's Jury to determine his criminality respecting the sin of Poesy, my verdict should be 'Guilty! A Poet of Nature's making!'

At the end of the letter he wrote, 'I should like to know who the author is, but whoever he be, please present him with my grateful thanks for the entertainment he has afforded me. The author was James Cririe, who at one period was Latin Secretary to the Society of Scottish Antiquaries. In 1788 he became Rector of the High School at Leith, and in 1795 he succeeded William Cruckshank as Classical Master of the High School in Edinburgh. He resigned in 1801 on being presented to the Parish of Dalton in Dumfriesshire. The degree of Doctor of Divinity was conferred on him by Edinburgh University in 1802. [13] Obviously he and Burns had not met during the poet's visits to the Capital.

Burns was always eager for news of the Capital. In a long letter of 2 February, 1790, *(CL 315)* he enquired, 'What has become of Borough Reform or how is the fate of my poor namesake Mademoiselle Burns decided?' The young woman referred to was Margaret Burns, a prostitute, whose beauty, fine figure and fashionable attire had attracted much attention. Her real name was Mathews and she was a native of Durham. She had come to Edinburgh in 1789, accompanied by a Miss Sally Sanderson, with whom she had set up a house of ill-repute in Rose Street. As a result of complaints by neighbours, the two 'madames' were brought before the magistrates, presided over by William Creech. They were convicted

Robert Fergusson.
A fellow poet, who died in 1774. Burns erected a tombstone over his grave.
Portrait by Alexander Runciman,
Scottish National Portrait Gallery.

of the offence with which they were charged, and 'banished forth of the city and liberties forever.' The sentence was later overturned by the Court of Session. The case created considerable interest and set tongues wagging. Needless to say Creech was extremely annoyed at the decision, and he became the butt of various squibs circulated at his expense. The unkindest cut of all, however, was when a London newspaper reported that 'Bailie Creech, of literary celebrity in Edinburgh, was about to lead the beautiful and accomplished Miss Burns to the hymeneal altar'. Creech was furious and only abandoned legal action on the promise of a retraction being printed in the next publication of the paper. A retraction duly appeared, but certainly not the one he expected. It ran thus; 'In a former number we noticed the intended marriage between Bailie Creech of Edinburgh, and the beautiful Miss Burns of the same place. We now have the authority of that gentleman to say that the proposed marriage is not to take place, matters having been otherwise arranged to the mutual satisfaction of both parties and their respective friends'. [14] How Burns must have laughed at this amusing situation.

Did Burns suspect that some of Edinburgh's prominent citizens had visited Rose Street, when he continued in the same letter?

'Which of their grave lordships can lay his hand on his heart and say that he has not taken the advantage of such frailty? Nay, if we may judge by near 6000 year's experience, can this world do without such frailty? O Man! but for thee and thy selfish appetites and dishonest artifices, that beauteous form, and that once innocent and still ingenuous mind might have shone conspicuous and lovely in the faithful wife and the affectionate mother; and shall the unfortunate sacrifice to thy pleasures have no claim on thy humanity?'

Burns took a swipe at Margaret Burns's detractors in a neat little quatrain:

> Cease ye prudes, your envious railing!
> Lovely Burns has charms – confess
> True it is, she had one failing:
> Had a woman ever less? *(CW 375)*

In the Spring of 1791, Hill sent Burns a present of books which the poet acknowledged by the gift of a ewe-milk cheese. In a lengthy letter *(CL 318)*, he recommends the cheese as a cure for indigestion which has plagued him for the last week. He humorously suggests that Hill might pass a slice of the cheese to some of his Edinburgh friends, whose digestions may suffer from various causes. In particular he mentions William Smellie, who printed the Edinburgh edition of his poems:

'There in my eye is our friend Smellie; a man positively of the first abilities and greatest strength of mind, as well as one of the best hearts and keenest wits that I have ever met with, when you see him, as, Alas! he too often is, smarting at the pinch of distressful circumstance, aggravated by the sneer of

Canongate Church.
It was in the church yard that Burns erected a stone to the memory of Robert Fergusson.
'Clarinda' is also buried here.

contumelious greatness –
a bit of my cheese alone
will not cure him; but
if you add a tankard of
brown stout and superadd
a magnum of right
Oporto, you will see his
sorrows vanish like the
morning mist before the
summer sun.'

During his first visit to Edinburgh
Burns found that the poet
Fergusson, who died in 1774,
was buried in an unmarked grave
in the Canongate churchyard.
Burns had been greatly influenced
by Fergusson's poems, and to
acknowledge his debt to his
brother poet, he petitioned the
managers of the Canogate Kirk

William Creech.
He published the first Edinburgh Edition of Burns's
poems. Portrait by Sir Henry Raeburn,
Scottish National Porttrait Gallery.

for permission to erect a headstone over Fergusson's grave. Permission was granted and
the work was given to Robert Burn, an Edinburgh architect, who designed the stone
and supervised its erection. In a letter to Peter Hill on 5 February, 1792, *(CL 321)* Burns
remitted the sum of £5.10/- and requested him to pay Burn's account. In the letter the
poet wryly observes:

'He was two years in erecting it, after I commissioned him for it, and I have
been two years paying him, after he sent me his account, so he and I are quits.
He had the hardiesse to ask for interest on the sum, but considering that the
money was due by one Poet, for putting a tomb-stone over another, he may,
with grateful surprise, thank Heaven that he ever saw a farthing of it.'

Burns was not the only person whose livelihood had been adversely affected by the
war with France. A number of businesses in Edinburgh had gone to the wall. Writing
to Hill in April, 1793, he expressed his concern:

'I hope and trust that this unlucky blast which has overturned so many, and many
worthy characters who four months ago little dreaded any such a thing – will spare my
friend. O! May the wrath and curse of all mankind, haunt and harass these turbulent
unprincipled misc [reants] who have involved a People in this ruinous business.'

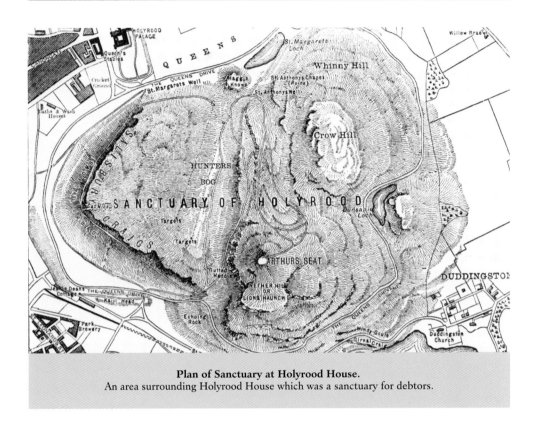

Plan of Sanctuary at Holyrood House.
An area surrounding Holyrood House which was a sanctuary for debtors.

During the summer of 1794, Hill, accompanied by David Ramsay of *The Edinburgh Courant* and a Mr. Cameron, who was a wholesale stationer and paper manufacturer, visited Burns in Dumfries. Following their visit, Burns sent Hill a kippered salmon in October and advised him:

> 'If you have the confidence to say there is anything of the kind in all your great City superior to this in true Kipper relish and flavour, I will be avenged of your slander by – not sending you another next season. – In return, the first party of Friends that dine with you (provided that your fellow- travelers and my trusty and well-beloved veterans in intimacy, Messrs. Ramsay and Cameron be of the party) about that time in the afternoon when a relish, or devil, becomes grateful; give them two or three slices of the Kipper, and drink a bumper to your friends in Dumfries.' *(CL 323)*

The poet's next letter to Hill *(CL 324)* was written while suffering the pangs of toothache. With the letter he enclosed a batch of epigrams, which seems to have been prompted by the 'hell o'a'diseases'. He wrote:

'I do not pretend that there is much merit in these Morceaux, but I have two reasons for sending them; primo, they are mostly ill-natured, so are in unison with my present feelings while fifty troops of infernal Spirits are riding post to post from ear to ear along my jawbones, and secondly, they are so short, that you cannot leave off in the middle, and so hurt my pride in the idea that you found any Work of mine too heavy to get through.'

It was probably the bout of toothache which prompted Burns to write his humorous 'Address to the Toothache'- [15] *(CW 553)*

> My curse upon your evenom'd stang,
> That shoots my tortur'd gums alang
> An' thro' my lugs gies mony a bang
>   Wi' gnawin' vengeance:
> Tearing my nerves wi' bitter twang
>   Like rocking engines.

The final letter which Hill received from Burns was dated 29 January, 1796. *(CL 325)* and accompanied a gift of the annual kipper. It was sent with the express condition 'that you do not, like a fool as you were last year, put yourself to five times the value in expence (sic) of a return.' The letter closed with a promise to write again in a week or ten days. Unfortunately the promise was never fulfilled, as the poet's health was then in ominous decline.

Hill Place, Edinburgh, today.

Peter Hill married Elizabeth Lindsay in 1783. She was the daughter of Sir John Lindsay and was considered to be Hill's social superior. In several of his letters Burns asks to be remembered to her and in one *(CL 316)*, he expresses the hope that she is 'as amiable, and sings as divinely as ever'. We learn from her grandson, however, that Mrs. Hill did not have a very high opinion of Burns. She looked with disfavour on the evenings he spent in the company of her husband, and regarded his visits to Edinburgh with a certain amount of aversion. On the other hand, Hill probably needed little persuasion to spend an evening in Burns's company.

Of the marriage there were seven sons and seven daughters. His eldest son, Peter took over the running of the business in 1813.

In 1805 Hill was appointed City Teasurer, and from 1809 to 1813, during Creech's provostship, he acted as Treasurer of Goerge Heriot's Hospital. In 1813 he was appointed Chief Collector of Burgh taxes, a post he discharged till near the end of his life. He died on 17 February, 1837, having reached the advanced age of eighty-three. His grandson recorded that 'he was prosperous through life till near the close, when he lost his means through over confidence in others'.[16]

Although it can only be conjecture, it seems possible that Hill may have got into financial difficulties when he purchased in 1809 a large area of ground opposite Nicolson Square and on it created Hill Place. Recent research has revealed that young Peter Hill, who took over the business in 1813, was admitted, as a debtor to the Sanctuary at Holyroodhouse. in 1826, when it appears that the firm ceased to function. [17] Further research, however, has failed to reveal the reason for Hill snr. 'losing his means' nor the extent and nature of young Hill's debt.

The same grandson wrote of his grandfather:

> '. . . . when Burns knew him he was a douce family man, diligent, temperate, and prudent; not a Bohemian, though with Bohemian likings and leanings; generous in his sympathies and practice, (Burns called him 'my liberal-minded friend'), and with a strong relish for the humorous aspect of things.'

ROBERT GRAHAM OF GARTMORE

Writing to Peter Hill on 2 February, 1790, Burns enquired, 'Does Mr.Graham of Gartmore ever enter your shop now? He is the noblest instance of great talents, great fortune, and great worth that ever I saw in conjunction.'
(CL 318)

Robert Graham of Gartmore was a cousin of the fourteenth Earl of Glencairn, Burns's patron, and it is more than likely that he was introduced to the poet by the Earl. His name is on the list of subscribers to the 1787 Edinburgh edition of the poems.

A.F. Tschiffely, biographer of Robert Graham's famous ancestor, R. B. Cunninghame Graham ('Don Roberto'), claims that 'Fox, Burns and Sir Walter Scott often stayed as honoured guests at Gartmore'.[1] While this may be true of Fox and Scott, there is no documentary evidence to prove that Burns was ever a guest there. Indeed from what is known of his journeys it is difficult to see when such a visit could have taken place.

Robert Graham possessed 'great talents' being poet, politician, laird, and successful merchant in

Robert Graham of Gartmore.
From a portrait by David Martin.

Jamaica. He is best remembered, however, for the lyric that has found a place in almost every anthology of English verse:

> If doughty deeds my ladye please,
> Right soon I'll mount my steed;
> And strong his arm, and fast his seat,

That bears frae me the meed.
I'll wear thy colours in my cap,
Thy picture in my heart;
And he that bends not to thine eye
Shall rue it to his smart.
Then tell me how to woo thee, love ;
O tell me how to woo thee!
For thy dear sake, nae care I'll take,
Tho' ne'er another trow me.

There follows another two stanzas each one ending with the same four lines as in the first stanza. Exactly when he wrote this lyric is not known, although it probably was between the years 1780 and 1790. Sir Walter Scott, in his *Minstrelsy of the Scottish Border* under the head, 'O Tell Me How To Woo Thee', writes:

'The following verses are taken down from recitation and are averred to be of the age of Charles I. They have indeed much of the romantic expression of passion common to the poets of the period whose lays still reflected the setting beams of chivalry, but since their publication in the first edition of this work the Editor has been assured that they were composed by the late Mr. Graham of Gartmore.' [2]

At first Scott was inclined to the opinion that the verses had been written by the famous James Graham, Marquis of Montrose, hence the reason why he placed them

Gartmore House near Aberfoyle, Perthshire.

in the reign of Charles I. Others thought they were the work of the Cavalier poet, Richard Lovelace, who belonged to the same period. It is a striking tribute to their merit to have been attributed to either source

To all Robert Graham's descendants he has been known as 'Doughty Deeds', the title of this single lyric that has placed his name among the immortals.

He was born at Gartmore House, Perthshire, in 1735, and could trace his descent from Robert II. He was the second son of laird Nicol Graham of Gartmore, who was a close friend of Walpole and a staunch supporter of the Hanoverian succession. The estate of Gartmore lay within the district of Menteith and bordered on the Highland Line. It was a short distance to the mountainous country where the lawless McGregors preserved a defiant independence, and from where Rob Roy had conducted his cattle-thieving raids on the lowland countryside.

Rob Roy McGregor.
A sort of Scottish Robin Hood but a cattle stealer and a torment to the authorities. From a painting by unknown artist, Scottish National Portrait Gallery.

Rob Roy was scarce five years dead when Robert Graham was born. As a boy he must have heard many tales of the noted freebooter (tradition has it that his father captured the McGregor on one occasion, but he escaped); and he would no doubt witness the measures taken by his father to defend the countryside against those who supported the Stuart cause.

It was a fairly common practice in those days for the sons of landed gentry to seek their fortune either in India or Jamaica, and many West of Scotland families who boasted a 'lang pedigree', were merchants, trading to Jamaica or planters on the island. In 1749, following three years at Glasgow University, where he was well grounded in the *Humanities,* young Robert Graham (he was barely seventeen years of age) decided to push his fortune in Jamaica. Within a year of landing on the island, and largely through family connections, he was installed as Receiver-General of Taxes, a post which he discharged faithfully and wisely until 1764, despite his tender years. In 1765 he was elected to the Assembly for the district of St. David's.

Throughout his life he embraced the Liberal politics of his family. His liberalism is evident in many of his letters and particularly in one which he wrote on 31 March, 1766, to Major- General David Graeme, Secretary to His Majesty, (perhaps a kinsman) :

> 'It is true I am one of those who in a Land of Slaves, struggle for liberty. I am not ashamed of it and on the contrary I glory in it, and wherever I am I hope shall retain so much of the Brittain (sic) as to show a dislike of oppression, and a willing though weak hand to mob tyranny.' [3]

Ardoch House.
The house is situated three miles West of Dumbarton on the banks of the Clyde.

In 1770, the state of his wife's health obliged him to return to Scotland, where he took up residence on the estate of Ardoch, near Dumbarton, which had been entailed upon him in 1757 by a kinsman, Mr. Nicol Bontine. Under the will of the testator, he was required to assume the name of Bontine. His elder brother, William, died in 1774 and, as he left no sons, Robert became heir to Gartmore. About this time he reassumed the family name of Graham, and within a few months his father, laird Nicol, died at the venerable age of eighty.

Robert Graham now found himself a great landed proprietor, with the two estates of Ardoch and Gartmore. In 1796, a year before his death, he inherited the estate of Finlaystone, on the death of the fourteenth and last Earl of Glencairn, and took the name of Cunninghame in addition to his own. Finlaystone, in Renfrewshire, lay on the south bank of the Clyde, across the river from Ardoch. His entire property now extended to well over 10,000 acres and was situated in Perthshire, Stirlingshire, Dunbartonshire and Renfrewshire – great fortune indeed!

He seems to have taken a warm interest in his old *alma mater*. His circle of friends included a number of professors at Glasgow University; and it is not surprising, that in 1785 he was elected Lord Rector, in succession to Edmund Burke. During his period of office, he founded the 'Gartmore Gold Medal', to encourage the study and knowledge of 'Political Liberty', an act that must have endeared him to Robert Burns.

His sojourn in Parliament was brief; (he represented Stirlingshire from 1794 to 1796) and introduced, unsuccessfully, a Bill of Rights, which to some extent foreshadowed the great Reform Bill of 1832, He was also very actively engaged in the reform of the internal government of the Royal Burghs of Scotland, and was Chairman of the Committee that had been formed in Edinburgh to combat the malpractices and abuses, that had, over the years, disfranchised the Burgesses' of their right to elect the Councils.

The neglect of Pitt to answer a letter sent to him in February, 1787, calling for redress of the Burgesses' grievances led to Graham addressing a lengthy public letter to him. The following extract is worth quoting:

> 'It would be injurious to the respect in which I hold your character to consider your silence as a mark of disapprobation of the proposed application to Parliament. I wish to account for it from the attention, you must necessarily bestow on the variety of business incident to your situation. But although this may apologise for the little regard you have thought proper to pay to solicitations of a numerous and respectable body of citizens, oppressed with grievances unheard of in a free country. I should certainly be wanting in the proper discharge of the duty I owe to the Burgesses' of Scotland if I could hesitate in again addressing you on a subject in which their interest and wishes are so nearly concerned . . . . As I persuade myself that the papers which I formerly transmitted to you are still in your possession, I shall not detail you by recapitulating their contents. But I must beg leave to observe that had they met with the respect which I am bold to say they merited, I should have had no occasion to trouble you with the present public address.' [4]

Here was no 'mealy-mou'd' approach to the King's First Minister. Obviously, Graham looked upon Pitt as his servant and not his master. Like so many of Burns's poems, it has a man to man approach and breathes an air of freedom and equality.

Robert Graham had not the robust constitution of his father. His long sojourn in the tropics, coupled with a fondness for rum and port, had impaired his health and for many years he suffered from gout, the scourge of the age. He died at Gartmore on 4th December, 1797, and was interred in the little burial ground in the estate.

When Burns went to Edinburgh and mixed with the highest society in Scotland, he soon realised that wealth and rank did not always go hand and hand with mental ability. On one occasion it galled him to see Lord Glencairn pay deference to a man of higher station, but of inferior intellect, and he wrote in his Commonplace Book, 'He showed so much engrossing attention to the only blockhead at table that I was within half a point of throwing down my gage of contemptuous defiance!' It was mortifying to him 'to see a fellow, whose abilities would scarcely have made an eightpenny tailor, and whose heart is not worth three farthings, meet with attention and notice that are withheld from the son of genius and poverty.' [5]

"Don Roberto",
famous kinsman of Robert Graham.

Burns did not suffer fools gladly, and so it must have been very refreshing for him to meet such a man as Robert Graham, who courted the Muse, and whose idea of political liberty was so much in accord with his own. One feels that when they met it would be as man to man, with wealth and property forgotten.

Although Robert Graham was not destined to have his name written large in the affairs of his country, he will be remembered, not as one of the richest lairds in Scotland, nor yet as politician, but, as Burns would have wished him to be remembered, as the writer of that exquisite lyric, 'Doughty Deeds.'

DAVID ALLAN

In 1788, an edition of Allan Ramsay's pastoral comedy, *The Gentle Shepherd*, met with instant success. This was due, in great measure, to the illustrations in the book by David Allan, the Scottish genre painter. He had continued to develop the relationship between Scots poetry and painting, first embarked on by Alexander Runciman, painter. and Robert Fergusson, poet, which had, unfortunately, been cut short by Fergusson's tragic early death in 1774.

In a letter to his Edinburgh friend, Alexander Cunningham, dated 3rd March, 1793, Burns expressed his admiration for the artist.

> 'Bye the bye, do you know Allan ?—He must be a man of very great genius.— Why is he not more known ? Has he no patrons; or do 'Poverty's cold wind and crushing rain beat keen and heavy' on him ? – I once, and but once, got a glance of that noble edition of the noblest Pastoral in the world, and dear as it was; I mean dear as to my pocket, I would have bought it; but was told that it was printed and engraved for Subscribers only. He is the *only* Artist who has hit *genuine* Pastoral costume----.'

Burns, indeed, was correct, for it was in the way that Allan portrayed peasant life and costume, that he excelled. There was a receptive market in the 18th century for contemporary genre scenes. David Allan skilfully exploited this interest in everyday life by producing some of the liveliest and humorous records of contemporary customs. For this he was dubbed the 'Scottish Hogarth'.

Considering the sickly and delicate nature of Allan's birth and subsequent misfortunes, it is remarkable that he ever reached adult life. He was born in Alloa on 13th February, 1744.

David Allan.
Self portrait.
In the collection of the Royal Scottish Academy.

"The Black Stool", also known as the "Cutty Stool" and "Stool of Repentence", it varied in size and shape from church to church, depending on the number and frequency of sinners. From a painting by David Allan. National Gallery of Scotland.

His mother was Janet Gullan, who came from Dunfermline, and his father was David Allan, who was shoremaster at the busy harbour of Alloa. Janet was a sick and ailing mother and David was born a very delicate baby, two months prematurely. Two days later his mother died. His father had great difficulty in finding a wet nurse for his little son. Several local mothers offered their services, but were found unsuitable due to the smallness of the baby's mouth. A wet nurse was found, however, but at some distance away. The infant was placed in a basket and taken on horseback, on a cold, raw February day, but unfortunately the horse slipped on the frozen snow, and basket and baby were thrown to the ground. It was said that the artist carried the mark of his bruises to the end of his life.

David was still only eighteen months old when the Second Jacobite Rebellion occurred. Prince Charlie and his army, swept southwards, and as it was uncertain where the Jacobite army were likely to cross the Forth, a battery of cannon was rushed to Alloa shore to prevent a crossing there. It was while it was there that it almost ended the life of the unfortunate David. His nurse had taken him out for an airing and led the child too near the guns for safety. When they were fired, the nurse and child were in grave danger, and both were fortunate to escape with their lives.

In due course he attended the parish school, which was under the supervision of the Minister and Kirk Session, and where the teaching was generally sound. The schoolmaster was a certain John Lamb, who had already been a schoolmaster in Clackmannan parish, but according to the Session Records, had proved troublesome and unsatisfactory. He moved to Alloa, where he caused further trouble and annoyance. This then was the pedagogue into whose keeping young David Allan was entrusted. Clad in a tartan gown and armed with a cane he held sway over a noisy class, where the discipline was poor and the teaching was consequently below standard. There is ample proof that David did not get a proper grounding in grammar, as his letters show serious lapses in correct spelling and punctuation. Even in simple composition he had failed to learn the use of syntax.

Being given a piece of chalk one day, he started to draw birds and beasts on the floor, and before long he attempted the outlines of human figures. As yet this new talent displayed by David merely amused the family and was not taken seriously. At school one day he sketched on his slate the master punishing some errant boys, and showed it to his fellow pupils. Allan Cunningham takes up the story:

> 'The startling laugh which this occasioned drew the attention of the dominie, who though half- blind, detected the resemblance; and incensed at being caricatured among his scholars, bestowed a smart chastisement on the culprit. He then complained to the father. Old Allan, when he heard of the talents and petulance of the boy, "knew not whether to rejoice or mourn".'

The Reel of Tullochgorum
by David Allan

As a result of this incident David was withdrawn from the school and his father was faced with the problem of what was to become of his gifted son. There was no local future for a lad like this, even though he had a gift for caricature. He need not have worried as a more influential friend was at work on David's behalf. It is generally believed that Lord Cathcart, who was keenly interested in the Glasgow Academy of Art, established by Robert and Andrew Foulis in the University of Glasgow in 1754, used his influence to secure a place for David at the Academy. He was also able to assure Mr. Allan that there would be little charge for David' training, as the Foulis Brothers undertook to pay so much to their young students, It was not an easy decision for

George Thomson.
Burns collaborated with Thomson in the Production of *Selected Scottish Airs* which contained 25 songs by Burns. Thomson sent him a five pound note to which Burns' replied that he was truly hurt by Thomson's gift and informed him that he would indignantly spurn all transaction if repeated again.

David's father to make; to send a boy of eleven, delicate in health and timid by nature to a strange city, but he had sufficient foresight to see that it was a unique opportunity for David to learn the rudiments of art in the first officially recognised Academy of Art in the whole country.

At the Academy the students were encouraged to study Dutch, Venetian and Renaissance paintings, of which Robert Foulis had built up a collection. They also came under the tuition of Italian and French teachers, as the Academy was based on continental lines. The fundamentals of art disciplines were not forgotten, however, and anatomy, perspective, geometry and classical rules of proportion were an important part of the Curriculum. Students probably went out into the surrounding countryside to gain experience in drawing direct from nature. It is recorded that the two outstanding students were David Allan and James Tassie (1735 - 1799), who, later created profile-portrait medallions, inspired by classical cameos. It is interesting to note that they became in course life-long friends. David Allan remained at the

Glasgow Academy of Art for twelve years, and emerged having received a sound art training. However, it was considered essential that he undertake the Grand Tour to round off his art education. His wealthy patrons, Lord Cathcart, Lady Francis Erskine, Lady Charlotte Erskine and Mrs. Abercrombie of Tullibody, combined to send the young artist to Rome to continue his studies.

Throughout his long stay in Italy (1767 – 1777) he developed his interest in genre alongside historical subjects. He executed a series of incidents in a Roman carnival, capturing the variety of social classes who participated. The series helped to establish Allan's contemporary fame, since they were etched by the English painter, Paul Sandby. Shepherds, a fortune teller and a fishmonger were among the many characters depicted by Allan. In Italy he was one of Gavin Hamilton's principal protégés; no relation of Burns's Gavin Hamilton - but a renowned Scottish Painter (1723 – 1798), who spent most of his time in Rome. In 1788 David Allan dedicated to Hamilton his illustrations to Allan Ramsay's *The Gentle Shepherd.* He acknowledged, 'a grateful

recollection of those advices with which you honoured me while I was studying painting in Rome.' During his stay in Italy he won the gold medal of the Accademia di San Luca, The subject set for the competition was an interpretation of a sketch of Gavin Hamilton's painting, *Hector's Farewell to Andromache,* The instructions for the competition are preserved in the Accademia and are presumably written by Hamilton, for they read like a description of his own picture.

In 1770 he returned to London, but failed to find success, and after two years there he settled in Edinburgh, where he succeeded Alexander Runciman as Master of the Trustees' Academy of Art in 1785. It was in this position that he came into contact with the Principal Clerk, George

Patrick Miller of Dalswinton.
He sent Burns a gift of ten guineas during the poet's visit to Edinburgh and later rented the farm from Ellisland to him. He had many interests and is credited with sailing one of the earliest steam ships on Dalwinton Loch.

Thomson, who was in the process of collecting songs for a publication of *A Select Collection of Original Scottish Airs*. In 1791, Thomson secured Burns's collaboration to write words for the songs, and a little later he enrolled the assistance of Allan to provide illustrations. First mention of Allan in the Burns / Thomson correspondence is when Thomson wrote to Burns in August, 1793, 'Mr. Allan has made an inimitable drawing from your ' John Anderson, my Jo', which I am to have engraved as a frontispiece to the humorous class of songs.' By 17 April, 1794, Burns had seen some of Allan's drawings, as Thomson wrote, 'Alan is much gratified by your good opinion of his talents. He has just begun a sketch of your 'Cotter's Saturday Night', and if it pleases himself in the design, he will probably etch or engrave it.' Burns replied the following month:

> 'I return you the plates, with which I am highly pleased. I would have returned them sooner, but I waited the opinion of a friend of mine who is positively the ablest judge on the subject I have ever met with . . . and he is quite charmed with Allan's manner. I got him a peep of *The Gentle Shepherd*, and he pronounces Alan a most original artist of great excellence . . . For my part I look upon Mr. Allan's choosing my favourite poem for his subject, to be one of the highest compliments I have ever received.'

George Thomson, who was not without his anxieties in the matter of rewarding Burns, once wrote, 'I felt anxious to show him my sense of his great liberality, by sending him a few presents such as I thought he could not well refuse. Accordingly I got the ingenious artist, David Allan to paint for him *con amore* the interesting scene of family worship from 'The Cotter's Saturday Night', which he thankfully received.' In the painting the eldest son, sitting beside his father, bears a remarkable resemblance to Burns. The poet and the artist never met, so Allan must have copied the features from the Nasmyth portrait. Burns was delighted with the gift and his response was enthusiastic:

> 'Ten thousand thanks, my dear sir, for your elegant present; though I am ashamed of the value of it, being bestowed on a man who has not by any means merited such an instance of kindness. – I have shown it to two or three judges of the first abilities here, and they all agree with me in classing it as a first rate production. – My phiz is *sae kenspeckle* that the very joiner's apprentice whom Mrs. Burns employed to break up the parcel (I was out of town that day) knew it at once. – You may depend upon my care that no person shall have it in their power to take the least sketch from it. – My most grateful compliments to Allan, that he has honoured my rustic Muse so much with his masterly pencil. – One strange coincidence is, that the little one who is making the felonious attempt on the cat's tail, is the most striking likeness of an ill-deedie,

damn'd, wee, rumble-gairie hurchin of mine, whom, from that propensity to witty wickedness and manfu' mischief, which, even at twa days auld I foresaw would form the striking features of his disposition, I named Willie Nicol, after a certain friend of mine, who is one of the Masters of a Grammar-school in a city which shall be nameless. – Several people think that Allan's likeness of me is more striking than Naysmith's for which I sat to him half a dozen times.'

Although Burns does not offer any complex critical opinion, his sense of how appropriate Allan's art was to what he himself was trying to do is clearly quite apparent, and also his realisation of their common interest. At the beginning of their co-operation Burns wrote to Thomson on the subject of Scottish song : 'In the sentiment and style of our Scottish airs, there is a pastoral simplicity, a something that one may call the Doric style and dialect of vocal music.' Allan's illustrations seem to reflect an attempt, on his part, to match this view In all, Allan did twenty illustrations for Thomson but they were never published in their entirety. Last mention of Allan is in a letter which Burns sent to Thomson in April, 1796. Although he was dying, he had not lost his appreciation of Allan's work: 'I am highly delighted with Allan's etchings . . .' Alas, both died within days of each other -- Burns on 21st July, 1796 and Allan on 6th August.

Had they both been spared to collaborate for many more fruitful years, it is interesting to speculate what may have been achieved. Both held a mirror to ordinary lives and customs., and caught the reflections in brilliant paintings, poems and songs. It is to be regretted that they came together in the twilight of their lives.

An interesting feature of the Bi-Centenary, in 1996, commemorating the death of Robert Burns, was the issue of four stamps by the Royal Mail. The stamps were designed by Andrew Wolffe, who decided to concentrate on the poet's

Postage stamp, value 60p, issued by the Royal Mail in 1996 to commemorate the Bi-centenary of Burns's death, shows a detail from "A Highland Dance" by David Allan.

193

words. 'Auld Lang Syne' is the subject of the 60p denomination and shows the opening line of the song, reproduced in the poet's own handwriting, alongside an illustration of Highland dancers, taken from an 18th century painting by David Allan, in the National Gallery of Scotland.

WEST HIGHLAND TOUR

'I have lately been rambling over
by Dumbarton and Inveraray'

THE REV. JAMES OLIPHANT

On 29th June, 1787, at the conclusion of his West Highland Tour, Robert Burns was made a freeman of the Royal Burgh of Dumbarton. According to Dr. George Grierson, who was Burns's travelling companion, the Dumbarton Magistrates were denounced publicly the following day by the Rev. James Oliphant, Minister of Dumbarton Parish Kirk, for conferring honours on the author of 'vile, detestable and immoral publications.' [1]

Oliphant's opposition was no doubt due to the fact that he had figured in Burn's satire, 'The Ordination', written the previous year, 1786 :

> Curst common - sense that imp o' hell,
> Cam in wi' Maggie Lauder;
> But Oliphant aft made her yell
> An' Russell sair misca'd her (CW 192)

Old High Church, Kilmarnock.
Oliphant was minister here from 1762 -1773, before his translation to Dumbarton.
The church is still standing and functioning as a church.

'The Ordination' is concerned with the presentation of the Rev. James McKinlay to the Laigh (low) Kirk, Kilmarnock, in 1785, by the Earl of Glencairn, patron of the parish. His induction was opposed by many of the parishioners, who resented the right of patronage then in operation within the Church of Scotland. Prof. T. Crawford in *Burns, a Study of the Poems and Songs,* describes it as 'one of the finest and freshest things Burns ever did.' While this is no doubt true, the poem requires too much explanation of local church politics and personalities, for ready enjoyment by a modern reader.

The Rev. James Oliphant was an Auld Licht, who possessed so powerful a voice, he could 'mak the kirk yell.' Following a charge in the Gorbals Church, Glasgow, he was called to the High Church, Kilmarnock. He laboured there with much acceptance until 1773, when he was transferred to Dumbarton.

Oliphant's anger over the appearance of his name in 'The Ordination' is understandable. His own induction to Dumbarton was not a smooth one, and no doubt the poem revived unhappy memories. The Town Council of Dumbarton were the patrons of the living and his introduction to the charge was not effected without considerable opposition. The New Lichts in the Presbytery were opposed to his induction and they sought to belittle his abilities. In order to annoy him and raise a protest against the Council, they bought up copies of his work entitled, *Catechism, for the use of Schools and young Communicants,* and employed several strong-lunged characters to go through the streets of the town, shouting, 'The whole works of the godly Mr. Oliphant, presentee to the Parish Kirk of Dumbarton, for the small charge of twopence.' None of the objections and protests was effective, however, and Oliphant was duly inducted to the charge, ultimately to become a pastor of very great influence in the town. The very catechism which his opponents had derided, was introduced and taught in almost every parish school in Scotland.

Although Oliphant was ultra-Calvinistic, he seems to have possessed a keen sense of humour, and it is a great pity that he and Burns were in opposite religious camps. It is very unlikely that they ever met, as Burns would be only a lad of fourteen when Oliphant left Kilmarnock, and it is almost certain that no meeting took place during the poet's visit to Dumbarton. Had they done so there is no doubt that, religion apart, they would have enjoyed each other's company. Both saw the humorous side of life and could enjoy a spicy story and a laugh. Burns has left us sufficient evidence of his wit and humour in his poems and songs. Fortunately, many of Oliphant's humorous sayings and doings have been preserved. When one reads them it is difficult to imagine this clergyman as a dour Calvinist and staunch guardian of Orthodoxy. The following are some examples of his nimble wit and humorous pulpit sayings. [2]

Preaching in a neighbouring church one Sunday morning, he had been warned before entering the pulpit, that certain members of the congregation had got into the habit of leaving the Church before the end of the service. Towards the end of his sermon, he announced that it was his custom to address a few words to saints and sinners in that order, but as he understood that the sinners were in the habit of leaving before the conclusion of the service, he would speak to the sinners first, knowing full well that the saints would sit out the service. Needless to say there were no sinners present that morning.

Part of a sketch by Paul Sandby, showing Old Parish Church, Dumbarton in 1747.
It was to this church that Oliphant was inducted in 1773. It was demolished in 1809 and the present church was erected in 1811 on the same site.

His scripture reading on one occasion was from the Book of Psalms, in which the Royal Psalmist says, 'I said in my haste all men are liars,' to which Oliphant quickly added, 'Deed David man, had ye leeved noo a days ye micht hae said that at your canny leesure an' said nae mair than the naked truth.' His comment on the Apostle Peter's statement, 'Lord we have left all and followed Thee,' was 'Brethren, the leavin'o' an auld cobble an a wheen o' auld nets was a puir a' for an inspired Apostle tae mak a brag aboot.'

On another Lord's day he was reading the chapter where Satan tempts Christ with an offer of the whole world, which was spread out before His vision, if He would only fall down and worship him. At this point Oliphant is reported to have cried out, "What a bouncin' auld vagabond! O the astoundin' cheek o' him! The foul fiend, wha hadnae as much grun as his twa cloots stood on, for tae offer to gi'e tae onybody the hail earth, which is declared in the Scripture to be the Lord's, wi' a' the fullness thereof.'

A member who had committed the sin of fornication, was named from the pulpit and ordered by Oliphant to mount the cutty stool and be rebuked. The offender, however, choose to remain in his own seat, no doubt thinking that the minister might be lenient and let him remain there. Three times he was called without response, until at length the minister was advised by an elder that the sinner was in his 'ain seat.' 'In his ain seat,' said Oliphant, in indignant wrath, 'Does he think I'm gaun tae mak a black stool in every corner o' the kirk? Na', na'; send him tae the ither end o' the hoose!'

His family did not escape his forthright comment – even in church. One Sunday, his daughter was exchanging telegraphic signals with a party of officers from Dumbarton Castle, who sat in the 'breist o' the laft.' Her father, who had observed what was going on, stopped the service and announced that the conduct of certain persons in Church that morning was most reprehensible, and warned that unless they behaved better he would name them from the pulpit. The offenders mended their ways for a short time, but gradually signals were renewed between Jenny and the young officers. Suddenly the service was interrupted by a roar from the pulpit, 'Jenny Oliphant, my glaiket, sair-misguided dochter, rise up frae the manse seat that ye're disgracin' and march quickly oot o' the hoose o' God that ye're profanin',' There is no record of the ensuing meeting of father and daughter, which is a pity, as it would have made interesting reading.

During the period when there was a very real threat of a French invasion, he urged from the pulpit that all young men of the parish should join the ranks of the Volunteers, and help save their country from the foreign foe, 'Some of your number may plead that you are not very hardy, and you are not fit for campaigning; well my advice is this – if you are not strong and tough enough to fight in the open, join the ranks, nevertheless, and when the day of battle comes, just jeuk ahint a hedge and pepper the French. I and my brethren will assist you in the closet, by earnestly praying that your courage may not fail in the hour of trial. With fighting men and praying ministers we may expect, with confidence, that all will go well with our cause.'

Towards the end of his long ministry in Dumbarton, because of infirmities of age and failing eyesight, he had as helper and assistant the Rev. James Barr. Apparently Oliphant became jealous of the young minister, who had won the regard of the congregation by his preaching. He confided to one of his elders, 'Mr. Barr's a clever preacher, nae doot; but we maun pairt wi' him. I'm afraid he's a barrier in the way o' my getting on sae weel wi' my folk were he oot o' the road. In fact he's lickin' the cream aff my milk.'

Ultra-Calvinistic though he was, it is obvious from the records of the period, that Oliphant did not allow the demands of the next world to interfere with the enjoyment of this. He was neither gloomy nor unbending, and his sense of humour often enlivened his conversation and way of life. Throughout his ministry he was noted for his good deeds, and when he died in 1818, his passing was mourned by his parishioners, who had, over the years, come to regard him with deep affection and appreciation.

He was buried in the Parish Churchyard of Dumbarton. His grave was on the right-hand side of the main entrance. It was originally marked by a table stone, but in a fairly recent renovation and refurbishment of the Church, all the gravestones surrounding the Church were removed. Fortunately Oliphant's was preserved and is now located at the rear of the building. The inscription on it reads;

Sacred to the memory of the Rev. James Oliphant, Minister of Dumbarton, who died on the tenth day of April, one thousand eight hundred and eighteen years, in the 84th year of his age and the 54th of his ministry. He was licensed to preach the Gospel by the Presbytery of Kintyre, in Islay, 19th May, 1760; ordained nearly a year in Gorbals of Glasgow: was ordained by the Presbytery of Irvine at Kilmarnock, and remained there until 23rd December, 1773, when he was ordained Minister of the Church and Parish of Dumbarton, where he continued to labour until removed by death…

JAMES KENNEDY

In the 1933 edition of the *Burns Chronicle*, the then editor, James C. Ewing, published a list of holograph letters addressed to Burns and found among his papers after his death. These formed part of the 'sweepings of his desk', sent by the Trustees in 1797 to Dr. James Currie as the prospective biographer of the poet. The list of over 300 letters, arranged in chronological order and prepared by Currie, or under his guidance, contains a précis of their contents. Unfortunately the list has been damaged so severely by damp that approximately half of each page of the précis has been destroyed. The list is in the Museum of the Burns Cottage. Some of the letters, included in the list, are still extant but the majority have never been traced. They probably were destroyed by the neglect and indifference of the Currie family.

The publication of the list in 1933 was followed by a further article in the *Chronicle* of 1939, again by James C. Ewing, in which he attempted by brief notes to relate the letters addressed to Burns and those written by Burns. Included in the list are two letters, numbered 118 and 126, addressed to Burns on 24th September, 1789, and 19th October, of the same year, from James Kennedy, Glenlee Mill, near New Galloway. Against this correspondent's name Ewing made this comment, 'James Kennedy appears to be unknown in Burnsiana.'

The minutes of Dumbarton Town Council, dated 14th November, 1785, record that:

> 'An invitation was extended to Mr. James Kennedy, presently teacher in Ayrshire, along with Mr. Robert Rainey as fit persons to take charge of the Publick School of this place for the year ensuing and do hereby elect these gentlemen as joint Teachers of said school for the year to Marts. next.'

The school at that time was held in a room in 'Walker's Close', a tenement building on the north side of the High Street. It continued there until 1789, when the scholars moved into a purpose-built school, a two-storey building near the south end of Church Street. English and Latin were taught on the lower floor and arithmetic, writing, mathematics and geography on the upper. [1]

Kennedy served as Joint Master of Dumbarton Grammar School until 28th May, 1789, when he 'deserted his charge'[2]. It was during the period of his appointment in Dumbarton that Burns visited the town on 29th June, 1787, when he was made an Honorary Burgess and Guild Brother. A close friendship seems to have existed between the poet and Kennedy while the latter was teaching in Ayrshire. This is borne out by a letter which Burns sent on 4th June, 1789, to John McAulay, Town Clerk of Dumbarton, thanking

Purpose built school in Church Street, Dumbarton.

him for the hospitality he had received during his visit. (CL 531) In the course of the letter he writes, 'It gives me the sincerest pleasure to hear by my old acquaintance Mr. Kennedy, that you are, in immortal Allan's language, 'Hale and weel, and living . Burns's introduction to the Dumbarton Magistrates and Town Officials was probably effected by Kennedy. His name appears on the list of subscribers to Burns's 1787 Edinburgh edition of the poems.

The fragments of Currie's précis that remain of the two letters which Kennedy sent to Burns from Glenlee Mill are as follows. Missing portions are indicated thus (-----).

> Letter No 118 dated 24th September, 1789
>> 'Had been almost sent "*to the stygian* ------
>> cure the school of Dunscore- but -------
>> dyke, that he may raise money to prov --------
>> is safely delivered.'
> Letter No 126 dated 19th October, 1789.
>> Makes further enquiries relative to Duns --------
>> Building is of more service than learn --------
>> Asks for his Greek Grammar -----

From the dates it will be observed that the two letters were written shortly after Kennedy left Dumbarton. Perhaps the reference that he 'had been almost sent *to the stygian----*' is an explanation of his reason for deserting his charge in Dumbarton. What the remaining fragment of the précis does indicate is that Kennedy was earnestly trying to enlist Burns's aid to secure him the school of Dunscore, the little village some eighteen miles from Dumfries. It lay within the parish of the same name as did Ellisland Farm, which Burns had leased in 1788.

The second letter of 19 October, 1789, makes further enquiries regarding Dunscore and Kennedy seems to have a building in mind. The phrase, 'building is of more service than learn-----' would appear to suggest that Kennedy a reply to his first letter.

Although it must be conjecture, it is possible that the complete sentence might have read, 'building is more service than learned *gentleman realises*'. The appointment of a schoolmaster at Dunscore would undoubtedly have required the blessing of the parish minister, the Reverend Joseph Kirkpatrick, who was also Burns's spiritual overlord. Kirkpatrick described Dunscore Parish for Sinclair's *Statistical Account of Scotland*. His report was not encouraging. On the subject of education it appears that the schools were badly taught – 'the encouragement being so inconsiderable, the parish cannot be supposed to have well-qualified teachers.'

If the conjecture is correct and Kirkpatrick was the 'learned gentleman', Burns must have found it difficult to advance Kennedy's case. He did not rate Kirkpatrick very highly. In a letter to Alexander Cunningham, dated 11 March, 1791, (CL *462*) he described him as 'one vast constellation of dullness', an opinion which was shared by his friend Robert Riddell, who said that 'the ignorance and stupidity of the minister is such, and so great a Mule is he, that no good can be done with him.' [3]

There is no record of Kennedy having secured the position; it seems most unlikely. If he had he would surely have come within the circle of Burns's friends at Ellisland and more would have been heard of him.

An interesting point emerges from the second letter. James Kennedy 'asks for his Greek Grammar', which he must have lent to the poet. This is perhaps the only indication that Burns displayed an interest in Greek.

James Kennedy is a somewhat shadowy figure. The facts, as established, are that he was a schoolmaster for a short period in Dumbarton, and an acquaintance of Robert Burns from his Ayrshire days. He and the poet exchanged letters, but beyond that very little is known about him.

DR. GEORGE GRIERSON

From an account, written by a Dr. George Grierson, of Glasgow, it would appear that he and a Mr. George Gairdner of Ladykirk accompanied Burns on his West Highland Tour in June, 1787. Grierson's report was first printed by the Rev. Peter Hately Waddell in his edition of the *Life and Works of Robert Burns*, published in monthly parts between 1867 and 1869. It bore the rather simplistic title of *Hints respecting Burns the Ayrshire Poet* and in 1867 was in the possession of John Reid of Kingston Place, Glasgow, which he made available to Waddell. The text of the Grierson MS reads:

WEST HIGHLAND TOUR
Burns at Inveraray and Dumbarton
by Dr. George Grierson.

Whoe'er thou art that lodgest here,
    Heaven Help thy wofu' case,
Unless thou com'st to visit Him,
    That King of Kings, his Grace.

There's Highland greed, there's Highland pride
    There's Highland scab and hunger;
If Heaven it was that sent me here,
    It sent me in an anger.

NB – The above lines were written at the Inn at Inveraray by R. Burns, on the pane of Glass, in the presence of George Grierson, in 1788.

Burns wrote an encomium on Mary McLachlan, the Innkeeper's daughter at Tarbert, ending with:

To fair Maria add McLachlan,
Quod Burns, a rhymer lad frae Mauchlin.

'George Grierson was with him when he wrote the stanzas on Miss McLachlan, in 1788, and he, a day or two after this, wrote an Invocation to the Sun, at Bannachra on the banks of Loch Lomond. – It was in June, 1788, when Burns made a young man, Duncan McLachlan, son of Mr. McLachlan of Bannachra, bring out the largest bowl of punch his house could furnish, and made all the ladies and gentlemen kneel down, till he would repeat *extempore*, at the dawn of Day, an Invocation to the Sun. The company were Dr. Grierson, Mr. McLachlan, junior,

Inveraray, showing the Castle and grounds on the right.

and the family, Mr. McFarlan from Jamaica, Mr. John Shedden, merchant, and Miss Shedden of Glasgow, Mr. Gardner of Lady-Kirk, and the two Misses Butters from Edinburgh. Next day, Messrs. Grierson Gardner and Burns left Arden in the evening, and in coming to Dumbarton met with a Highlandman riding with his bare-back – on a bare-back horse. Burns pursued the Highlandman, till he was thrown from his horse into a thorn tree, and Burns's face was all bloody, he having fallen from his horse and cut his face. They came that night safe to Dumbarton – when the magistrates did them all the honour of conferring the freedom of their city [on them]; and Oliphant preached the next day, being the Fast-day, against the parties foresaid, and found great fault [with] the magistrates for conferring honours on the author of *vile, detestable and immoral* publications.'

From original, entitled *Hints respecting Burns the Ayrshire Poet*,
By G Grierson, in possession of John Reid,Esq., Kingston Place, Glasgow.

Of the company that were present on that convivial gathering at Bannachra, the following have been traced. John Shedden is listed in *Jones' Directory of Glasgow* for 1787 as a merchant residing on the west side of Dunlop Street, Glasgow, with Miss Shedden, his unmarried sister. Mr. Gardner (sic) of Ladykirk, was in fact George Gairdner, who had inherited the Ladykirk estate in 1780 from his father, William Gairdner. The two Misses Butter were Elizabeth, (born 1767) and Margaret, (born 1775), daughters of Henry Butter of Pitlochry, whose town-house was in George Street, Edinburgh. The other members of the company have not been traced.[1]

In 1787 Archibald McLachlan was the tenant-farmer at Bannachra, and no doubt was related to 'Peter McLauchline (sic) of Bannachray', who is listed as a subscriber to the *Edinburgh Edition*. Perhaps the reason for Burns's visit was to pick up Peter's subscription.

On his return from the West Highland Tour, Burns presided at a meeting of St. James' Masonic Lodge, Tarbolton, of which he was Deputy Master. The entry in the minute book, in Burns' own hand, records:

> 'Mauchline 25 July, 1787.
> This night the Deputation of the Lodge met in Mauchline, and entered Brother Alexander Allison of Barnmuir, an apprentice. Likewise admitted Bros. Professor Stuart of Cathrine, and Claude Alexander, Esq., of Ballochmyle, Claude Neilson, Esq., Paisley, John Farquhar Gray, Esq., of Gilmiscroft, and Dr. George Grierson, Glasgow, Honorary Members of the Lodge.
>
> Robt. Burns, DM'

The only other oblique reference to Grierson is to be found in Burns' journal of his Highland Tour, which he undertook with William Nicol in 1787. On Sunday, 26 August, he and Nicol dined with advocate, John Munro and his daughter Isabella at Auchinbowie House, situated about three-quarters of a mile south west of Bannockburn. Burns's entry in the journal reads:

'Dine at Auchinbowie – Mr. Munro an excellent, worthy, old man – Miss Munro an amiable, sensible, sweet young woman, much resembling Mrs. Grierson.' This is, undoubtedly, a reference to Grierson's wife, as Burns at that time had not met James Grierson of Dalgoner, the only other person of that name who became acquainted with the poet.

It seems reasonable to assume that Grierson and Burns were on very friendly terms at that time. Waddell states that an important series of letters, addressed to Grierson from Burns, was in the possession of John Reid of Glasgow, but were destroyed when the Clyde burst its banks and inundated the Kingston area in 1831.

It would appear the Grierson MS was written some time after the actual journey took place, as Grierson gives the date as 1788, whereas the tour was undertaken the previous year. He must have been misled in his recollection of the exact year – a not uncommon fault when recalling past events. Dr. James Adair, who accompanied Burns on his second trip to Harvieston in 1787, and John Syme, who was the poet's travelling companion on the tour of Galloway in 1794, obviously experienced the same difficulty. Both furnished

The Great Inn, Inveraray.
It was here on a window pane that Burns scratched his scathing epigram. Apart from the addition of the entrance porch, the building is very much the same as in the time of Burns's visit.
(N.B. This is now called 'The Argyll Hotel').

Currie with accounts of their respective journeys, and although their reports are substantially correct on the main facts, they contain inaccuracies in some of the dates. Grierson's version of the lines written by Burns on a pane of glass at the Great Inn, Inveraray, differs from the text usually given in any of the printed works, but the lapse of time may have accounted for the variation. The window pane was in the possession of the Argyll family for many years, but its present whereabouts is unknown. It is thought that it was given out to an exhibition and never returned.[2]

Very little is known of Grierson. His name appears on the list of subscribers to the 1787 Edinburgh Edition as 'Mr. George Grierson, Glasgow.' He subscribed for 36 copies of the poems, easily the largest Glasgow subscription, and from this may be gathered that his interest in the poet and his works extended beyond that of a normal subscriber. An enquiry to Edinburgh University revealed that there are five entries in the medical matriculation records for a George Grierson from 1777 – 1783, although there is no trace of him as a medical graduate. Assuming that he was 18 years of age when he first matriculated in 1777, he would be about 27 or 28 at the time of the West Highland Tour, and about the same age as Burns. It is interesting to note that at that time there were no restrictions on anyone practising as a doctor without having graduated.

Old print of the Tolbooth and MacKenzie House of Dumbarton.
It was probably within the Tolbooth that Burns received his Burgess Ticket.

An aura of mystery hangs over the whole tour, and the absence of a journal by Burns makes the subject most perplexing. In letters written to friends he is annoyingly vague, and gives the minimum of information about the places he visited and the people he met. We are, therefore, indebted to George Grierson, of Glasgow, for his rather curious and plain-worded document, which certainly helps to shed more light on the tour of the West Highlands, which Burns undertook in 1787.

Riverside Church, Dumbarton.

DUMFRIES

**'There was Maggie by the banks o'Nith,
A dame wi' pride enough'**

JOHN LEWARS

On 26th December, 1789, a young man of twenty entered the service of the Excise as a gauger at Linlithgow. His name was John Lewars and he was following in the footsteps of his father, also John Lewars, who, at the time of his death on 22nd April, 1789, was Supervisor of Excise at Dumfries. Within six months young John was transferred to the Dumfries Excise Collection. He had two sisters living in Dumfries Mary and Jessie. Mary had married William Hyslop, a local builder, and it is possible that John's early transfer was on compassionate grounds, in order to provide for his younger sister, Jessie, who was then only eleven years of age. [1]

The Rev. Charles Rogers in *The Book of Robert Burns* states that 'Jessie, after her father's death in 1789, took up her abode with her brother, who occupied a small dwelling at Mill Brae or Mill Vennel (now Burns Street) Dumfries.' There appears to be some doubt, however, as to when the Lewars occupied the house at Mill Brae. A court action was raised by a Samuel Blunt on 2nd April, 1792, to remove John and Jessie Lewars from their 'high Lodging, cellar and garret lying in the High street of Dumfries.' It is possible that John and Jessie Lewars did not take up residence in Mill Brae until sometime in 1793, following their removal from High Street.[2]

Mill Brae (now Burns Street).
Burns's house is on the left, and one of the small dwellings on the right
was occupied by John Lewars and is sister, Jessie.

One of Lewars' fellow officers was Robert Burns, who had taken up duty in the Dumfries Division the previous year. Although Lewars was ten years younger than the poet, a warm friendship quickly sprang up between them, no doubt it was further cemented in April 1793 when Burns and his family moved into a house in Mill Brae, opposite the one occupied by the Lewars.

A Register for the Dumfries Excise Collection for 1791 shows that Lewars' first station was in the 2nd Itinerancy. He remained in that post until 1799 when he was transferred to the 1st Itinerancy, Burns old circuit, and like the poet, it involved him in riding some two hundred miles per week. In an Ages and Capacities Register for 1794 he was described as a 'good officer' and marked 'a', i.e. fit for promotion. Official records also reveal that he was reprimanded in 1795, but no reason is given, which seems to suggest that the offence was of a minor nature.

Jessie Lewars.
Younger sister of John Lewars, she became Burns's ministering angel in his final illness. In return he wrote for her 'O wert thou in the cauld blast' An engraving by H. Robinson from *The Land of Burns.*

On 29th February, 1792, Lewars took an active part in the seizure of the smuggling brig, *Rosamond*, on the Solway Firth. The incident was reported in the Glasgow and Edinburgh newspapers the following week. A highly coloured account of the episode was given by Lockhart in his biography of Burns, published in 1828:

> 'On the 27th of February a suspicious looking brig was discovered on the Solway Firth, and Burns was one of the party whom the superintendent conducted to watch her motions. She got into shallow water the day afterwards, and the officers were enabled to discover that her crew were numerous, armed, and not likely to yield without a struggle. Lewars, a brother exciseman, an intimate friend of our poet, was accordingly sent to Dumfries for a guard of Dragoons; the superintendent, Mr. Crawford, proceeded himself on a similar errand to Ecclefechan, and Burns was left with some men under his orders, to watch the brig and prevent landing or escape. From the private journal of one of the

excisemen (now in my hands) it appears that Burns manifested considerable impatience while thus occupied, being left for many hours in a wet salt marsh with a force he knew to be inadequate for the purpose it was meant to fulfil. One of his comrades hearing him abuse his friend Lewars in particular, for being slow about his journey, the man answered that he also wished the devil had him for his pains, and that Burns, in the meantime, would do well to indite a song upon the sluggard. Burns said nothing; but after taking a few strides among the reeds and shingle, rejoined his party, and chanted to them the well known ditty, 'The Deil's run awa' wi' the Exciseman.' *(CW 467)*

Lewars and Crawford eventually returned with a combined force of forty four Dragoons. By this time the brig had drifted to the English side of the Solway, which was mostly dry sand. When the crew saw the Dragoons and the Excisemen wading out to the ship in three columns, one led by Burns, they gave up the fight and made their escape toward the English shore.
Lockhart concludes his account:

'The vessel was condemned, and, with all her arms and stores, sold by auction next day at Dumfries; upon which occasion Burns, whose behaviour had been highly commended, thought fit to purchase four carronades, by way of trophy. But his glee went a bit further - he sent the guns, with a letter, to the French Convention, requesting that body to accept them as a mark of his admiration and respect. The present and its accompaniment, were intercepted at the custom house at Dover.'

Lockhart gave as his source, 'the private journal of one of the excisemen, (John Lewars) now in my hands.' Later it was revealed that he had been indebted for this document and two others to Joseph Train, antiquary and Supervisor of Excise at Castle Douglas, who had furnished Sir Walter Scott with material for his Waverley Novels. It appears that Train had passed the *Rosamond* documents to Sir Walter, who had handed them over to Lockhart, his son in law, then in the course of writing his biography of Burns. In a letter (undated) which Train sent to Robert Canuthers of the *Inverness Courier*, he stated that Lockhart's account was based on three documents which he (Train) had received from John Lewars' widow; (1) the original diary of a Mr. Walter Crawford, a riding officer of the Excise, who had been present at the seizure of the brig; (2) an account of the seizure and sale of the vessel in the handwriting of Burns himself, and (3) a document written by Mr. John Lewars, who was also present at the capture, 'detailing the circumstances of Burns having purchased the four carronades at the sale.' Train also stated that Sir Walter 'applied to the Custom House authorities, who, after considerable search, found that they had been seized at the Port of Dover, as stated by Mr. Lewars in his memorandum.' [3]

For over a hundred years Lockhart's story of the carronades was treated with the utmost scepticism by subsequent biographers. This was due, in the main, to the absence of the three documents mentioned by Train. Round about the centenary of Scott's death (1932), a large number of manuscripts, which had lain at Abbotsford for over a century, were transferred to the National Library of Scotland, among them were three documents concerning the schooner *Rosamond*; (1) the journal of Walter Crawford .. (2) two large sheets in Burns's handwriting, setting forth the expenses incurred in repairing, guarding and laying up the vessel, and (3) a notice of the sale, to which was attached an inventory, apparently in John Lewars' hand, of the sails, spars, rigging and furnishings, with a brief summary of the amounts realised in the auction. Unfortunately Lewars' account of the purchase of the carronades by Burns, and their despatch to France, was not among the documents recovered. The discovery of two of the three manuscripts cited by Train, would seem to indicate, however, that Lewars' account was also among the papers handed to Sir Walter.

The origin of 'The Deil's Awa' also has been the subject of much doubt and speculation down the years. The most sensible assessment, made to date, is by Prof James Kinsley in his notes on the song. He recounts the story, as told by Lockhart, and then proceeds:

> 'We are rightly suspicious of such tales of spontaneous composition, which are frequent in the Burns myth but the wait by the Solway may have been the occasion of the song later revised and set. Cromek says that Burns was called on for a song at an Excise Dinner in Dumfries and 'handed these verses extempore to the President, written on the back of a letter,'[4] a more unlikely tale than Lockhart's. Editors have read Burns's letter to John Leven (March 1792, CL 614) as confirmation of Cromek's note 'Mr. Mitchell, mentioned to you a ballad, which I composed and sung at one of his Excise Court dinners; here it is' This is the source of Cromek's note, perhaps, but Burns does not say that the song was composed at the dinner.'[5]

We doubt if the recovery of Lewars' journal would settle this argument.

About 1795 Burns wrote a poem called 'The Hue and Cry of John Lewars'. He preceded the verses with a note:

> A poor man ruined and undone by Robbery and Murder. Being an aweful (sic) WARNING to the young men of this age, how they look well to themselves in this dangerous, terrible WORLD.

A thief and a murderer! stop her who can!
    Look well to your lives and your goods!
Good people, ye know not the hazard you run,
    'Tis the far famed and much noted Woods

While I looked at her eye, for the devil is in it,
    In a trice she whipt off my poor heart:
Her brow, cheek and lip in another sad minute,
    My peace felt her murderous dart.

Her features, I'll tell you them over, but hold!
    She deals with your wizards and books;
And to peep in her face, if but once you're so bold,
    There's witchery kills in her looks.

But softly I have it her haunts are well known,
    At midnight so slily I'll watch her;
And sleeping, undrest, in the dark, all alone
    Good lord! the dear Thief how I'll catch her! (cw 468)

The note and the poem would appear to be a bit of playful satire on Burns's part, as the verses were almost certainly written on a love affair of John Lewars. The original MS is in the Burns Museum at Alloway. A footnote, thought to be in John Syme's hand, states, 'John Lewars, Land Surveyor in Dumfries; Miss Woods, Governess at Miss McMurdo's boarding school.' Apparently Miss Woods was not the only object of Lewars' affection. In a letter which Burns sent to John Gillespie, an Excise colleague of Burns, and an unsuccessful suitor of Jean Lorimer, (Burns's 'Chloris'), he mentions that, 'The great rivals now with Miss Jeany are our brethren Officers, Messrs. Lewars and Thomson. They are both deeply in love, but the lady does not favour the one or the other.' (CL 572)

John Syme described Lewars as a Land Surveyor. It is well known that many Excisemen had subsidiary occupations, and evidently Lewars augmented his Excise income by undertaking surveying work. This is corroborated from a manuscript in Dumfries Burgh Records. It is docketed 'Proposal by J. Lewars for publishing a map of the Town and Borough Roads of Dumfries, 1796/16 May 1796. Read in Council to lye (sic) on the table.'

When Burns died on 21st July, 1796, Jean, his widow, was in no position to carry out the many duties attendant upon such a melancholy event. On the day of the funeral she gave birth to a son, later christened Maxwell in honour of Burns's physician,

Dr. William Maxwell. In Jean's extremity, John Lewars and his sister Jessie proved true and devoted friends. Jessie took care of the children, while John undertook many of the essential tasks, writing letters to friends and relatives informing them of Burns's death. Indeed it is from one of those letters that we learn of the reconciliation that took place between Mrs. Dunlop and the poet a short time before his death. Their correspondence, which had brought much joy and satisfaction to both, had been terminated eighteen months previously by Mrs. Dunlop, who presumably had taken offence at some remark made by Burns in one of his letters. Eleven days before he died he sent her a heart rending letter of farewell. *(CL 218)* Lewars' letter to Mrs. Dunlop, written on the day following the poet's death, contains the only evidence that she had replied. Preserved in Edinburgh University Library, it reads:

> 'MADAM --- At the desire of Mrs. Burns I have to acknowledge the receipt of your letter, and at the same time to inform you of the melancholy and much regretted event of Mr. Burns's death. He expired on the morning of 21st, after a long and severe illness. Your kind letter gave him great ease and satisfaction, and was the last thing he was capable of perusing or understanding, The situation of his unfortunate widow and family of most promising boys, Mrs. Dunlop's feelings and affection for them will much easier paint than I can possibly express, more particularly when Mrs. Dunlop is informed that Mrs. Burns's situation is such that she is expected to ly in dayly. I am certain that a letter from Mrs. Dunlop to Mrs. Burns would be a very great consolation, and her kind advice most thankfully received. I am, with the greatest respect, your most obedient and very humble servant.
>
> JNO. LEWARS,
> Dumfries, 22rd July, 1796.'

Lewars married Barbara Howe of Gretna in 1799 and there were two children of the marriage. For reasons unknown, he quit the Excise in 1807 and rented the farm of Lauder at Caerlaverock. Perhaps he was tired of the drudgery of riding round the various parishes of the 1st Itinerancy in all weathers, or had he become disheartened that the promotion, for which he had been recommended in 1794, had failed to materialise? No reason is recorded in official records.

Apparently his venture into farming was not a success as we find him back in the Excise in 1817. His subsequent movements in the service would seem to indicate that he was employed for several years as relief supervisor, Kincardine on Forth 1817, Linlithgow 1817, Dunkeld 1818, Inveraray 1818, Montrose 1819 and Dumfries 1820, where he remained until his retiral in 1824, on a pension of £160 per annum, a goodly sum in those days. He died two years later, aged 57, at his home, Rydedale Cottage, Troqueer. [6]

John Lewars' place in Burnsiana has been somewhat overshadowed by his younger sister, Jessie, who nursed the poet in his last illness, and was the subject of several poems and songs by Burns, including the incomparable, 'O wert thou in the cauld blast.' (CW 567) John Lewars' place in the Burns story, however, is equally secure. Although he was ten years younger than Burns, he quickly won the poet's friendship and respect, He appears to have been a young man of some education and above the average of the common gauger. Burns once described him as 'a particular friend of mine', and 'as a young man of uncommon merit, indeed by far the cleverest fellow I have met with in this part of the world.' (CW 678) Lewars reciprocated Burns's affection by devoted service to him and his family during his illness and after his death. For this he will always be fondly remembered.

Burns house, today.

ALEXANDER FINDLATER

On 27th August, 1789, Robert Burns wrote to Mr. David Blair, Gunsmith, Birmingham:

> **I have for some time had in view to commence acting Excise Officer. I say acting, for I have had a Excise Commission by me nearly these two years…I believe I am now appointed to a Division in the middle of which I live, and may perhaps enter on business in a week or ten days.** (CL 502)

On 10th October his name appeared on an official list of Excise Officers, with a note to the effect that he was on active duty. Burns lost no time in translating the good news into verse. In his 'Epistle to Dr. Blacklock', the blind Edinburgh poet, written from Ellisland on 21st October, he said:

> But what d'ye think, my trusty fier?
> I'm turned a guager   Peace be here!
> Parnassian queires I fear, I fear
>   Ye'll now disdain me,
> And then my fifty pounds a year
>   Will little gain me. (CW 371)

Before he could take up his appointment, legally, he had to be sworn into the service. This took place on 27th October, as is shown by the minute of the Justices of the Peace Quarter Sessions for Dumfriesshire:

> 'At Dumfries the twenty seventh day of October one thousand, seven hundred and eighty nine years. Quarter Sessions of the Peace Sedurunt (sic)
> George Maxwell of Carruchan, John Welsh, Sheriff substitute, William Lawson of Girthead, Thomas Goldie of Craigmuire and John Bushby of Kempleton, who made choice of the said George Maxwell to be their Praeses.

Mr. Findlater & Mr. Burns qualified	'Alexander Findlater Supervisor of Excise & Robert Burns, officer of Excise both in Dumfries Collection qualified themselves, the first as an extraordinary officer of the Customs & the other as an Officer of the Excise by taking and swearing the oath of allegeance (sic) to His Majesty King George the Second (sic) & other oaths appointed by law and subscribing the same with the Assurance. And the Justices adjourn their Quarter Session till the Third Tuesday of November next.' [1]

Portrait of **Alexander Findlater,**
by an unknown artist.

Alexander Findlater, whose name appears on the minute, was at that time acting Supervisor of the Dumfries Excise District and Burns's immediate superior. He proved to be one of Burns's most loyal friends and defended the character and reputation of the dead poet against the calumnies of those early biographers, who sought to paint Burns, in his Dumfries years, as a person 'perpetually stimulated with alcohol.' [2]

The name *Findlater* is of French derivation, *Fin-la-terre*, signifying 'the land's end,' and is a very apt description of the locality which bears the name. It is situated in the Parish of Fordyce, on the shore of the Moray Firth, about one mile east of Cullen. Resting on a peninsula is the ruin of Findlater Castle, a stronghold of the Ogilvies in the reign of James II and from which the Earls of Findlater derived their title. The title became extinct in 1811.

Alexander Findlater was born at Burntisland on 11th September, 1754, the fourth son of James F. Findlater, Excise Officer, and Helen Ballantine. Many of his ancestors were ministers of the Church of Scotland, and he was called after his grandfather, the Reverend Alexander Findlater, first minister of Hamilton after the Revolution Settlement. [3]

Findlater was admitted to the Excise in 1774 and his first station was at Cupar, Fife in 1777, thereafter at Camelon, 1778, Falkirk 1782, and Glasgow (Glasshouse), 1784. On 10th October, 1786, he was recommended for Examiner and Supervisor. From December, 1787 until June 1791, when he was appointed officially as Supervisor of Dumfries, he acted as Supervisor, first for John Lewars, senior, who died in 1789 and thereafter for John Rankine, who died in 1791. Presumably both these officers had been off duty prior to their deaths, hence the reason for Findlater's temporary appointment. [4] In a character register of 1794 he was described as 'a good officer.'

From a letter written by Burns to Findlater on the day following their appearance before the Justices of the Peace, it would suggest that the two had become acquainted sometime prior to Burns's entry into the Excise. The letter also reveals that Findlater had furnished the Scottish Board of the Excise, no doubt on request, with a favourable testimony of Burns's character. Here is the text of Burns's letter:

'I believe I mentioned something to you yesterday of the character that Mr. Corbet told me you had given of me to our Edinburgh Excise folks, but my conscience accuses me that I did not make the proper acknowledgements to you for your Goodness. Most sincerely and gratefully do I thank you, Sir, for this uncommon instance of kindness & friendship,

I mean not by this as if I would propitiate your future inspection of my conduct No, Sir; I trust to act, and, I *shall* act, so as to defy Scrutiny, but I send this as a sheer tribute of Gratitude to a Gentleman whose goodness has laid me under very great obligations, and for whose character as a Gentleman I have the highest esteem. It may very probably never be in my power to repay, but it is equally out of my power to forget, the obligations you have laid on.

Sir, your deeply indebted and very humble servant,
Robert Burns.' (CL 539)[5]

Copy of letter from Burns to Alexander Findlater,
29 October, 1789.
Courtesy of National Library of Ireland.

The Mr. Corbet, mentioned by Burns was William Corbet, a fellow Exciseman in the Dumfries Collection from 1789 to 1791. Apparently he had learned that Findlater had spoken highly of Burns to his superiors in Edinburgh, and had passed the information on to Burns. This William Corbet should not be confused with the other William Corbet, who was one of the General Supervisors of Excise for Scotland.

Burns's first posting in the Excise was to the 'Dumfries first Itinerancy,' as it was called. His salary was £50 per annum, plus an indeterminate sum out of fines collected from defaulters whom he reported. His Excise station comprised fourteen circuits, technically termed *rides*, which involved him travelling two hundred miles per week on horseback in all weathers. He had to provide and maintain a horse, and pay all travelling expenses out of his meagre income. It is not surprising, that before he was six months in the service, he was angling for a more lucrative and less arduous station. In a letter to his elderly correspondent, Mrs. Dunlop written in March, 1790, he gave the first hint of his intention to give up the farm at Ellisland and rely solely on the Excise for a living. He wrote:

> 'My farm is a ruinous bargain, and would ruin me to abide by it. The Excise, notwithstanding all my objections to it, pleases me tolerably well, and is indeed my sole dependence.' *(CL 184)*

Ellisland Farm.
Burns described it as a "ruinous bargain" and gave it up in September, 1791,
the Excise becoming his sole source of income.

On 25th July, 1790, Burns was transferred to the Dumfries Third or 'Tobacco' Division a footwalk, which increased his salary to £70 per annum and relieved him of the necessity of keeping a horse. It was known as the 'Tobacco Division', although it does not appear in any of the Excise records under that name. It obviously got its title by virtue of the fact that fifty-two tobacco dealers and retailers were situated within its bounds. In addition there were nine victuallers, one chandler and a bricklayer, all of whom came under Burns's surveillance. In area it covered about one third of the town of Dumfries and involved him in no more that four miles of walking. [6]

At this time it seems evident that Findlater was doing his best to advance Burns's prospects. Although the poet had been little more than a year in the service, Findlater had formed a high opinion of his character and ability, and was confident that Burns was capable of carrying out the duties of any post within the Excise. Following a meeting at Stirling, at which Burns's future in the service appears to have been discussed, Findlater sent the following letter to William Corbet, General Supervisor of Excise, Stirling:

> 'Dear Sir,
> Mr. Burns informs me that, in Consequence of a communication between you and some of his friends, he has stated his case to you by letter and exprest (sic) his wishes, on account of his family, of being translated to a more beneficial appointment; And as at our last interview at Stirling you hinted a desire of being certified of the propriety of his Character of the Revenue, I shall, abstracted from every Consideration of his other talents, which are so universally admired, in a few words give you my Opinion of him. He is an active, faithful and zealous officer, gives the most unremitting attention to the duties of his office (which, by the bye, is more than I first lookd for from so eccentric a genius) and, tho' his experience must be as yet small, he is capable, as you may well suppose, of atchieving (sic) a much more arduous task than any difficulty that the theory or practice of our business can exhibit. In short being such as I have described and, believe me, I have not o'erstep't the modesty of *truth* he is worthy of your friendship; and if your recommendation can help him forward to a more eligible situation, you will have the merit of conferring an Obligation on a man who may be considered a credit to the profession. I am, Dear Sir, Your most Obedient humble Servant.
>
> A. Findlater. [7]
> Dumfries,
> 20th December 1790.'

Just one month later, on 21st January 1791, Burns was placed on the list of those eligible for promotion to Examiner and Supervisor. It seems reasonable to assume that Findlater's letter was an influential factor.

Although a warm friendship existed between Burns and his Supervisor, it was not allowed to interfere with official business. Findlater's professional integrity was such, that he was strict in the surveillance of all officers under his control. In June, 1791, he had occasion to take Burns to task over a faulty entry in one of his ledgers. An extract from Burn's reply shows how concerned he was about the imputation against his character, and also how attentive he was to his duties:

> 'I know, Sir, & regret that this business glances with a malign aspect on my character as an Officer; but as I am really innocent in the affair & as the gentleman is known to be an illicit Dealer, & particularly as this is the single instance of the least shadow of carelessness or impropriety in my conduct as an Officer, I shall be peculiarly unfortunate if my character shall fall a sacrifice to the dark manoeuvres of a Smuggler.' *(CL 540)*

The year 1792 was one of mixed fortune for Burns. On 26th April he was promoted to the Dumfries Port Division, the best assignment in the District. His prospects seemed good; now he could look forward to being a Supervisor, which would ultimately come his way by seniority, while beyond that was the prospect of an appointment as a Collector which would give him, 'besides a handsome income, a life of complete leisure.' In December, however, someone reported him to the Scottish Board of Excise as a person disaffected to the Government, and an enquiry was ordered into his conduct.

Perhaps it was fortunate for Burns that the man chosen by the Board was, William Corbet, the General Supervisor, already mentioned. He came to Dumfries to carry out an on the spot investigation, an indication that the Board took a serious view of the case, since they were dealing, not with an ordinary humble subordinate, but with an officer who was also a national celebrity. Findlater testified that Burns 'was exact, vigilant, and sober, that in fact he was one of the best officers in the District.' [8] If we are to believe John Syme, Distributor of Stamps in Dumfries, and a close friend of Burns, Corbet's mission became something of a social occasion. In a note to Alexander Peterkin he said, 'Mr. Corbet admonished Burns but found no grounds save some witty sayings, Mr. Corbet, Mr. Findlater, Burns and I dined together once or twice on the occasion.' [9] Writing later of this affair, Findlater said :

> 'I may venture to assert that when Burns was accused of a leaning to democracy and an enquiry into his conduct took place, he was subjected, in consequence thereof, to no more than perhaps a verbal or private caution to be more circumspect in future. Neither do I believe his promotion was thereby affected, but had he lived, it would have gone on in the usual routine.' [10]

Findlater's testimony that Burns 'was one of the best officers in the District' was fully justified two years later, when he was chosen from some twelve officers in the Dumfries

District to act as Supervisor for Findlater, who was absent from duty for nearly four months because of illness. It also confirmed that he was capable of discharging the arduous and responsible duties of Supervisor, and indicates that his promotion prospects had not been jeopardised.

The only poem which Burns addressed to Findlater was a somewhat broad verse epistle sent from Ellisland one Saturday morning, along with a present of eggs. Although the poem contains only five stanzas, it illustrates, once again, Burns's mastery of the verse epistle and his wonderful sense of humour:

Dear Sir,
Our Lucky humbly begs
Ye'll prie her caller,new laid eggs:
Lord grant the Cock may keep his legs,
    Aboon the Chuckies;
And wi' his kittle, forket clegs
    Claw weel their dockies!

Had Fate that cursed me in her ledger,
A Poet poor, and poorer Gager,
Created me that feather'd Sodger,
    A generous Cock,
How I wad craw and strut and roger
    My keeklin Flock!

Buskit wi' mony a bien, braw feather,
I wad defied the warst o' weather,
When corn or bear I could na gather
    To gie my burdies
I'd treated them wi' caller heather,
    And weel knooz'd hurdies.

Nae cursed Clerical, Excise
On honest Nature's laws and ties;
Free as the vemal breeze that flies
    At early day,
We'd tasted Nature's richest joys,
    But stint or stay.

But as the subject's something kittle,
Our wisest way's to say but little;

John Syme.
His great friend in Dumfries.
From an engraving by J T Kelley in
The Land of Burns.

And while my Muse is at her mettle,
I am most fervent,
Or may I die upon a whittle!
Your friend and Servant

ROBT BURNS *(CW 378)*

Following his death in 1796, Burns's reputation suffered severely at the hands of his early biographers. Robert Heron in 1797 and Dr. James Currie in 1800, both painted him as a habitual drunkard in his latter years, which, unfortunately, became the accepted legend for more than a century. In 1814, the copyright of Currie's first edition expired, and the following year an attempt was made by Alexander Peterkin, a Scottish solicitor, to disprove some of the false charges made by Heron, Currie and others.

Although he printed Currie in full, the real value of the work lies in his ninety eight page preface, which included among others a letter contributed by Alexander Findlater, testifying to Burns's true character. The great significance of Findlater's evidence is that it comes from one who had known the poet intimately during the last six years of his life - a period which a biographer, a century later, was so misguided to describe as 'a story of decadence.' [11] The following is an extract from Findlater's letter, written from Glasgow on 10th October, 1814:

'My connection with Robert Burns commenced immediately after his admission into the Excise, and continued to the hour of his death. In all that time, the superintendence of his behaviour as an officer of the revenue, was a branch of my especial province, and it may be supposed I would not be an inattentive observer of the *general* conduct of a man and a poet, so celebrated by his countrymen. In the former capacity, so far from its being 'impossible for him to discharge the duties of his office with that regularity which is almost indispensable', as is palpably assumed by one of his biographers, and insinuated not very obscurely even by Dr. Currie, he was exemplary in his attention as an Excise officer, and was even jealous of the least imputation of his vigilance ... Having stated Burns's *unremitting attention to business*, which certainly was not compatible with perpetual intoxication, it follows, of course, that this latter charge must fall to the ground: and I will further avow, that I never saw him, which was very frequently while he lived at Ellisland, and still more so, almost every day, after he removed to Dumfries, but in hours of business he was quite himself, and capable of discharging the duties of his office, nor was he ever known to drink by himself, or seen to indulge in the use of liquor in a forenoon, as the statement, that he was *perpetually* under its stimulus, unequivocally implies.... I have seen Burns in all his various phases, in his convivial moments, in his sober moods, and in the bosom of his 'family ; indeed, I believe I saw more of him than any other individual had occasion to see, after he became an Excise officer, and I never beheld anything like the gross enormities with which he is now charged. That when set down in an evening with a few friends whom he liked, he was apt to prolong the social hour beyond the bounds which prudence would dictate, is unquestionable; but in his family, I will venture to say, he was never seen otherwise than attentive and affectionate to a high degree. Upon the whole, it is much to be lamented that there has been so much broad unqualified assertion as has been displayed in Burns's history, the virulence indeed with which his memory has been treated, is hardly paralleled in the annals of literature.'

In February, 1834, following the publication of Allan Cunningham's *Life of Burns*, which came out as a preface to the edition of the works, Findlater sent a long letter to the editor of the *Edinburgh Magazine*. The letter also appeared in the *Glasgow Courier* in March of the same year. In it he took issue with Cunningham who claimed that Burns had been harshly treated by the Government and the Board of Excise. He also successfully debunked some of 'Honest Allan's' flight's of fancy. Although Findlater was then eighty years of age, his letter showed that when recalling events of some forty years past, his memory of Burns and the Excise was still very clear. With the subsequent publication of the Works, Findlater again sent a letter to the editor of the *Glasgow Courier*, which appeared in January, 1835. Once more he found it necessary to correct Cunningham's colourful fabrications. As these letters are not easily accessible to readers they appear on pages 230-235.

Findlater remained as Supervisor at Dumfries until 1797, when he was promoted to one of the prestigious posts of General Supervisor for Scotland in succession to William Corbet. He served in this capacity until 1806, when he took over as Collector at Haddington, a move which suggests that the post at Haddington was more rewarding than that of General Supervisor. In 1811, he again succeeded Corbet as Collector at Glasgow, then considered the plum post in Scotland. He held this position until 1825,

Burns joined the Dumfries Volunteers,
during his service in the Excise,
and wore the uniform as shown.

when he retired at the age of seventy one after fifty years service. The minutes of the Board of Excise bear frequent witness to the confidence which the Board placed in him, over the long period of his service. [12]

He was twice married. His first wife was Susannah Forrester, daughter of a writer in Falkirk, whom he married in 1778. There were five children of the marriage. Susannah died in 1810 and was buried in Greyfriar's Churchyard, Edinburgh. Sometime thereafter, (date is unknown), he married Catherine Anderson and from this marriage there were three children.[13] Findlater lived out the remainder of his fife in Glasgow, where he died on 3rd December, 1839, at the grand old age of eighty five. He was buried in the old Anderston Burying Ground in North Street, Glasgow. In 1923 the inscription on the original headstone was found to be almost illegible, and a new granite memorial stone was erected by the Sandyford Burns Club, which bore the following inscription:

To the Memory of
ALEXANDER FINDLATER
Supervisor of Excise at Dumfries
afterwards
Collector of Excise at Glasgow
Born 1754   Died 1839
The friend of ROBERT BURNS in life
His vindicator after death
Erected by Sandyford Burns Club, 1923 [14]

Photograph taken at the dedication of the **Findlater Memorial Plaque in Linn Cemetery** on 5th June, 2002. It shows Alexander Findlater a descendant, who along with his wife and two daughters, travelled from Somerset for the occasion.

"Alexander Findlater,
friend and champion of
Robert Burns"
This tombstone was erected by
The Sandyford Burns Club
in 1923 at
Anderston Burying Ground
and was subsequently removed to
The Linn Cemetery
on the redevelopment of
Anderston mid 1960s.
Dedicated 5th June 2002

Plaque attached to Findlater Memorial Stone.

In the massive road redevelopment which took place in the Anderston area in the mid 1960s, the headstone was removed to the Linn Cemetery, where it stood neglected and almost forgotten: but not quite, as once again the Sandyford Burns Club came to its rescue. In 2002 the Club decided that it should be cleaned and restored, and this work was undertaken by artist and craftsman, Colin Hunter McQueen. The Club also decided that a plaque should be placed on the stone. The Dedication took place in Linn Cemetery on 5th June, 2002, before a gathering of Burnsians and friends. The company were delighted to welcome Alexander Findlater, a descendant, with his wife and two daughters, who had travelled from the south of England to be present at the ceremony. [15]

In a letter which Burns sent in January, 1794, to Robert Graham of Fintry, one of the Commissioners of Excise who had befriended him, he paid this tribute to his immediate superior:

'Mr. Findlater, my Supervisor, who is not only one of the first, if not the very first of Excisemen in your Service, but also one of the worthiest fellows in the universe.'

Burns was never to know how truly prophetic his tribute was to become.

GLASGOW COURIER

JANUARY, 29.1835.

LITERATURE

Cunningham's Life of Burns
Mr. Findlater to the editor of the *Glasgow Courier*

'Sir, You cannot, I dare say, have failed to observe that few of our Scottish poets have had so many biographers and writers of remarks and strictures on their works, life, and conduct, as Robert Burns. Some have lauded him to the skies, while others have treated him with an extreme degree of harshness and severity. On the whole, however, the former sentiment seems latterly to prevail, and, as these discussions have been handled by abler pens than mine, I, by no means, intend to obtrude my opinion on his merits.

An idea, however, having gone abroad that he was illiberally and cruelly treated by the Board of Excise, which, it is broadly insinuated, arrested his promotion, crushed his spirits, injured his health, and hurried him to an early grave, and, knowing this opinion to be erroneous, I mean to combat it but, while I do so, I will take no credit to myself for a generous and chivalric attempt, *exclusively*, to rescue the memory of the Commissioners of Excise (now, believe, all in the dust) from so unjust an aspersion. Being, in another shape, implicated myself, and my veracity called in question, and, this, for having stated (as recorded in Lockhart's Life of Burns) that, when the investigation relative to his political principles took place, 'he was subjected to no more, perhaps, than a verbal, or private caution, and to be more circumspect in future; and that neither did I believe that his promotion was thereby affected, but that, had he lived, it would have gone on in the usual routine. This is 'the head and front of my offending.' In a review of this work in a celebrated periodical, the editor, with much urbanity, as well as good feeling, does not express any doubt of my veracity, but only the extent of my knowledge on the subject, as, after a prefatory compliment, he only says, '*We know better*'. With this, the most fastidious would have had no fault to find. But, in the late life of the poet, by Allan Cunningham, it is carried a degree further. He says p.282 (after quoting what I had said about a private caution):

> 'Burns knew best how this was an order to act, and not to think; and whatever might be men and measures, to be silent and obedient seems a sharp sort of private caution'

He further adds, after expressing his doubts of a story given of Burns purchasing, and sending to the French Directory, four guns, captured in a smuggling vessel:

> 'I suspect the story is not more accurate than, that when accused of a leaning to Democracy, he was subjected to no more than, perhaps, a verbal or private caution, to be more circumspect in future.'

If Mr. Cunningharn had been fair and polite, I would have been *silent*, and, perhaps, submissive; but this is so highly coloured as imperatively to call on me for a vindication, which, I am sorry to say, will unavoidably lead me into a technical and, of course, disagreeable discussion of excise forms of business, not at all likely to be interesting to the public; but being brought before that dread tribunal in so questionable a way, I am obliged to have recourse to a similar mode of explanation. I have to mention then, that, the excise business, even in rebukes and censures to officers, is managed in the most regular and systematic manner; and the following are the degrees, beginning with that for a slight offence: First, a *verbal caution*. This is not much regarded by young and thoughtless officers, who, in a slang way, say, it breaks no bones, that is, it does not affect the character, *no record thereof being kept*: immediately, however, these assume a more tangible, and latterly an appalling shape, as the second degree is an admonishment; third a sharp admonishment: fourth, a reprimand: and fifth, a severe reprimand; all narrating the cause of the censure, and this last concluding with a caveat, that, if the offender does not in future pay more regard to his instructions, he will be suspended or discharged. These are transmitted to the respective Supervisors, to be registered and delivered to the offenders. Nor is this all a complete register thereof, for all Scotland, is kept by the General Examiner, at the head office, which is examined on every occasion when an officer's character falls to be considered, particularly when any application is made for promotion. Now, if Burns had been subjected to any or all of these, except the first I must, *ex-officio* have known of it, as it could not have been concealed from me: and I, therefore, consider the authority for what I have stated, on this subject, to be of the most unquestionable and decisive description, such, indeed, as nothing but the most obstinate prejudice will resist: and hence, it is apparent, why *no record* of this business could be found in the excise office, as stated in 'Lockhart's Life', and more pertinaciously and virulently insisted on by Cunningham (p. 282). In truth, there was not much to put on record; chiefly an order from the Board of Excise, to a superior officer, to investigate the complaint, which he having, of course, performed and reported the result, was directed in return, to caution the Bard, as before stated. In this view of the case I think I may safely appeal to every dispassionate mind, whether any public Board could have exhibited more liberal and humane conduct than appears here. The mildest form of censure is directed not even a trace of the transaction to be found; and, in a short time, so totally forgotten, that Burns finds himself not only continued on the list for promotion, but, on the very first opportunity that occurred in Dumfries, is actually employed to officiate as a

Supervisor, and, I say without hesitation, would, if he had lived, have been promoted in his due course: and, that, at a shorter period of service than any of his predecessors. Nay, he himself, though a good deal alarmed at first, was at length satisfied at this, and writes to his friend, Mrs. Dunlop, Dec., 29, 1794, that being now employed to officiate as a Supervisor, he considered his political sins to be forgiven him. Another charge of cruelty has also been brought forward against the Board, that of refusing his full salary during his illness, which a little explanation will set rights. A few years previous to this period, an addition of £15 per annum had been made to the salaries, accompanied with a condition of being stopped to officers not doing duty. This still existed in Burns's time, and his was no worse treatment than others in similar circumstances of indisposition. It is here incumbent on me to mention, that Commissioner Graham, regretting, I have no doubt, his inability to comply with the Poet's wishes as to the full salary, sent him a donation of £5, which, I believe, nearly, or totally, compensated the loss.

Upon the whole, therefore, I think I have a right to assume, that the charge of the Poet having his promotion blasted, his spirits crushed, and himself hurried to an early grave by the cruelty and oppression, or, as Cunningham more graphically, perhaps, designates it, *the racks of the excise*, must fall to the ground. Indeed, so much the contrary is the fact, that instead of obstructing, all his superior officers I have conversed with on the subject were anxiously desirous to see him promoted, and would have lent their every aid to accomplish it. But, alas! the Poet was not fated to see this, and fell a victim to distress and premature death, from other causes than those now ascribed by his biographers. Let the noble, the proud, the great, and affluent, who ought to be the patrons of genius, consider this and blush!

I ought, perhaps, to close here, as I am neither disposed nor qualified to take on me the office of critic, but the notice of a few trifling mistakes in 'Cunningham's Life' will hardly, I presume, come under that designation. At p. 271, Burns is described as having 'his excise labours extended over a long and barren line of sea coast, upon which he was compelled to keep watch for many darksome hour galloping from point to point, to prevent the disembarkation of run goods' &c I cannot suppose willful misrepresentation here, but the author has either been misled or very ill-informed as after Burns removed into Dumfries from Ellisland, he never kept a horse, nor had any occasion for one in his business; he had no charge whatever of the Dumfriesshire coast was not compelled to watch the darksome hours, and still less to gallop from point to point to prevent the landing of run goods, Indeed, except in the isolated emergency of the empty smuggling vessel, brought so prominently forward, and one or two occasions when cargoes of rum from the West Indies were legally landed near Annan, where Burns attended as Port officer, for which he had an extra salary, he never had any occasion, save for his own pleasure, to go beyond the precincts of the town of Dumfries.

It is painful to enter upon the next article I have in view. At p. 344, is:

> 'Presented a melancholy spectacle; the poet dying, his wife in hourly expectation of being confined; four helpless children wandering from room to room, gazing on their miserable parents, and little of food or cordial kind to pacify the whole or sooth the sick.'

If *effect* has been studied here the author has succeeded *a merveille*, but this must not deter me from stating what came under my own observation, and agrees with my own knowledge. It is unnecessary, no doubt, to explain that food is a tangible subject, and what every body understands; but the cordial is not so easily defined, being probably, in the language of romance, either wine or some other more highly and deliciously concentrated modification of the grape. In common parlance, however, the family of the bard wanted none of the necessities of life, during all the period of my acquaintance with him, and few people, I believe, had better opportunities of knowledge on this subject then myself, or were more frequently in his house, particularly after he came to reside in Dumfries, and in the latter days of his life. On the night, indeed immediately preceding his decease, I sat by his bedside, and administered the last morsel ever swallowed, not certainly in the form of medicine, which at that period was totally relinquished as unavailing, nor of the cordial of romance; but what was better fitted to allay his thirst and cool his parched and burning tongue.

I might extend these animadversions further, but having, I presume, accomplished the object I had in view, I desist. *Quid multis verbis?*

I am, Sir,
Your most obedient servant,
A. Findlater.
Glasgow, North Wellington Place.
February, 1834

Cunningham's Life of Burns

To the Editor of the Glasgow Courier.

'Sir   When I wrote and sent you a few observations on Cunningham's Life of Burns, at the time of the publication of his first volume, I considered them sufficient to set an often discussed question (thread bare I wot) at rest. That such was the effect with most of Burns' living relatives, as well as many of his friends, I have great reason to believe, but it appears that this was not the case with some of his posthumous, or, as I may designate them, ultra fastidious friends, particularly his present Biographer, who still perseveres in his unrelenting hostility (I should be loth to use a harsher term) towards the

Commissioners of excise. He now however, takes a wider and higher range including the government of the country (at the period in question under the premiership of Wm. Pitt) in one indiscriminating and sweeping denunciation of 'eternal dishonour', (vol. 7, p.191) and as he still continues to assail my veracity, who certainly had far better opportunities of knowing the facts than Mr. Cunningham could possibly have access to, I consider it incumbent upon me to repel his insinuations and for this purpose I have again to trouble you with a few further remarks, requesting the insertion thereof in your respectable paper. There is little requiring animadversion in his 5th vol. p. 21, when he begins to nibble, (to use a piscatory phrase) and start an objection to an assertion of mine that Burns kept no horse after he came to reside in Dumfries. And will it be believed, that the only argument adduced in contradiction to this is, that Burns, in proceeding to accompany some friends into the country, uses the expression, 'I took my horse' as if any man, were about to ride, would not say the same thing or use some such terms, were it the Pope's horse, or the sorriest hack in Christendom and my attention, forsooth, is particularly directed to this circumstance, as of irrefragable importance. But enough of this foolery; and I proceed to notice, that in vol.7, p.222 still in the view of invalidating my testimony, he has a note at the bottom, importing that the Poet, in a letter to Mr. Erskine on the subject of an enquiry into his conduct had given a full history of that *dark* transaction, as he terms it a mode of phraseology Mr. Cunningham seems partial to, thereby rendering truth subservient to *effect*. 'Dark transaction' is sublime, and doubtless infinitely more dignified than any plain or simple epithet, however genuine or appropriate, would have been, and may perhaps, recall to a romantic imagination reminiscences of the olden time, when republican Venice was in her glory, and her dismal halls the theatres of many dark and atrocious deeds. But I have wandered from my subject, infected, I suppose, by the romantic mania, and hasten to remark, that the letter in question was, in all likelihood, written by the Poet while still smarting under his castigation, and under mistaken apprehensions of impending disasters. I say mistaken apprehensions, because on grounds of this kind I am accused of giving Burns the lie (p.238). This I deny, but contend that he overrated in some degree the consequences as likely to result from the situation he found himself placed in, nor is it much to be wondered at, all things considered he, perhaps the most irritable of the 'genus irritable', hitherto totally unaccustomed to official censure, and his very inexperience tending to increase his alarm. Mr. Cunningham here asks a very unnecessary, I had almost said childish question. Whether I denied that the Collector was commissioned to enquire into Burns' political offences? and I give him the full benefit of the admission, by declaring that I would hardly think of denying a fact so well known, and so frequently discussed. By way of giving effect to the whole, he states a circumstance of Burns receiving an official letter with a large seal, of which I know nothing ; and only have to observe thereon, that if the Board of Excise corresponded in this way with Burns, it was a very singular and unique case, as in every other they have no correspondence whatever with that rank of officers, but through the medium of superior officials. Before concluding, I must admit, that Mr.C. in his first vol, (p.326,) notwithstanding all this, manifests a more kindly feeling towards me, by considering me 'incapable of misrepresentation', which, though savouring of inconsistency, I am bound to acknowledge; and, after what I have briefly stated now, and, formerly, I shall give neither myself nor him any further trouble ; and as my veracity is pretty well known to many of my fellow citizens here, among whom I have sojourned for nearly a quarter of a century, and whose good opinion I am still anxious to retain though now retired as a public functionary, I take my leave of him with the old saying, 'In mea virtute me involvo.'

I am, Sir, your obedient Servant,

A.Findlater,

Glasgow, January, 1835'

WILLIAM CORBET

The person to whom Robert Burns wrote more letters than any of his other correspondents, was Mrs. Frances Dunlop of Dunlop (1730-1815). Following the publication of the Kilmarnock Edition in 1786, she took a keen interest in the poet, and throughout their long correspondence she became self appointed maternal adviser, confidante, critic and censor. She was particularly keen to advance Burns's position in life, and from time to time offered him suggestions on possible future careers. At one stage she gave him advice on purchasing a career in the army, and later, she had the fanciful notion that he might become a professor of agriculture. More practical, however, was the influence she exerted on Burns's behalf, following his entry into the Excise. She enquired in a postscript to a letter 16th February, 1790, 'Do you know a Mr. Corbet of the excise ? Could he be any use to you in getting on ? Pray tell me' [1]

Burns lost no time in replying. Four months in the service, riding round fourteen circuits, in all weathers, had no doubt convinced him that there were more rewarding and less arduous posts in the Excise. He had begun to realise too that the farm of Ellisland was 'a ruinous bargain', and that his future livelihood lay with the Excise. His reply left no doubt as to his aspirations:

> 'You formerly wrote, if a Mr. Corbet in the Excise could be of use to me. If it is a Corbet, who is what we call one of our General Supervisors, of which we have just two in Scotland, he can do everything for me. Were he to interest himself properly for me, he could easily by Martinmas, 1791, transport me to Port Glasgow, Port Division, which would be the ultimatum of my present Excise hopes. He is William Corbet, and has his home, I believe, somewhere about Stirling.' *(CL 184)*

The Mr. Corbet to whom Mrs. Dunlop had referred, was indeed William Corbet, who then held the important position of General Supervisor of the Excise for Scotland. His rise in the service had been meteoric. He was an Expectant in 1772 when only sixteen years of age. Following a spell as a supernumerary at Glasgow, he was outdoor officer at Dumbarton and Bonhill from October 1774 to July 1776, when he returned to Glasgow. He was officiating Supervisor at Dumbarton from June, 1779 to June, 1780, again returning to Glasgow, where he was appointed Examiner on 21st, August, 1783. He was promoted Supervisor at Stirling on 24th June, 1784, and the following year he was entrusted with one of the prestigious posts of General Supervisor for Scotland. [2] In this capacity he was to prove a very good friend to Burns.

When Mrs. Dunlop wrote again one April, she disclosed her relationship with Corbet, 'I am glad to hear you say Corbet can do all you want as I once had an intimate connection with his wife, which by accident I hope just now to renew'[3] Three days later he received another letter from her, which seemed to dash all hopes of securing Corbet's interest. Obviously she had lost no time in contacting Mrs. Corbet, as the following passage from her letter shows 'I have this moment a letter from Mrs. Corbet, in which she tells me her husband is soon to be taken from his present line to be appointed to a Collector's office.'[4] Mrs. Dunlop's fears, however, proved momentary. While Corbet had indeed been named to succeed to the more remunerative position of Collector of Excise at Glasgow, it was not until 1797 that he took up the post, on the retiral of the previous incumbent.

On 28th July, 1790, Burns was transferred to the Dumfries Third or 'Tobacco' Division– a footwalk, which relieved him of the necessity of keeping a horse. It would not be unreasonable to assume that the transfer may have been partly due to Corbet's influence.

Apparently Mrs. Dunlop did not let up in her efforts to promote Burns's prospects. She wrote to him on 5th August, enclosing a letter she had received from Corbet. It was not until October that Burns returned the letter with the comment, 'I enclose you Mr. Corbet's letter. I have not seen him but from the gentleman's known character for steady worth, there is every reason to depend on his promised friendship.' *(CL 191)* While the content of Corbet's letter is not known, it seems fairly obvious that he had promised to look with favour on Burns's promotion to a Port Division.

About this time, Burns wrote direct to Corbet in response to an invitation conveyed through his Supervisor, Alexander Findlater. The copy of the letter is taken from Burns's transcript in the Glenriddell MS and dated by him as 1792, but it has been conjecturally dated October, 1790, which places it in a more chronological sequence. Burns wrote:

> 'Mr. Findlater tells me that you wish to know from myself, what are my views in desiring to change my Excise Division -- with the wish natural to man, of bettering his present situation, I have turned my thoughts towards the practicability of getting into a Port Division – as I know the General Supervisors are omnipotent in these matters, my honoured friend, Mrs. Dunlop of Dunlop, offered me to interest you on my behalf.' *(CL 598)*

While Corbet may have promised to consider Burns favourably, apparently he was not prepared to accept him solely on a friend's recommendation. Sometime in November he had a meeting with Findlater at Stirling, when Burns's future was evidently discussed. Five days before Christmas, Findlater sent a letter to Corbet in which he gave an assessment of Burns's character and ability[5] (see text of Findlater's letter on page 223). It was probably as a result of Corbet's meeting with Findlater, and the Supervisor's letter, that Burns was able to say to

Mrs. Dunlop, in a letter, written in November, 1790, 'I heard of Mr. Corbet lately. He, in consequence of your recommendation, is most anxious to serve me.' (CL 192)

On 27th January, 1791, Burns was placed on the list of officers recommended for promotion to Examiner and Supervisor. It is almost certain that Corbet was responsible, following the excellent reference he had received from Findlater. Appointment was then by seniority, and it is sad to reflect that when Burns died on 21st July, 1796, he was but one year away from being promoted Supervisor at Dunblane. The officer immediately below him on the list, got the appointment on 1st August, 1797. [6]

Corbet's name does not appear anywhere in the Burns / Dunlop correspondence until 3rd February, 1792, when Burns wrote:

> '... as to Mr. Corbet, I have some faint hopes of seeing him here this season; if he come it will be of essential service to me, --- Not that I have any immediate hopes of a Supervisorship; but there is what is called, a Port Division, here, and entre nous, the present incumbent is so obnoxious, that Mr. Corbet's presence will in all probability send him adrift into some other Division, and with equal probability will fix me in his stead.' (CL 197)

Towards the end of the same month Burns wrote to Maria Riddell, informing her that he had 'just got an appointment to the first or Port Division, as it is called, which adds twenty pounds per annum more to my salary.' (CL 661) Evidently Corbet had visited Dumfries and, as predicted by Burns, sent the previous holder of the Port Division 'adrift', and appointed the poet in his stead. Further corroboration of Corbet's part in the promotion seems evident from a letter which Burns sent him in September. Apparently Corbet had written to Burns and the following is an extract of the poet's reply:

> 'Never did my poor back suffer such scarification from the scourge of conscience, as during these three weeks that your kind epistle has lain by me unanswered ... At last by way of compromise, I return you by this my most grateful thanks for all the generous friendship and disinterested patronage, for which, now and formerly, I have had the honour to be indebted to you; and as to Rhymes, another edition, in two Volumes, of my Poems being in the Press, I shall beg leave to present a copy to Mrs. Corbet, as my first, and I will venture to add, effectual mediator with you on my behalf'.

The period following the French Revolution was one of fear and mistrust, with spies everywhere, reporting even private conversations. The government, fearful of a similar uprising in Britain regarded all sympathisers with the French struggle for liberty as conspirators, whose aim was to destroy law and order and inaugurate a reign of terror. Burns became suspect because of his radical opinions, freely expressed both publicly and privately.

Although his radicalism went no further, perhaps, than parliamentary reform in the highly charged atmosphere of the time, it is not surprising that someone, who had possibly felt the lash of his scorn, denounced him as a disloyal servant of the Crown.

The threat of an investigation threw Burns into a panic and immediately he sent off a letter to Robert Graham of Fintry *(CL 435)*, one of the Commissioners of the Scottish Board of Excise, whom Burns had first met at Blair Castle, during his tour of the Highlands in the autumn of 1787. Graham replied with a kind letter, in which he tried to calm Burns's fears and also outlined the various charges that had been levelled against him. This was followed by a long letter from the poet, answering the specific charges. One passage is significant:

Maria Riddell.
Portrait by Sir Thomas Lawrence.

> 'As to REFORM PRINCIPLES, I look upon the British Constitution, as settled at the Revolution, to be the most glorious Constitution on earth, or that perhaps the wit of man can frame; at the same time, I think, and you know, what High and distinguished characters have for some thought so, that we have a good deal deviated from the original principles of the Constitution, particularly, that an alarming System of corruption has pervaded the connection between the Executive Power and the House of Commons.' *(CL 437)*

Graham laid the letter before his fellow Commissioners and, although the above passage was no more than the truth, they, no doubt, realising that they were dealing with a celebrity and not an ordinary common gauger, instructed Corbet to conduct an on the spot investigation.

It appears that the investigation was conducted over a dinner table in company with Alexander Findlater and John Syme, Distributor of Stamps in Dumfries, and a close friend of the poet. In that pleasant atmosphere Corbet could find no grounds for the charges, 'save some witty sayings.' [7] Burns, however, in a letter to the Earl of Mar revealed that:

'Corbet was instructed to document me --- 'that my business was to act; not to think; and whatever might be Men or Measures, it was for me to be silent and obedient' Mr. Corbet was likewise my steady friend; so between Mr. Graham and him I have been partly forgiven.' *(CL 690)*

An article on William Corbet by Professor J. De Lancey Ferguson in the 1931 issue of the *Burns Chronicle*, contains a number of inaccuracies. He suggested that the Colonel Corbet, who took part in the Battle of Jersey in 1781, was Collector Corbet who befriended Burns. He quoted as his source of information, the diary of Joseph Farington, RA, who recorded that he had dined with Corbet's brother in Glasgow and picked up the following bit of information: 'Coll Corbet ... was the Officer who succeeded to the command of the troops engaged in the Island of Jersey after Major Pearson was killed'.

The error was corrected by James C. Ewing in the *Burns Chronicle* of 1937, who proved conclusively that 'Coll' was an abbreviation for 'Colonel' and referred to Colonel James Corbet, who, at the time of the conflict in Jersey, was Captain of the 95th Regiment. In 1795 he became Lieutenant Colonel of the First Regiment of the Royal Glasgow Volunteers, and the same year, led his men in the bloodless Battle of Garscube. He was seventh laird of Tollcross and elder brother of Cunninghame Corbet, a Glasgow 'Tobacco Lord'. An Excise Ages and Capacities Register for 1792, often referred to as the 'Character Book', contains the following entry: 'Wm. Corbet, General Supervisor; an Active good officer; age 37; employed 21 years; No. of family, 10'. This entry, alone, is sufficient to disprove any suggestion that he was the officer who took part in the Battle of Jersey.

In the same article De Lancey Ferguson stated:

> 'Some confusion has resulted from the fact that another man of the same name had an Excise appointment in the West of Scotland. This William Corbet, then Supervisor of Excise at Dumbarton, on 26th February 1780, took part in a drunken raid on the lodgerooms of Dumbarton Kilwinning Masonic Lodge No 18; and probably it was this same Corbet whose death is recorded (in contemporary newspapers) as having occurred at Irvine on 29th September 1793.'

It is clearly evident from the record of service, already detailed above, that William Corbet who is the subject of this article, was acting Supervisor at Dumbarton from June 1779 until June 1780, and it was he who took part in the ' drunken raid' on the local Masonic Lodge. The service record of the other William Corbet, who died at Irvine, shows that he was never at any time stationed at Dumbarton. [8]

From a minute of Dumbarton Kilwinning Lodge No 18, we learn that the raid occurred on 23rd February, 1780, and not 26th February, as stated by De Lancey Ferguson. As the minute is the only evidence available, it is printed here in full:

> 'At Dumbarton, the Twenty sixth day of February, 1780. Convened the Depute Master and a competent number of Brethren; It having been reported to the Lodge, that upon the 23rd inst., William Corbet, acting Supervisor of Excise in Dumbarton, attending with some other officers of Excise, had, in searching the house of Thomas Phillips, attacked the Door of the Lodge and by force and threats against the said Thomas Phillip's serving maid, actually gained possession thereof, and after ransacking the different presses therein, had broke open or other ways with false keys, procured access to the private closet where the Box containing the records and other papers belonging to the Lodge lay; which Closet they also ransacked and went away leaving the same open and exposed to the public: The Lodge, considering this unprecedented conduct on the part of the said William Corbet and his accomplices, are of the opinion that the same ought to be checked in future and for that purpose they unanimously Agree and Resolve to prosecute him before the Sheriff of Dunbartonshire and authorise the Secretary to present a Complaint against him in the name of the Depute Master and Wardens for the Masters as representing the whole Brethren. Concluding against the said William Corbet for such punishment as he shall think the said offend merits.
>
> William Hunter DM'

In those days it seems to have been the practice of Lodge 18 to rent a room in the house of one of its members. According to Donald MacLeod in his *History of the Castle and Town of Dumbarton*, the Lodge had moved from house to house in search of suitable accommodation, and had finally rented the upper storey of the property belonging to Thomas Phillips in the Cross Vennel. Phillips must have been suspected of some evasion of Excise Duty, which obviously warranted a search being made of his premises. Whatever Corbet and his officers were looking for, a locked door would certainly arouse their suspicion that something was being concealed inside Under these circumstances it is not surprising that they forced an entry. That Corbet's action was justified is strengthened by the fact no censure appears against him in official Excise records in connection with this affair.

Where De Lancey Ferguson got the information that it was 'drunken raid' is a mystery, as the minute makes no mention of any of the Excisemen bring under the influence of drink. Had this been the case it is almost certain that it would have been mentioned, as the mood of the members was obviously one of indignation and outrage at the violation of their lodgeroom. The decision to proceed with a court action against Corbet also indicates how intense was their anger. It would appear that the action was never raised, as no mention is made of

Deacon Brodie.
Portrait by Kay.

the incident in subsequent minutes, which seems to suggest that Corbet had acted within his powers and no case could be found against him.

In 1788, when Corbet was General Supervisor, he was named at the trial of the notorious Deacon Brodie. Some sources describe him as a 'friend' of Brodie, while others speak of him as a 'connection'.[9] That they were on friendly terms is certainly beyond dispute. William Brodie was a prototype of Dr. Jekyll and Mr. Hyde. By day he was a respectable cabinet maker, Deacon of the Incorporation of Wrights and much respected member of Edinburgh Town Council. By night he was a case hardened burglar, incurable gambler and frequenter of the city's low haunts. In his capacity as tradesman, he was often employed by his fellow citizens to carry out repair work on their shops and houses, which enabled him to acquire a detailed knowledge of the interior of each one. It also gave him an opportunity to take wax impressions of the keys of the premises, which usually hung on a hook behind the front door. With duplicate keys it was easy for Brodie and his accomplices to carry out a number of thefts from lockfast premises within the city. These crimes had baffled all attempts by the authorities to solve them, due to the absence of clues and with no apparent explanation as to how the thieves had gained entry.

Emboldened by these successes, Brodie decided upon a robbery on the grand scale. The plan was to break into the Scottish Excise Office, then located in Chessel's Court, off the Canongate. To help him carry out this audacious raid he used his friendship with Corbet to gain access to the Excise Office. Evidence brought forward at Brodie's trial revealed that Corbet, who had his headquarters at Stirling, made a journey once or twice a week to Edinburgh for the purpose of depositing or drawing money at the Excise Office. Brodie made a point of meeting Corbet and accompanying him into the office, which gave the Deacon an opportunity to study the layout of the premises. Brodie also paid several visits on the pretext of enquiring for Corbet, and on one of those visits he managed to take an impression of the key of the outer door, which was hanging on a nail nearby.[10] It is well known how the robbery went badly wrong; how Brodie was caught, found guilty and publicly hanged. There is no doubt that Corbet

The Old Excise Office, Chessel's Court, Canongate, Edinburgh.
Built in 1748 as mansion flats, it later became an hotel,
before being taken over by the Scottish Excise.

was completely innocent and unaware of Brodie's sinister intent. Like everyone else in Edinburgh he was taken in by the 'respectable' Deacon.

William Corbet was born on 15th December, 1755, probably in Glasgow. An extract from the Old Parish Register of Bonhill, Dunbartonshire for the year 1775, reads:

> 'July 22nd
> Mr. William Corbet, officer of the Excise, and Miss Jean McAdam, both in this parish, came this day and intimated their purpose of marriage desiring the same might be regularly proclaimed in the Kirk of Bonhill three times next Sabath (sic) day, which was done, were married at Glasgow.'

There were ten children of the marriage. Corbet was appointed Collector at Glasgow in July, 1797, and held that post until his death at Meadowside, Partick, on 16th September, 1811. He was buried in Ramshorn Churchyard. During his service in Glasgow he resided at 14 Miller Street, next door to the Excise office, which in 1811 was No. 13. He was a member of the Board of Green Cloth, one of the most exclusive of the many convivial clubs which flourished in Glasgow at that time.

Obviously Corbet was an officer who was highly regarded by the Board, and it is therefore surprising to learn that he was suspended from duty for virtually four months in 1795. [11] The reason for the suspension is not known, but his name must have been cleared, otherwise he would not have been appointed Collector at Glasgow in 1797. An extraordinary feature of his service is that he received his first appointment at the age of 16, was acting Supervisor at Dumbarton at age 24 ; promoted Supervisor at Stirling at age 29; became General Supervisor for Scotland at age 30, and at age 42 was probably one of the youngest officers ever to be appointed Collector at Glasgow. [11]

He is best remembered, however, as the 'warm and worthy friend' of Robert Burns; the man who gave the poet a helping hand to promotion, and remained his 'steady friend' following the investigation into his political conduct in 1792.

Chessel's Court, today.
Tho Old Excise Office has been restored to its original use as a dwelling house.

JAMES GRAY

In November 1791, Robert Burns and his family moved from Ellisland Farm to a first floor flat at the foot of the Stinking Vennel in Dumfries. Young Robert was then five years of age, and showing early promise of becoming an excellent scholar. Burns had done his best to teach him at home, but the move into town had made it possible for the boy to receive a formal education. Dumfries at that time was well endowed with schools. Three had been established for the teaching of English, one for arithmetic, book keeping and mathematics, and one for writing. The Grammar School which was *the* school in the town, taught Latin and mathematics and had a roll of about one hundred pupils. The Latin master was, *ipso facto*, rector and had a salary of £20 per annum. He also had a dwelling assigned to him, a privilege which no other master enjoyed. In addition to his salary he received a fee of five shillings per quarter from children of those other than Burgesses, whose children were taught free of charge. He also received 'an offering' from all pupils at Candlemas each year.[1]

It is not known which school young Robert first attended. Burns mentions him in a letter to Mrs. Dunlop, dated September, 1792, as ' indeed the mildest, gentlest creature I ever saw. He has the most surprising memory and is quite the pride of his schoolmaster' (CL 200), It would appear, however, that Burns was anxious for Robert and his younger brothers to attend Dumfries Grammar School. In March, 1793, we find him petitioning the Provost, Bailies and Town Council:

> 'The literary taste and liberal spirit of your good town has so ably filled the various departments of your schools, as to make it a very great object for a Parent to have his children educated in them. – Still, to me a Stranger, with my large family and very stinted income, to give my young ones that education I wish, at the High School fees which a Stranger pays, will bear hard upon me. Some years ago your Town did me the honour of making me an Honorary Burgess. Will your Honours allow me to request that this mark of distinction may extend so far, as to put me on a footing of a real Freeman of the Town, in the Schools.' *(CL 553)*

His request for free schooling was readily granted, and sometime in 1793, young Robert took his place as a pupil of the Grammar School, which stood on the Greensands, adjacent to Buccleuch Street. It was demolished about 1804 to make way for a new Bridge over the Nith.[2] The granting of this concession to Burns seems to suggest that he still enjoyed the respect of his fellow citizens, and that his social standing in the town had not been affected by the accusation of political heresy, made four months previously.

House where Burns lived, Bank Street, Dumfries.

Burns's first house in Dumfries
– a first floor flat in the Stinking Vennel.(now Bank Street).

On 13th May, 1794, a notice appeared in the *Dumfries Weekly Journal* that 'this day Mr. James Gray was admitted Rector of the Grammar School of Dumfries, in the room of Mr. James Wait, who has resigned.'

James Gray was very much the Scottish 'lad o' pairts.' He was born at Duns Berwickshire in 1770. His father was a shoemaker and an elder in the local Antiburgher Church. Young James became an apprentice to his father, but had an obvious bent for learning and a desire to improve his position in life. Before entering the trade of shoemaker he had acquired a knowledge of the classics under the parochial schoolmaster, William Cruickshank, whose nephew of the same name, was Latin master of the High School in Edinburgh, and a close friend of Burns. Young James was keen to acquire a liberal education and spent his leisure time in study. Even when he was twenty years of age, he was to be found each day during his dinner hour, attending the local grammar school, which was then under its efficient teacher, Mr. James White. A Mr. James Cleghorn, who was a pupil in the school at the time, has left this early description of Gray :

> 'Among the earlier things I can remember was the appearance of James Gray in the school, with a leather apron rolled up round his waist. He came in amidst all our staring and took a seat by himself, not belonging to any class, turned up his books, and in a few moments after was upon the floor repeating some Latin

authors to our master, which he did always easily and without interruption, and I therefore suppose quite well. Indeed it was the opinion of us all that he was a better scholar than White himself. When the task was over he left the school, and returned at the same hour to perform the same part the day following.'

About 1790 he gave up the trade of shoemaker to become usher assistant to Mr. White.[3] It must have been a courageous step to take, as the job was poorly paid, and this seems to indicate that he was determined to pursue an academic career. His decision was justified in 1794 when he was appointed rector of Dumfries Grammar School. The fact that he was then only twenty four years of age, suggests that his reputation as a teacher had extended beyond the little town of Duns.

Gray's appointment brought young Robert Burns under his charge and led to a friendship with the poet. Over the two years remaining until Burns's death in 1796, they met regularly, and it is not surprising that his literary tastes recommended him to the poet. They also rubbed shoulders in the Royal Dumfries Volunteers, formed in 1795 as a defence against a possible French invasion. Gray proved a loyal friend, and after Burns's death, he defended the character and reputation of the poet against the calumnies in the works of the early biographers.

He was not long in the post of Rector when young Robert's ability came to his notice. Writing to Gilbert Burns many years later, he said:

> 'The boy attended the grammar school of Dumfries and soon attracted my notice by the strength of his talent and the ardour of his ambition. Before he had been a year at school, I thought it right to advance him a form, and he began to read Caesar, and gave me translations of that author of such beauty as I confessed surprised me. On enquiry I found that his father made him turn over his dictionary till he was able to translate to him the passages in such a way as he could gather the author's meaning, and it was to him that he owed that polished and forcible English with which I was so greatly struck.'

As Rector, Gray was able to observe and appreciate the help and direction Burns gave to his children in their studies. In the same letter to Gilbert Burns, he continues:

> 'He was a kind and attentive father, and took great delight in spending his evenings in the cultivation of the minds of his children, Their education was the grand object of his life, and he did not, like most parents, think it sufficient to send them to public schools. He was their private instructor and, even at that early age, bestowed great pains in training their minds in habits of thought and reflection, and in keeping them pure from every form of vice. This he considered as a sacred duty, and never, to the

period of his last illness, relaxed in his diligence. With his eldest son, a boy of not more than nine years of age, he had read many of the favourite poets, and some of the best historians in our language, and what is more remarkable, gave him considerable aid in the study of Latin.' [4]

Gray served with much success at Dumfries Grammar School until 2nd September 1801, when he was appointed one of the masters of the Royal High School of Edinburgh. The school had an acknowledged reputation for learning, although it was also notorious for its severity and harshness. Lord Cockburn, who commenced as a pupil in 1787, recalls in *Memorials of His Time*, that 'out of the whole four years of my attendance, there was probably not ten days in which I was not flogged at least once.' Flogging was considered an indispensable concomitant to learning in those days.

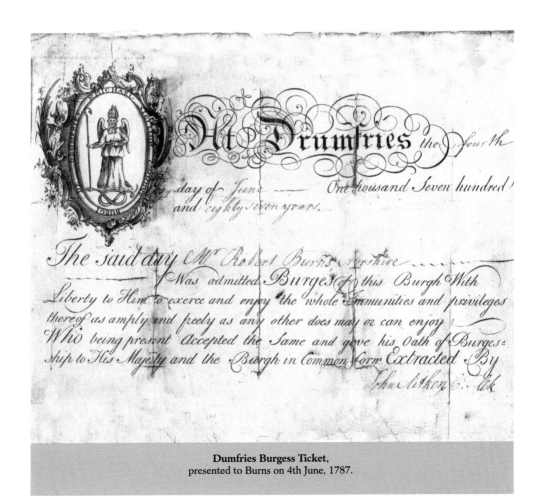

Dumfries Burgess Ticket,
presented to Burns on 4th June, 1787.

248

Benjamin Mackay, who at a later period became one of the classic masters, visited the High School in 1803, and left an account of his visit. Of James Gray he wrote:

> 'He then had a large class, which appeared in admirable order. When we entered he was standing on the floor with his back to us, teaching with extraordinary energy and enthusiasm, his questions being put with great rapidity, force, and precision, and answered in the same style. The pupils had evidently imbibed much of the spirit and manner of their master. He seemed anxious not only to make his pupils good scholars, but to fill their minds with great ideas. He was an exceedingly warm hearted, benevolent, and enthusiastic man. Though not robust, he had a wiry active frame, jet black hair, and keen black eyes. There was something like the inspiration of genius in everything he said and did.' [5]

One of Gray's pupils recalled his impressions of his schoolmaster:

> '.... he was a curious compound, and if I was noting down my impression of him I could not fail to mark the sense of his high toned and chivalrous honour, his abhorrence of what was base and mean, his kind-heartedness (so often conjoined with irascibility) and his power of attaching his pupils to him.' [6]

We are grateful for those pen pictures, which give us an insight to Gray's appearance, character and ability as a schoolmaster. His apparent irascibility seems to have been more than compensated by his other virtues, and perhaps the most significant testimony is the esteem in which he was held by his pupils.

During his residence in Edinburgh his home became a rendezvous for the literati, among whom was James Hogg, the Ettrick Shepherd. Gray is credited with giving Hogg generous support in his early struggles to establish him as a man of letters. When Hogg came to write 'The Queen's Wake', Gray was included. The poem is written in the style of the old Scottish ballads, and consists mainly of a series of metrical tales. Seventeen bards of Scotland, are represented as contending for prizes before Mary Queen of Scots and her court at Holyrood. Gray is introduced as the fifteenth bard:

> The next was bred on southern shore,
> Beneath the mists of Lammermoor,
> And long, by Nith and crystal Tweed,
> Has taught the Border youth to read.
> The strains of Greece, the bard of Troy,
> Were all his theme and all his joy,
> Well toned his voice of wars to sing.,
> Its hair was dark as raven's wing;

> The eye, an intellectual lance;
> No heart could bear its searching glance;
> But every bard to him was dear;
> His heart was kind, His soul sincere. [7]

When Hogg founded and edited the literary weekly journal, called *The Spy,* Gray and his wife gave him their support. In his memoir Hogg wrote, 'I began it without asking, or knowing of any assistance, but when Mr. and Mrs. Gray saw it was on foot, they interested themselves in it with all their power, and wrote a number of essays for it.' The journal lasted for just one year. It is interesting to note that the stirring Border song, 'Lock the Door Lariston' first appeared in *The Spy,* found its way into the London papers, Gray being credited as the author. The error was later corrected by Hogg, who, of course is the author.

Both belonged to a group of very capable young men, which included John Gibson Lockhart and John Wilson ('Christopher North'). All were regular contributors to *Blackwood's Magazine,* and together they concocted the anonymously published, *Translations from an Ancient Chaldee Manuscript,* which, in effect, was a vicious attack, in biblical language, on the *Edinburgh Review* and the Whig establishment.[8]

It was almost inevitable that Gray should become acquainted with 'Clarinda' (Mrs. Agnes McLehose) during his stay in the Capital. Although she and Burns parted for the last time in December, 1791, we know from her journal, that for the remainder of her long life, she cherished fondest memories of the poet. No doubt she would be eager to meet and talk

New Dumfries Academy,
built at the beginning of the nineteenth century.

with someone who had been closely associated with Burns during the last years of his life in Dumfries. There are several references in her journal of her great desire to meet Burns in Heaven. The hope of eternal bliss found expression in the last verse of a poem which she sent to James Gray, in response to his request for a copy of 'Lines on a Linnet':

> 'Philosophers deem Life's joys all a dream: But I ne'er heard its woes were eternal, Bliss eternal above, we all hope to prove; Leave the others to regions infernal.' [9]

Gray's most important role in the Burns story, however, is undoubtedly the letter which he wrote for Alexander Peterkin in defence of Burns's character. It was included in a *Review of the Life of Robert Burns, and Various Criticisms on his Character and Writing*, written by Peterkin and published in 1815. Also included was a testimony by Alexander Findlater, Supervisor of Excise in Dumfries. (see page 226) Both men had been closely associated with Burns during his latter days in Dumfries. It is to their eternal credit that they were the first to challenge the legend, started by Heron, Currie and early reviewers, that Burns drank himself into an early grave.

In the opening paragraph of his letter, Gray deplores the fact that the critics who had denigrated Burns, had done so purely on second hand reports:

> 'The truth is that not one of the periodical writers who have thought fit to pronounce judgement in so decisive a tone, on the moral conduct of the Poet, had the means of forming a fair estimate of his character. They had heard certain reports injurious to his reputation, and they received them without examination as established facts. It is besides to be lamented, that the most respectable of his biographers (Dr. Currie) has in some cases suffered himself to be misled by the slanderous tales of malice or party spirit.'

After paying tribute to Dr. Currie for the generous service which he rendered to Burns's widow, Jean, and the family, (approximately £1200 was raised for their benefit from the publication of the works) Gray makes his purpose clear:

> 'I love Dr. Currie, but I love the fame of Burns more; and no authority, how respectable so ever, shall deter me from a bold declaration from the truth. The poet of the Cotter's Saturday Night, who felt all the charms of the humble piety and virtue, which he had so delightfully sung, is here charged with vices which would reduce him to a level with the most degraded of his species. "He is a habitual drunkard he spends his time in society of the lowest kind he is the sport of uncontrolled passions he is polluted by contamination, over which delicacy and humanity draw a veil". On each of these charges I shall hazard a few remarks and as I knew him during that period of his life,

emphatically denominated his evil days, *I am enabled to from my awn observation*. It is not my intention to extenuate his errors, because they were combined with his genius; on that account they are only the more dangerous, because the more seductive, and deserve the more severe reprehension; but I shall likewise claim, that nothing may be set down in malice against him.'

Gray also pointed out, in the following paragraph, that if Burns had been continually besotted with drink, as some of his critics had stated, he could not have produced the large number of song lyrics during the closing years of his life; nor could he have supervised the education of his children as has already been noted.

'Not many days passed during his stay in Dumfries, in which he did not compose some piece of poetry or some song, destined to delight the imagination and soften the heart for ages to come. It was during the last years of his life that he erected the most lasting monument of his genius, by composing those numberless lyrical effusions that enrich Mr. Thomson's collection; which for simplicity, pathos, truth to nature, and a fine adaptation to the heart stirring melodies of our native land, are unrivalled in any language. It came under my own view professionally, that he superintended the education of his children with a degree of care that I have never seen surpassed by any parent in any rank of life whatever. In the bosom of his family, he spent many a delightful hour in directing the studies of his eldest son, a boy of uncommon talents. I have frequently found him explaining to this youth, then not more than nine years of age, the English poets, from Shakespeare to Gray, or storing his mind with examples of heroic virtue, as they have in the pages of our most celebrated historians. I would ask any person of common candour if employments like these are consistent with habitual drunkenness?'

In 1816, publishers Cadell and Davies wished to publish a new and improved eighth edition of Currie's work, and invited Gilbert Burns to edit it. He was expected to furnish a considerable amount of new biographical material and also some hitherto unpublished poems and letters. Gilbert accepted the assignment and named his fee at £500 -- £250 for the eighth edition, and another £250 if sales should warrant a second printing. It is reported that the figure of £500 was fixed on the instigation of James Gray, as Gilbert confessed that the terms were such that 'he could scarcely muster impudence enough to name' [10] while Cadell and Davies agreed to the figure, they considered Gilbert's terms as 'certainly a good deal higher than we calculated.' [11]

Gilbert soon found himself in an unenviable position. He knew that he had little that was new or important to add to the canon, and although he was anxious to clear his brother's name, he was warned by Cadell and Davies that he must not do anything which would discredit Dr. Currie's portrait of the poet. In his dilemma he approached William Wordsworth, through James Gray, for his advice as to how he should deal with Currie's Life.

Wordsworth issued a pamphlet in the form of a *Letter to a Friend of Robert Burns* (Gray), in which he conveyed to Gilbert his 'actions upon the best mode of conducting a defence of his injured brother's reputation.'

In a letter which Gilbert wrote to George Thomson on 25th June, 1816, he said, 'I am very much pleased with Mr. Wordsworth's letter to Mr. Gray . . . I do not doubt that what Mr. Wordsworth proposes in regard to the publication of my brother's work might have a good effect, but it would require so much arrangement and so much writing on my part as I think I cannot go through with it,' Gilbert chose to let the *Life of the Poet* by Dr. Currie reappear without alteration, but attempted a brief appendix to correct some of the misrepresentations contained in it. The appendix was duly submitted to the late Dr. Currie's friend, William Roscoe, who appears to have been the literary arbiter, and following upon Roscoe's reply, the appendix was altered by timid Gilbert,' so as to make as little allusion to Dr. Currie's work as a sense of my duty to my brother's memory will allow.' [12]

Gilbert's sense of duty to his brother's memory at least allowed him to include in his appendix letters from Alexander Findlater and James Gray. Their testimonies in Peterkin's edition had convinced him that Dr. Currie had done injustice to the port's memory. Gray recast his original letter for Gilbert; two passages of which have already been quoted. It is interesting to note that he reiterated his determination to do everything in his power to restore Burns's maligned reputation. The following passage is worth quoting:

> 'What I have written is from my own observations, and whether my efforts shall be successful or not in clearing away the moral darkness with which his reputation has been obscured, I shall at least have the consolation that I have done my utmost to restore to him that good name of which he has been so cruelly, and in my opinion, so unjustly robbed. For twenty years I have heard calumny added to calumny, and in a number of periodical works, some of them of great authority. I have seen pictures drawn, in which I should never have recognised Robert Burns. I have conversed on the subject with many of his most intimate friends, and am happy to say that their opinions coincide with mine. I have been necessarily led to censure one or two passages in Dr. Currie's valuable and ingenious work, as I consider them the source and authority of the numerous anonymous slanders and misrepresentations that have since appeared.' [13]

Bearing in mind that the above passage was written by one who knew Burns intimately, it is, perhaps, the most damning indictment of the baleful influence of Currie.

In 1820, James Pillans, Rector. of the High School, was appointed to the Chair of Humanity in the University of Edinburgh, and James Gray, who was then senior master, became a candidate for the vacancy. He was passed over, however, in favour of a Mr. Carson, one of his colleagues, and seems to have expressed keen disappointment at the decision. By way of compensation he was appointed sole teacher of Greek, but this arrangement did not work out so well as anticipated, probably due to the opposition of the other masters, and after a year's trial was rescinded. The school reverted to its former practice, whereby each master was allowed to teach Greek, and Gray was granted an annuity of £100 per annum in lieu of the privilege. [14]

Edinburgh Town Council were the patrons of the High School and it may well be that Gray was rejected because he had incurred the wrath of some of the Whig councillors by his anti-Whig views, expressed with such partisan fervour in the *Chaldee Manuscripts* its attack on the *Edinburgh Review* and the Whig establishment shocked and outraged literate Edinburgh, and Gray may have made some enemies in the process.

Whatever the reason for him not being appointed Rector, it would appear that in the period following, Gray was unhappy and unsettled, and in December, 1822, he secured the appointment of Principal of Belfast Academy. Apparently the post did not fulfil his expectations as he remained in it for just one year. [15] Although he had been brought up among Presbyterian dissenters, it is reported that at an early period in his life, he had considered qualifying as a minister of the Church of Scotland. His earlier inclination to enter the church, was again given serious consideration, and on 21st December, 1823, he was ordained into the Irish Episcopal Church by the Bishop of Down and Connor, Within three years he left Ireland to become a chaplain in the service of the East India Company, stationed at Bhuj in Kutch, on the north west coast of India.

His manner of living in India was in complete contrast to the busy life he had led in Edinburgh. In a letter to an Edinburgh friend he wrote:

> 'My life is as retired and uniform as possible. The greatest part of my day is spent in absolute solitude. Never was there such a contrast in two periods of the history of any individual as in my present and my Edinburgh life. I who lived so many years in the whirlwind of human beings, now see few people but my own native servants gliding into my apartments with noiseless steps.'

Over and above his duties as a military chaplain, Gray studied Hindustani and Kutchee in order to converse with the natives. The Kutchee language was said to be a dialect of the Sanscrit, with a mixture of Sindy and Guzerattee. Because it was oral and not a written language, many regarded it as a patois. Gray, however, set himself the difficult task of compiling a vocabulary and grammar. When he achieved this he began a translation of the four gospels into written Kutchee. In addition, he voluntarily undertook the education of the young King of Kutch, which hitherto had been entirely neglected. [16]

It was while engaged in translating the gospels into Kutchee, that James Gray died on 25th September, 1830. Many tributes were paid to him. The Governor of Bombay declared that his death was a 'public loss', and was also quoted as saying 'he was ashamed to think that none of the chaplains, from ignorance of the native language, could occupy his place, and that his zeal in the cultivation of the native literature was most exemplary.' The young King of Kutch spoke with great respect and affection of his former tutor, and erected a handsome monument to his memory in Bhuj. [17]

Gray was an accomplished classicist in an age which placed great emphasis on the teaching of Latin and Greek. He was also a poet of no mean merit and in 1823 he published *Sabbath among the Mountains*, which ran to three editions. [18] It originated from a visit to the Rev. Robert Story at Rosneath in Dunbartonshire, where he met the Rev. Dr. Thomas Chalmers, who was to lead the seceding ministers out of the General Assembly of the Church of Scotland at the Disruption in 1843, In the poem he describes with much feeling and power, 'The happy recollection of a day of rest spent in their society, with all its lovely accompaniments of mountain scenery, rustic worship, and the habits of peasants, whose lot has been so remotely cast from a tumultuous world,' The poem contains the following lines on the Rev. Robert Story:

> The pastor of the people was beloved
> In cottage and in hall, where'er he moved.
> The aged loved him as a favourite son,
> The young a brother, all a faithful one.
> Of manners simple and devoid of guile,
> Even infants brightened to his kindly smile;
> Of active fancy, and of judgement clear,
> Of life unspotted, and of truth sincere. [19]

James Gray was twice married. His first wife, whom he married about 1795, was Mary Phillips, eldest daughter of Peter Phillips, farmer at Longbridgemoor, Annandale. There were five sons and three daughters of the marriage. Most of the family appear to have accompanied their father to India, as two of his sons entered the service of the East India Company and one became a surgeon in India. Of his daughters, two married men serving in the East India Company. It is interesting to note that Mary Phillips's youngest sister, Margaret, married James Hogg, the Ettrick Shepherd, in 1820. [20] Mary Gray died in 1806, shortly after the birth of her last child. Gray remarried in 1809, his second wife being Mary Peacock, intimate friend of Clarinda. It was probably through Clarinda that they met. A friend in India said that she had 'an amicable disposition, and well informed mind, well calculated to be an ornament in any society she moved in, but in India, where talents and pleasing manners are not always to be found, she was invaluable.' There were no children of the second marriage. Mary died in India sometime before her husband. [21]

No portrait is available of James Gray, although a drawing of him was done during his lifetime. When Robert Cromek, author of *Reliques of Robert Burns*, undertook a second tour of Scotland in 1809, he was accompanied by the artist, Thomas Stothard, R.A. In a letter which he sent to his wife in August, 1809, he said, 'We have now the portraits of Mrs. Burns (the mother), Gilbert Burns, Lord Woodhouselee, Mrs. Burnett, Mr. Gray of the Hgh School, John Murdoch, Robert Burns junior and Niel Gow, the celebrated fiddler.' Cromek also mentioned a number of scenes drawn by Stothard. The tour was financed by Cadell and Davies with the object of publishing an illustrated edition of Burns. Following Cromek's death in 1812, however, the plan seems to have been abandoned. The only practical result of the tour was the publication in 1814 of twelve scenes, engraved by Cromek from Stothard's drawings. The rest of the portfolio was never published.

We know from an unpublished manuscript of the life of Robert Cromek, written by his son, Thomas H. Cromek in 1864, that the drawings were in the possession of Cromek's sister, Ann, who refused to hand them over to her nephew, despite repeated requests. The collection was offered for sale at Christie's in 1845 and the drawings dispersed. The portraits of James Gray and John Murdoch were sold to a purchaser called Hogarth. Their present whereabouts is unknown, if indeed they are still extant. [22] It is a great pity that the original project was not fulfilled. The portraits of Burns's mother, Gilbert Burns, Robert Burns junior, then a young man of twenty four, John Murdoch, and of course, James Gray, would have been an invaluable addition to Burnsiana.

The whole of James Gray's life was devoted to the service of others, first as schoolmaster and latterly as military chaplain. His removal to Ireland and ultimately to India, must have occasioned genuine regret among his many friends in Edinburgh. In India he became something of a Christian Missionary. He was not content just to carry out his duties as chaplain, but undertook the translation of 'the barbarous languages of India,' as an aid to improving the lot of the natives and educating the young King of Kutch. Everything he did in life seems to have been imbued with a sense of high moral purpose. Scholarly by nature and an accomplished linguist, he was also blessed like Robert Burns, with compassion for his fellow man. His defence of Burns was one of the first blows struck in the struggle to free the poet from the gross misrepresentations of Currie, Heron and others, a struggle that still continues even today.

NOTES ON SOURCES

John Murdoch

1   Essay by John Strawhorn in *Burns Now*, ed. Kenneth Simpson, 1994.
    p 29 (n13) Strawhorn states that Burns's first schoolmaster's name was
    Adam Campbell and not William Campbell, as erroneously given elsewhere.

2   A.M. Boyle, *Ayrshire Book of Burns Lore*, 1988, p.101.

3   William Will, 'John Murdoch, Tutor of Robert Burns', *Burns Chronicle* 1929, p.61.

4   Dr. James Currie, *The Works of Robert Burns, 1800, 4 Vols.* Quotes letter
    from John Murdoch to Joseph Cooper Walker, Vol.1, pp. 89-98.

5   Ibid.

6   Ibid.

7   James Mackay, *Burns, a Biography of Robert Burns*, 1992, p.33

8   W. Scott Douglas. *The Works of Robert Burns*, 1891, 6 Vols., Vol IV, p.21
    and James Mackay, Ibid p. 34.

9   W. Scott Douglas, ibid, *Vol. IV, Appendix C*, p 357. Letter from
    Gilbert Burns to Mrs. Dunlop, usually referred to as Gilbert's Narrative.

10 Ibid.

11 Currie, op. cit., Murdoch's letter, p. 89.

12 Ibid, pp. 95-97.

13 Op. cit., Gilbert's Narrative, pp.356-357.

14 Currie, op. cit., Murdoch's letter, pp. 92-93.

15 Chambers/Wallace, *Life and Works of Robert Burns, 4 Vols.* 1896, Vol.1, p 34(n).

16 Op. cit., Gilbert's Narrative, p 359.

17 Will, op. cit., p 64.

18 Will. Ibid.

19 Chambers / Wallace, op. cit., Vol 1, p.34 (n).

20 Will, op. cit.,p 68.

David Sillar

1   Alan Cunningham, *The Works of Robert Burns with his Life, 1834,Vol. 1*, p 61.

2   David Lowe, *Burns's Passionate Pilgrimage, 1904*, p 27.

3   Currie, op cit, Vol. 1, p109.

4   *Poems of Robert Burns ed. Morrison, 1811 Vol. II*, pp 257- 260.

5   Ibid.

6   John Gibson Lockhart, *The Life of Robert Burns*, ed. with Notes and
    Appendices by W. Scott Douglas, 1914, Vol.I, pp 54-55 (n).

7   Currie, op. cit., pp 106-7.

8   James C. Dick, *The Songs of Robert Burns, 1903*, p 362 (n 31).

9   John McVie, *Burns and Stair, 1927*; p 60.

10 Lowe, op cit, pp 167-180.

11 Lockhart op cit., p 43 (n).

12 Gilbert's Narrative op. cit., Vol IV Appendix C., p. 360.

13 Currie op. cit., Vol.III, Appendix pp 4-5.

14 James Kinsley, *The Poems and Songs of Robert Burns, Vol. III*, pp 1039 - 40.

15 James Paterson, *The Contemporaries of Robert Burns, 1840*, p 55 (n).

16 Currie, op. cit.. Vol. pp 110- 111. 115.

17 John D. Ross, ed. *Burnsiana, 1897*, Vol II, pp 99- 105.

18 Paterson, op. cit., p 44.

19 Both letters are held by Irvine Burns Club, who bought them in 1975, from the Revd. D. W. Sillar, a great, great grandson of David Sillar.

20 McVie, op. cit., p 45.

21 John McVie. 'David Sillar, A Vindication', *Burns Chronicle, 1959*, p 39.

22 Paterson op. cit., pp 55-57.

23 McVie, op. cit.,pp 38-41.

24 Paterson, op. cit., 62- 63.

25 McVie, op. cit., p 40.

26 Dr. Sillar's Burgess Ticket is in the possession of Irvine Burns Club.

Dr. John Mackenzie, MD.

1   Charles Rogers, *Book of Robert Burns, 1889/91*, The Grampian Club, Vol. II , p 28.

2   Ayrshire Archeological and Natural History Society, 1985, *Mauchline Memories of Robert Burns*, p 237.

3   Josiah Walker, *Poems of Robert Burns with an Account of his Life, 1811*, Vol.II, pp 261-3.

4   Maurice Lindsay. Robert Burns, 1954, p 43.

5   Chambers / Wallace, *The Life and Works of Robert Burns, 1896*, Vol, I, p 378 (n).

6   Ibid, Vol I, p 363 (n).

7   Josiah Walker, op. cit., p. 264.

8   Dr. Charles Rogers, op. cit., p 32.

9   Letter of Dugald Stewart to Dr. James Currie in *The Life of Robert Burns, 1800*, Vol 1, pp 141-2.

10 Josiah Walker, op. cit., p 264.

11 J. Cuthbert Hadden, *The Life of George Thomson, 1898*, p 29.

12 James C. Ewing, 'Burns House in Mauchline', *Burns Chronicle, 1916*, p 56.

13   F. B. Snyder, *The Life of Robert Burns, Appendix B*, p 501.

14   *Mauchline Parish Register.*

15   A.A.N.H.S., op.cit., pp 254-5

16   J. C. Ewing, 'The Mackenzie Extension', *Burns Chronicle, 1920*, p 136.

17   'Purchase of Dr. Mackenzie's House', *Burns Chronicle, 1917*, p 117.

18   A.A.N.H.S., *Ayrshire at the time of Burns, 1959*, p 292.

19   'Dr. John Mackenzie', *Burns Chronicle, 1918.*

20   Henry Ranken, 'Burns and Irvine', *Burns Chronicle, 1905*, pp 49-63.

21   William Findlay, *Robert Burns and the Medical Profession, 1898*, p 20.

22   John McVie, *Robert Burns and Edinburgh, 1969*, p 42.

'Epistle to Dr. John Mackenzie'

1   Quoted by W. Scott Douglas in *The Works of Robert Burns, 1891, Vol I*, p 319 (n).

Saunders Tait

1   W. Scott Douglas, *The Works of Robert Burns, 1891*, 'Gilbert's Narrative'.
     Vol IV, Appendix C, p 354.

2   *Kay's Edinburgh Portraits, Popular Letterpress Edition. 1885*, Vol. II, pp 119-120.

3   Franklyn B. Snyder, *The Life of Robert Burns, 1968*, pp 499-503.

4   W. E. Henley, *'Life, Genius, Achievement' The Poetry of Robert Burns, 1896*,
     Vol IV, p 254 (n).

5   John McVie, 'The Lochlie Litigation', *Burns Chronicle, 1959* p 69 - 87.

Captain Richard Brown

1   W. Scott Douglas, *The Works of Robert Burns, 1891*.'Gilbert's Narrative',
     Vol IV, Appendix C, p 360.

2   Allan Dent, *Burns in his Time, 1966*, pp 103, 109.

3   *Lloyd's Register of Shipping, 1789.*

4   'In Defence of Burns', *Burns Chronicle, 1910*, p 148.

John Rankine

1   Chambers/Wallace, *The Life and Works of Robert Burns, 1896*, Vol I, p 120.

2   Ibid, p 119.

3   J. De Lancey Ferguson, 1964, p 77.

4   Donald A. Low, *The Critical Heritage, 1974*, p 81

5   David Lowe, *Burns's Passionate Pilgrimage, 1904*, p 32.

6   Ibid, pp 33-34,

7   Chambers/Wallace, op. cit., p 120.

8   Ibid.

9   A.B.Todd, *Reminiscences of a Long Life, 1906*, p 47.

10   Chambers/Wallace, op. cit., p 98.

11   Thomas Stewart, ed.Poems ascribed to Robert Burns, the Ayrshire Bard, 801, p 60.

James Smith

1   John Taylor Gibb *'More Mauchline Topography' Burns Chronicle , 1896*, p 80.

2   Catherine Carswell, *The Life of Robert Burns, 1951.* p 162.

3   Robert T. Fitzhugh, *Robert Burns, his Associates and Contemporaries, 1943,*
       'The Train Manuscripts', p 58.

4   Mr. Clinton V. Black, Archivist, Spanish Town, Jamaica, confirmed in 1985 that there
       is no record of Smith's death or burial in Jamaica, either in manuscript or printed
       sources.

5   W.H. Cromek, Reliques of Robert Burns, 1808, p.20 (n).

The Belles of Mauchline

1   David Sillar to Robert Aiken in *Poems of Robert Burns, Edinburgh*, 1811. VolIII, pp 257-60.

2   Ibid.

3   W. Scott Douglas. *The Works of Robert Burns, 1891*, 'Gilbert's Narrative',
       Vol IV, Appendix C, p 359.

4   Ayrshire Archeological and Natural History Society, *Mauchline Memories of
       Robert Burns, 1985*, p254.

5   Ibid.

6   Dr. Charles Rogers, *The Book of Robert Burns 1889-91*, The Grampian Club, Vol II, p.
27.

7   Andrew Edgar, *Old Church Life in Scotland, 1885*, pp. 269-70.

8   J.F. Mitchell, 'Burns's Excise Associates', *Scottish Genealogist, 1959*, Vol VII, No 2, p 15.

9   *Mauchline Parish Register.*

10   Ibid.

11   Dr. Charles Rogers, op. cit. Vol I, pp 82 - 90.

12   John McVie, *Robert Burns and Edinburgh, 1969*, p 52.

13   Chambers/Wallace, *The Life and Works of Robert Burns, 1896: Vol I*, p 138 (n).

14   Ibid.

15   Ayrshire A. N. H. S. op. cit. p 257.

16   Ibid p 245.

17   John Taylor Gibb, 'More Mauchline Topography', *Burns Chronicle,1896*, pp75-6.

19   Dr. Charles Rogers, op. cit. Vol II, p 106.

20   *'The Ronalds of the Bennals'.* (CW 76).

John Richmond

1   John Strawhorn, ed. *On an Ayrshire Farm, 1823-1824*, Ayrshire A. N. H. S., 1974, p 47.

2   William Jolly, *Robert Burns in Mossgiel, 1881*, pp 74-75.

3   *Mauchline Kirk Session Register.*

4   Allan Cunningham, *The Works of Robert Burns with his Life, 1834*, Vol II, pp 65-66.

5   James C. Dick, *The Songs of Robert Burns, 1903*, Notes p 445.

6   Andrew M. Boyle, *The Ayrshire Book of Burns Lore, 1985*, p 107.

7   Chambers/Wallace, *The Life and Works of Robert Burns, 1896, Vol II*, p 407.

8   Letter (unpublished) by Rev Archibald Lawrie to Dr. James Currie, cited by
        James C. Ewing in *'John Richmond : Mauchline Friend of Burns',in Burns Chronicle,*
        1925, p 56.

9   Letter, 7,9,1787, Gavin Hamilton to John Richmont (sic), cited by James C Ewing in
        Burns Chronicle, 1925, pp 56-57.

10   Robert T Fitzhugh, *Robert Burns, his Associates and Contemporaries, 1943,*
        'The Train Manuscript' pp 54 - 55.

11   A. B. Todd, *Poetical Works, with Autobiography, 1906*, p30.

12   Dr. Charles Rogers, *The Book of Robert Burns, 1889-91*, The Grampian Club',
        Vol II, pp 165-168.

13   J. De Lancey Ferguson, *Pride and Passion , 1964*, p 90.

John Lapraik

1   James Paterson, *The Contemporaries of Burns, 1840*, p 17.

2   George F. Black. *The Surnames of Scotland, 1946*, p 416.

3   Chambers/ Wallace, *The Life and Works of Robert Burns 1896*, Vol I, p 158 (n).

4   C.P.Bell 'The Lapraik Family in Muirkirk' *Burns Chronicle, 1915*, pp 99-100.

5   Black op. cit.

6   J.G.A.Baird, *Muirkirk in Bygone Days, 1910*, pp 31-32.

7   Ibid, p28-29.

8   Paterson, op.cit.: p I8.

9   John Rankine, *The Law of Land Ownership in Scotland, 4th edition*, 1909, p 218.

10   Dr. James Currie, *The Works of Robert Burns, 1800*, Vol III, Appendix, I. p 7.

11   John G. Lockhart, *The Life of Robert Burns*, edited with notes and appendices by
        W. Scott Douglas, 1914, Vol. I p 100 (n).

12   James Johnson, *The Scots Musical Museum,. 1790*, Vol III. p 205.

13   R.H.Cromek, *Reliques of Robert Burns, 1808*, p 263.

14   W.E. Henley and T.F.Henderson *The Poetry of Robert Burns, 1896*, Vol I, p380 (n).

15   Thomas Crawford, *Burns, a Study of the Poems and Songs, 1960*, p 89.

16   Davidson Cook, 'Imposing on Burns'. *Burns Chronicle, 1920*, pp 142-146.

17   Paterson, op. cit.. Cunningham cited p 25.

William Fisher ('Holy Willie')

1   D. I. Lyall, *Mauchline in Times Past, 1986*, p 15.

2   Rev. William Auld, comp. *Account of Parish of Mauchline, for Statistical Account of Scotland, 1782*, Vol II p 115.

3   Dr. Charles Rogers, *The Book of Robert Burns, 1889-91, Vol I*, p 198.

4   Rev. J. C. Glennie, 'Gavin Hamilton and the Kirk Session of Mauchline', *Burns Chronicle, 1970* pp 20-30.

5   Ibid.

6   Rev. Andrew Edgar, *Old Church Life in Scotland, 1885*, p 203.

7   W. Scott Douglas, *The Works of Robert Burns, 1891, Vol I*, pp 240-241.

8   Allan Cunningham, *The Works of Robert Burns 1839 edition*, Headnote to 'Holy Willie's Prayer', Vol 1, p 16.

9   Allan Cunningham, *The Works of Robert Burns 1834*, Vol I, p299.

10   Dr. Charles Rogers, op.cit. Vol I, 199, and Rev. Andrew Edgar, op. cit., p 299.

11   Edgar, op. cit. pp 227-228.

12   W. Scott Douglas, op,cit, Vol II p 243, and James Kinsley, *The Poems and Songs of Robert Burns 1968*, Vol III pp 1308-9.

13   Quoted by Dr. Charles Rogers, op.cit. Vol I, pp 200-201.

14   Dr. Charles Rogers, op. cit, Vol I, p 203.

15   A. B. Todd, *Reminiscences of a Long Life, 1906*, pp 56-57.

16   Ibid.

17   From Ardrossan ad Saltcoats Herald, issues 10 and 17 July, 1858, and reported in *Mauchline Memories of Robert Burns*, pp 248-249.

18   A.B. Todd, op cit. p 56.

19   Franklyn B. Snyder, *The Life of Robert Burns 1968*, p 109.

Thomas Walker

1   James Paterson, *The Contemporaries of Burns, 1840*, p 142.

2   Chambers/Wallace, *The Life and Works of Robert Burns, 1896*, Vol I, p 177.

3   Allan Cunningham, Quoted by W. Scott Douglas, *Works of Robert Burns, 1891*,Vol1, p 348.

4   Paterson, op. cit., p 71.

5   W. Scott Douglas, op. cit., Vol I, p 349.

6   Chambers/Wallace, op. cit. VoI p 402.

7   Paterson, op.cit., p 73 (n).

8   Ibid, 135.

9   Ibid, 137.

10 A.M. Boyle, *Ayrshire Book of Burns Lore, 1986*, p 111.

The Crochallan Fencibles

1   Robert Chambers, *Traditions of Edinburgh, 1967*, p 162.

2   Ibid, p 163.

3   Ibid, p 164.

4   Quoted by Marie W. Stuart, *Old Edinburgh Taverns, 1952*, p 55.

5   Chambers, op.cit., pp 165-166.

6   Robert Kerr, *Life of William Smellie, Vol I*, pp 502-503.

7   Kay's *Edinburgh Portraits, Popular Letterpress Edition*, 1885, Vol I.

8   Franklyn   B, Snyder, *The Life of Robert Burns, 1968*, p 209.

9   Kerr, op. cit. Vol II, p 350.

William Nicol

1   Dr. Charles Rogers, *The Book of Robert Burns, 1889-91*, The Grampian Club, Vol II, pp 128-129.

2   William Steven, *The History of the High School of Edinburgh, 1849*, Appendix VI, p 95.

3   James Mackay, Burns, a *Biography of Robert Burns, 1992*, p 332.

4   Robert T. Fitzhugh, (ed) *Robert Burns, his Associates and Contemporaries, 1943*, pp 65-67.

5   Ibid, pp 97-98.

6   *Lord Cockburn, Memorials of His Time*, (ed) W. Forbes Gray, 1946, p 100.

7   William Wallace, *Burns Dunlop Correspondence, 1898*, p 287.

8   William C. Maclehose, *The Correspondence of Burns and Clarinda 1843*, Letter No 18.

9   Dugald Stewart, Letter to the Editor of The Lounger, reprinted by Dr. James Currie in *Life of Robert Burns, 1800, Vol I*, p 146.

10 W. Scott Douglas, *The Works of RobertBurns, 1891*, Vol IV, p 284.

11 John G. Lockhart, *The Life of Robert Burns, 1914*, Vol I, p 230 (n).

12   Letter from Josiah Walker to Robert Burns, in Dr. Currie, op. cit., Vol II, p 99.

13   Letter from Dr. Couper of Fochabers to Dr. Currie, op. cit., Vol I, pp 184-185.

14   Story appeared in *Chambers' Edinburgh Journal, Vol VIII*, p405.

15   Bishop Skinner's letter is printed in *Burns Chronicle, 1944*, p 35.

16   Chambers/Wallace, *The Life and Works of Robert Burns, 1896*. Vol II, p 188.

17   Chambers/Wallace, Ibid, Vol II, p198 (n). See also Dr. Charles Rogers, op. cit., Vol II, p 136.

18   James Mackay, *Burns Lore of Dumfries and Galloway, 1988*, pp 124 and 154.

19   Chambers/Wallace, op. cit., Vol III, p 200.

20   Hilton Brown, *There was a Lad, 1949*, p 37.

21   Chambers/ Wallace, op. cit., Vol III, pp 395-396.

22   Chambers/Wallace, op. cit., Vol IV, p 61.

23   *Edinburgh Town Council Records, Vol CXVII*, pp 63 – 64.

24   John McVie, *Robert Burns and Edinburgh, 1969*, p 44.

25   Robert Heron, *Memoir of Robert Burns, as printed first in The Monthly Magazine, 1797*, cited by Hans Hecht in Robert Burns, 1959, p 271 (n 59).

26   *Edinburgh Town Council Records, Vol XV*, fol 118.

27   William Steven, op. cit., p 96.

28   Edinburgh University Library.

29   *Robert D. Thornton, James Currie, the Entire Stranger and Robert Burns, 1963*, p387.

30   David Daiches, *Robert Burns and his World, 1971*, p 64.

'Lang Sandy' Wood

1   Maurice Lindsay,*The Burns Encyclopaedia, 1959*, Heron's Memoir printed in full, p 123.

2   *Dr. Alexander Carlyle of Inveresk, The Autobiography (ed) John H. Burton, 1910*, p 226 (n).

3   Ibid, p 226-227.

4   Sir Walter Scott, to John G. Lockhart, *Memoirs of Sir Walter Scott, 1837*, Vol I, p 15.

5   *Kay's Edinburgh Portraits, Popular Letterpress Edition, 1885*, Vol I, p 116.

6   Ibid, pp 115-119.

7   Op cit, Vol I, p 116.

Peter Hill

1   Robert Chambers, *Traditions of Edinburgh, 1967* edition, pp 103-104.

2   *Lord Cockburn, Memorials of His Time*, ed. W. Forbes Gray, 1946, p 105.

3   Chambers/ Wallace, *The Life and Works of Robert Burns, 1896*, Vol II, p 266.

4   W. Scott Douglas, *The Works of Robert Burns, 1891*, Vol IV, p 137.

5   Catherine Carswell, *The Life of Robert Burns, 1951*, p 239.

6   Lord Cockburn, op cit,. p 104 (n).

7   W. Forbes Gray, 'An Ancient Trade: Some Old Edinburgh Bookshops',
        The Scotsman, 5 November, 1937.

8   Ibid.

9   James C. Ewing, 'Robert Burns's Literary Correspondence, 1786-1796',
        Burns Chronicle,1933.

10   Robert Chambers, quoted by W. Scott Douglas, op cit., Vol V, p 138.

11   Revelation, Chapter 7, verse 17.

12   John McVie, Robert Burns and Edinburgh, 1969, p 46, and Maurice Lindsay,
        The Burns Encyclopedia,1959, p 59.

13   Chambers/Wallace, op cit, Vol III, p 164.

14   James Kinsley, The Poems and Songs of Robert Burns, 1968, Vol III, p 1483.

15   George Wilson, Robert Burns and his friend Peter Hill, 1890, p 2,
        and Dr. Charles Rogers, The Book of Robert Burns, 1889/91, Vol I, p 334.

16   George Wilson, Ibid, p 2.

Robert Graham of Gartmore

1   A.F. Tchiffely, Don Roberto, the Life and Works of R.B. CunninghameGraham, 1937, p 9.

2   Sir Walter Scott, Minstrelsy of the Scottish Border, 1931, p 485.

3   R.B. Cunninghame Graham, Doughty Deeds, 1925, p 56.

4   Ibid, p 145.

5   Chambers/Wallace, Life and Works of Robert Burns, 1896, Vol II, p 86.

David Allan
Bibliography

James Mackay, The Complete Letters of Robert Burns, 1967.

Duncan McMillan, Scottish Painting, The Golden Age, 1986.

Murdo Macdonald, Scottish Art, 2000.

Paul Harris and Julian Halsby, The Dictionary of Scottish Painters,1998.

T. Crowther Gordon, David Allan of Alloa, 1951.

Allan Cunningham, Lives of the Painters, Sculptors and Architects, 1839.

The Rev. James Oliphant

1   James L. Hempstead, 'Burns's West Highland Tour, the Grierson MS',
        Burns Chronicle, 1974, pp 30-37.

2   Joseph Irving, The History of Dunbartonshire, 1857, pp 373-374. (n).
        and Donald Macleod, Past Worthies of the Lennox, 1894, pp 3-8.

James Kennedy

1 Fergus Roberts, *The Grammar School of Dumbarton*, reprinted from the Lennox Herald, 1948, p 5.

2 Ibid, p 18.

3 Robert Riddell, *Addenda to the Statistical Account of Scotland*.

Dr. George Grierson

1 James Mackay, Burns, *A Biography of Robert Burns, 1992* p.

2 James L. Hempstead, *Robert Burns and Dunbartonshire, 1997* pp 11, 13.

John Lewars

1 J. F. Mitchell, 'Burns's Excise Associates' *Scottish Genealogist 1959*, Vol VII, No 2. pp 15-16.

2 Dumfries Burgh Records, MS, '*Summons of Removing, 1792*', dated 2 April, 1792.

3 Henry W, Meikle, 'Burns and the Capture of the Rosamond,' *Burns Chronicle, 1934*. See also F,.B. Snyder, 'Burns and the Smuggler Rosamond', *Modern Language Association of America, Vol I*, No 2, June, 1935.

4 Robert H. Cromek.1808, p 148.

5 James Kinsley, *The Poems and Songs of Robert Burns, 1968*, Vol III, p 1408.

6 James Mackay, *Burns, a Biography of Robert Burns,1992*, p 530.

Alexander Findlater

1 Cited by F. B. Snyder , *The Life of Robert Burns, 1968*, p 317.

2 Dr. James Currie, *The Life of Robert Burns, 1800*, Vol I, p 220.

3 J.F.Mitchell, 'Burns's Excise Associates,' *Scottish Genealogist, 1959, Vol IV*, 2, pp 4-5.

4 Ibid.

5 Clark Hunter, 'From Rotary to Robert Burns', *Burns Chronicle, 1962*, p 3.

6 Graham Smith, *Robert Burns the Exciseman, 1989*, p 62.

7 J.C. Ewing and Andrew McCallum, 'Robert Graham (12th) of Fintry', *Burns Chronicle, 1931*, p 52.

8 John Sinton, *Burns, Excise Officer and Poet, 1897*, p 28.

9 Robert T Fitzhugh, *Robert Burns, the Man and the Poet, 1971*, p 226.

10 See Findlater's letter to editor of *Glasgow Courier, 29 January, 1835*,p 21.

11 W. E. Henley, 'Life, Genius, Achievement', *The Poetry of Robert Burns, 1896*, Vol IV, p 334.

12 J. F. Mitchell, op. cit., pp 4-5.

13 Thomas Bain, 'Alexander Findlater', *Burns Chronicle, 1924*, pp 74-75. See also Dr. Charles Rogers, *The Book of Robert Burns 1896*, Vol I, p 197.

14 'Memorial to Alexander Findlater,' *Burns Chronicle, 1924*, p 77.

15 'Dedication of Alexander Findlater Memorial Plaque, *Burns Chronicle, Autumn, 2002*.

William Corbet

1 William Wallace, Burns/Dunlop Correspondence, 1898, p241.

2 John F. Mitchell, (comp) *Card Index of Members of Scottish Excise Department, 1707-1830*, Scottish Record Office.

3 Wallace, op. cit. p 248

4 Wallace, ibid, p 249.

5 J.C.Ewing and Andrew McCallum, 'Robert Graham (12th) of Fintry', *Burns Chronicle, 1932*, p 52.

6 John Sinton, Burns, *Excise Officer and Poet, 1896*, p 55.

7 Robert T. Fitzhugh, *Robert Burns, the Man and the Poet, 1971*, p 226.

8 Mitchell, op cit.,

9 *Kay's Edinburgh Portraits, Popular Letterpress Edition*, 1885, Vol I, p 176, and William Roughead, *Notable Scottish Trials, 1906*, p 33.

10 William Roughead, Ibid, p 142.

11 Graham Smith, *Robert Burns the Exciseman, 1989*, p 60.

James Gray

1 William McDowall, *History of Dumfries, 3rd ed., 1906*, p 677.

2 James Mackay, *Burns Lore of Dumfries & Galloway, 1988*, p 63.

3 William Steven, *The History of the High School of Edinburgh, 1849*, Appendix VI, pp 103-4.

4 Dr. James Currie, *The Works of Robert Burns with an Account of his Life, 8th ed. 1820*, edited by Gilbert Burns, Appendix V. pp 436-7.

5 William Steven, op. cit., p 158.

6 Charles Cowan, *Reminiscences, 1878*, printed for private circulation, p 21.

7 Dr. Charles Rogers, *The Book of Robert Burns, 1889-91*, Vol I, pp 253-4.

8 James C Ewing, 'George Thomson, John Wilson and Gilbert Burns's Appendix No V', *Burns Chronicle, 1905*, p 28.

9 Raymond Lamont Brown, *Clarinda, 1968*, pp 68 and 216.

10 Chambers/Wallace, *The Life and Works of Robert Burns, 1896*, Vol IV, p 297.

11 Duncan McNaught, 'The Earnock Manuscripts', Letter Cadell and Davies to Gilbert Burns, 5.7.1816, and letter Gilbert Burns to Cadell and Davies, 20.2.1816, *Burns Chronicle, 1898*, p 16.

12 James C Ewing, op. cit. pp 22-89.

13 Duncan McNaught, op, cit., Letter James Gray to Wiliam Roscoe,
     28, 9. 1817, *Burns Chronicle, 1898* pp 31-32.

14 William Steven, op. cit., pp 205-206 and Appendix VI, p 104.

15 Charles Cowan, op. cit., p 22.

16 William Steven, op cit., p 105.

17 Dr. John Wilson, *Memoir of Mrs. Margaret Wilson of the Scottish Mission, Bombay, 4th ed.,
     1844*, pp 239-40.

18 William Steven, op cit., pp 106-107,

19 Robert H. Story, *Memoir of the Life of the Rev Robert Story, 1862*, p 63.

20 Dr. Charles Rogers, op cit., pp 236-237.

21 Mrs. C. Elwood, *Narrative of a Journey Overland to India and Residence there,
     1825-1828, Vol II*, p 111.

22 See 'Cromek and Stothard's 1809 Burns Tour' by Davidson Cook in *Burns
     Chronicle*, 1918, and 'Cromek and Stothard on Tour' by James C. Ewing
     in *Burns Chronicle, 1949*.

PICTURE CREDITS

Mr. Sam Gaw p.40; Irvine Burns Club pp.45, 62, 65; Dumbarton Burns Club p.47;
Mr. Peter Westwood p.55; Scottish National Portrait Gallery pp.74, 158, 163,
164, 166, 175, 177, 183; National Gallery of Scotland pp.85, 92, 139, 170, 188;
Mr. David Smith, Dumfries Howff Club pp.89, 248 (bottom right); Mr. James L.
Hempstead p.122; Mr. Ron Howard p.179; Mr. Ian McLean p.184; Royal Scottish
Academy p.187; National Library of Ireland p.221; Mr. James MacKay p.227; Burns
Chronicle pp.228, 229; S. G. Jackman p.244

All endeavours have been made to credit illustrations. For any that have been
omitted the author wishes to apologise.

Index

Index

Index